At Freedom's Limit

At Freedom's Limit

ISLAM AND THE POSTCOLONIAL
PREDICAMENT

Sadia Abbas

FORDHAM UNIVERSITY PRESS   *New York*   2014

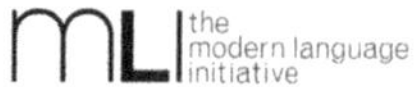

THIS BOOK IS MADE POSSIBLE BY A COLLABORATIVE GRANT FROM THE ANDREW W. MELLON FOUNDATION.

The system used for transliteration is LOC for Urdu with minor modifications.

Library of Congress Cataloging-in-Publication Data

Abbas, Sadia.
  At freedom's limit : Islam and the postcolonial predicament / Sadia Abbas.
      pages cm
  Includes bibliographical references and index.
  ISBN 978-0-8232-5785-0 (hardback)
  ISBN 978-0-8232-5786-7 (paper)
  1. Islam—21st century. 2. Islam—20th century.
I. Title.
BP161.3.A235 2014
306.6'97—dc23

                                        2013050012

Printed in the United States of America

16 15 14   5 4 3 2 1

First edition

Kamal,
For teaching me the possibilities of unconditional care
in human relationships.

Biju,
For being there and just being.

Papa,
Who taught me to argue.

R.A.,
Who made a beautiful promise and, far more
remarkable, is keeping it.

"What is conceivable can happen too,"
Said Wittgenstein, who had not dreamt of you

William Empson

یہ کہاں کی دوستی ہے کہ بنے میں دوست ناصح

yeh kahā<u>n</u> kī dostī hai ke bane hai<u>n</u> dost nāṣiḥ

What manner of friendship is this, that friends have
    turned to preaching

Mirza Ghalib

I sing, I sing, I sing, I sing,
I sing just to know that I'm alive

Nina Simone

CONTENTS

Color plates follow page 148

ACKNOWLEDGMENTS

A book such as this requires the patience of those who deal with its author. So let me begin by thanking all those who have loved and played and talked with me over the past few years for their fortitude and good humor and their only occasional impatience. It has been an extraordinary time, and with the merciful forgetfulness that accompanies the end of a project, and without which the beginning of any new one would be impossible, I'll say that it was all—every minute of despair and uncertainty, of exhaustion and also the exhilaration that accompanies thinking and reading and writing—worth it.

I am very grateful to all those who have contributed their insights and questions in personal conversation and in more public venues. The English department at Williams College and the comparative literature department at SUNY Buffalo gave me an opportunity to present parts of Chapter 3 and asked challenging and useful questions. Haverford College invited me to present sections from the final chapter. I benefited from conversations with the faculty, participants, and audience. A young Pakistani student asked me a question. The inadequacy of my answer to him continues to push me to think carefully about the questions motivating this book. The graduate students and faculty in the comparative literature department at UCLA were a stimulating audience to whom I presented materials from Chapter 2, as was the audience at the Columbia Literary Theory Seminar and at the *boundary* 2 conference at UCLA where I presented material from the same chapter.

Stathis Gourgouris shared rigorous thinking, loud laughter, and gave a timely introduction to Helen Tartar, who is amazing and upon meeting whom I realized I was meant to work with her. I'm glad she thought so too. Tim Roberts has also been a terrific and patient editor.

Bruce Robbins invited me to speak and to respond at the Columbia Literary Theory Seminar and was a supportive and cheerful interlocutor. David Lloyd asked me an extraordinarily important question one brunch in New York; Marjorie Levinson, in passing and with characteristic ease, made a remarkable, ostensibly throwaway observation over drinks at ACLA in New Orleans. Both had effects that ramified throughout the book. Hiram Perez and Maliha Safri gave talks that helped transform my thinking. Hiram's ethical intellect and profound decency are an inspiration. Those lingering conversations, in the hallways of the English department at the University of Michigan, with Vivasvan Soni were a terrific boost to thinking. Michael Schoenfeldt made thinking about early modern literature a pleasure. Aamir Mufti gave encouragement and applied good pressure at every step, demanding that I write a better book. Gayatri Spivak provided unobtrusive and profound encouragement at many key moments. Faisal Devji has read the work and been a supportive interlocutor and a great person to laugh with. Eduardo Cadava gave wonderful and characteristically generous feedback on several chapters, and we had some greatly stimulating conversations. Rajeswari Sunder Rajan was very encouraging about the work along the way. Tony Bogues gave quiet and perceptive support and comments.

Those heated conversations over Szechuan food with Christian Parenti have become one of my favorite New York rituals. Samah Selim taught me anew the possibilities of a thinking engagement with the world and joined in the fun of watching bad films. Paul Amar came to a talk as a member of the audience and stayed as a friend and collaborator. He has written to me from every corner of the world with a demand that I present my work better and be better at making sure that I do what I should than just about anyone. There's steel behind that ever-ready smile. Thank you. Here's to work over many years and in many places.

Ali Mir has responded to my queries and offered to help at every stage. It took discipline not to take more advantage of him. At a crucial stage, when I was extraordinarily pressed for time, Bilal Hashmi took over the transliterations (all mistakes are mine) and looked up references and did research, making wonderful suggestions along the way.

Fran Bartkowski, Bruce Franklin, Barbara Foley, Jack Lynch, and Laura Lomas have been extraordinary colleagues and friends. All five made settling into work a joy. Having Bruce and Barbara across the hall has been great. I'm tempted to change my teaching schedule just so I can linger in the halls discussing the history of world politics with Bruce again—it's amazing that either of us got anything done. Laura has been thoughtful and supportive in numerous ways. Jack's emails have a certain amazing, Augustan craft. Although I haven't needed to send him a random query for a while, sometimes I just want to make one up to get one of those again. I don't quite know what to say about Fran. She has been an extraordinary mentor, read every chapter, created an environment where thinking is possible without stress, and has modeled a remarkable collegiality, showing that one does not have to sacrifice tough-mindedness to be a warm and profoundly kind and generous person. Janet Larson was very welcoming when I arrived and made the transition much easier. Gabriel Miller was a supportive interim chair and a principled, funny, and kind presence. Manu Chander and Patricia Akhimie joined the department later; we have had great fun hanging out, and I can't thank them enough for those rides in. Since Ameer Sohrawardy joined the department, those occasional random jokes in Urdu do light up the corridors. Madelyn Munoz-Bertram is steady as a rock and holds things together. Thank you so very much, Maddy. Thomas Moomjy found some crucial references when I had no time at all. He and Sara Grossman were wonderful TAs. All my students have kept me engaged and (I like to think) honest. My undergraduate students at Newark have been a challenging inspiration. I have *loved* working with them while writing this book. They have made so much of it worthwhile.

When Unver Shafi gave me permission to use an image of his magnificent painting, *The Two Souzas*, for the cover of this book, I would have, had joints permitted, turned a whole bunch of cartwheels. Talking to him has made me have to think even harder about painting. I look forward to our future collaborations.

Some teachers cannot be forgotten. Miss Maimoona, the Urdu and class teacher in class 2, way back in Mama Parsi days, left an indelible memory of teacherly grace and kindness on a child recently returned from Singapore, learning to read Urdu for the first time. Mrs. Islam in classes 7 and 8 was insistent and encouraging and still wants to know what I'm doing to live up to her expectations when I go back. I hope she's not too disappointed. Terry Tyler allowed me to cultivate a joy in language at college. This book takes nothing from my dissertation, except some sentiments from the acknowledgments. Yet I cannot overstate my debt to my teachers at graduate school, William Keach,

Stephen Foley, and Neil Lazarus, particularly to Bill (as his students know him). Bill, who permitted all sorts of risk and was delighted when I argued, who is a tough-minded reader, and a warm and generous teacher and colleague. Speaking with him is still exhilarating. Friends though we have become, I remain (proudly) his student.

There are school friends from Karachi with whom friendship has survived a quarter of a century of moving and displacement: Feryan Ahmed, Ismail Mirza, Karim and Marianne, Yasir Husain, Sameeta Ahmed, and last, but never least, Sameer Rabbani, who remembers my birthday and who has always known how I'm feeling just by looking at me. In New York, I have relied on Carmen. Some friends have given moments of much-needed relief from the hothouse world of the academy. Shehnaz and Manisha have been great. Steven, who introduced me to the beauty of Harlem and Washington Heights. Naumann, who reminds me of home and has helped with the production of this book, who is sardonic and protective in equal, if sometimes carefully hidden, measure, and Ilya with whom I have learned to share Greece as well—to more days in Athens and Mytilene and, soon, Ikaria, buddy. Despina (humblingly) taught me the irrelevance of words—although we share hardly a fifth of a language between us, she has shown and wordlessly expressed tremendous care and insight. Walking to Café Neo before she retired and, now, down to the harbor in the evening when I get to the village, being met with those extraordinarily caring shrieks of joy to the complete bemusement of all the tourists around, has become one of the high points of every summer. And, of course, she's one of the best cooks I've ever met. John Slavin and Julie Copeland, friends from Australia, felicitously met in Greece, shared an unforgettable three days in Umbria, hunting for Peruginos and providing much-needed relief and pleasure at a crucial moment in the writing of this book. Azra Apa's (Azra Raza) place has become home; I have met new, beautiful friends there and taken comfort from her generosity and support and from her passionate knowledge of Urdu literature, as I have from Bibi's (Amera Raza) astuteness, indefinable grace, and attentive gentleness.

Two members of my family had a crucial role in my intellectual formation. My Muslim nationalist and fundamentalist (the two are not synonymous, of course) father came to Pakistan on a bus at the age of fifteen, rejecting his Congress-supporting father's views, following a dream of a Muslim homeland. His quest informs almost every page of this book. He bought me an encyclopedia when I was three and debated what I suppose I can only call moral theology with me throughout my adolescence. We fought passionately as I developed a different ideology and rejected his views on women. Yet his contradictions, quicksilver intelligence, and wit—which not nearly enough people get to see—have been more central to such ability as I have to think and argue and even banter than anyone else, which is why I think he chuckled with wry and respectful understanding when many, many years later he finally accepted the ineffectiveness of disowning someone who didn't care to be owned.

My maternal grandfather, who read all night, let me read in the crook of his arm long after lights went out in the rest of the house. He snuck me money for books and took me to Hyderi where he bought me secondhand books from a thelā—on which frayed and stained copies of Alberto Moravia and Andre Gide jostled the tattered, technicolor glories of *Urdu Digest*—and jalebīs from the shop next to it, andarse kī golīyān from somewhere deep in the city, and spicy fried fish from a corner in Karimabad, thus giving me at the same time my passion for street food. He was a remarkable, reticent, generous, and conservative man who died in terrible circumstances, betrayed and abandoned by all who should have fought to protect him from the cruelty to which he was subjected by those closest to him. I like to think that, had he lived, he would have loved the fact that I had written this book, even as he told me yet again that I had made a terrible mistake by not joining the Pakistani Civil Service.

Dimitris Krallis, Sarita See, Sangeeta Kamat, Kamal Ahmed, and Biju Matthew have taught me the possibilities of reinvention in friendship. Sarita made a life-changing suggestion, sent pictures of food from different corners of the globe, Skyped for hours from Ann Arbor, L.A., Manila, Baguio, and Singapore, and listened carefully as I worked out my ideas on the Baroque. Dimitris was an unbelievably present friend through a health crisis. Over the years, looking over Molivos bay at moonlight, or competing with the awful music at the beach bar, talking about ideas, tunelessly singing atrocious songs, and squabbling on the winding roads of Lesvos, we have become more like siblings (who actually like each other) than friends. Sangeeta opened her home to me and talked endlessly about ideas and came for a couple of intense and timely walks. Biju provided food on demand, was present in unbelievable ways, heard every page, pushed, argued, never lost faith, put up with my arguments, and whether in Hyderabad, Shanghai, or New York *always* answered the phone. I cannot name that debt, so I'll write about the joy of landing in New York and calling from the taxi, knowing that I have one more home and hare masāle kī machlī to be had on (frequent) demand. And Kamal, friend for a quarter of a century now, how do I write of his generosity and care? Perhaps best to focus on the giggle-making joy of his indescribably bad jokes and the absurdity of our conversations and play, on the wordless comfort of cooking together, and on those beautiful bus rides from Siena to Rome and San Gimigniano. I don't know what I would have done without him. Knowing that I could rely on him no matter what made this book possible.

Ashnfara and Alejandra were exceptionally generous in making me welcome in their father's life. Lucia and Javier rolled with me on the floor when I couldn't handle yet another sentence with too many appositives. R. A. Judy came into my life late in the composition of this book, *because* of the composition of this book. It is richer because of our conversations and his careful readings and profound attention. Sharing a study has been wonderfully intellectually volatile; we have argued passionately and pushed each other in exhilarating ways. And there's not much left to ask for when the man, who ran Fanon reading groups for the Black Panther party and studied philosophy at Al-Azhar, combines breathtaking erudition with an ability to eyeball the mixings for a pie crust and still make perfect peach pie, hot biscuits, and *kisra* from scratch and *almost* perfect *seekh* kebabs.

The Argument

The subject of this book is a new "Islam." This Islam begins to disclose its shape in 1988 around the Rushdie affair, the collapse of the Berlin Wall in 1989, and the first Gulf War of 1991. It is consolidated in the period following September 11, 2001. This Islam is a name, a discursive site, a flexible and simultaneously constrained signifier, indeed a geopolitical *agon*, in and around which some of the most pressing aporias of modernity, enlightenment, liberalism, and Reformation are worked out. In the formation that has clustered at this site, there are for Islam many metonyms: the veiled or "pious" Muslim woman, the militant, the minority Muslim injured by Western free speech. There are also a number of antagonists: the literary author, "progressive" feminists, "secular" Muslim intellectuals—a group that may include believing Muslims committed to reimagining Muslim law and practice in all of its heterogeneity—and presumptively "apostate" Muslims who have no interest in religion. Increasingly, customary and nonjuridical versions of lived Islam are antagonists too.[1]

This Islam draws upon a colonial history of the reorganization of religion, even repeats it in the former metropolises of Empire but works also to erase that colonial genealogy. In its many articulations it draws on the reconstitution of society, custom, and sentiment in colonial modernity. It draws on, and in some cases, continues the Cold War exacerbation and exploitation of the colonial reorganization and stabilization of religion, culture, and identities. As a conceptual object it exists most powerfully in the circuits of the Western academy, where it is increasingly a crucial node in the current academic debates invested in reimagining secularism and in the body of work that is sometimes known as the turn to religion, and where its most significant proponents are located. Even as this Islam gains increasing traction in cultural production, from television shows to movies to novels, the most intricate contestations of Islam so construed and perpetuated are to be found in the work of writers and painters.

This signifier allows for the stabilization and even reimposition of colonial cartographies; at the same time, it enables a series of erasures of contiguities and political intimacies and facilitates all sorts of amnesia regarding imperial and colonial history, racial brutality, the many instantiations of Muslim civilization, and *poeisis* in manifold Muslim historical, devotional, and aesthetic traditions. It also facilitates, perhaps even institutes, a number of (multiply exculpatory) cleavages—to name just a few: between the United States and the United Kingdom, between Islam and the "West," the U.S. and British governments and varieties of Islamism, the CIA and ISI, Muslim devotion and aesthetic traditions on the one hand and "authentic" / "orthodox" Muslim practice on the other. Yet thinking with and through this Islam reveals that against a variety of national histories and colonial and postcolonial cartographies are archaeologies that keep folding into the present, sometimes becoming particularly visible like geological strata after an earthquake.

The theme of freedom is central to this Islam even when it is not explicitly invoked. If a neoliberal empire and its quiescent media have on (opportunistic) occasion valorized the figure of the author, the feminist, the secular Muslim as ciphers of "freedom," some critics of Empire explain, understand, even celebrate their perceived others, the injured Muslim, the militant, the pious woman. It is thus that the figure of the slave who does not want to be free comes to be important in the new anthropology of Islam. The centrality of this figure is examined at some length in the first chapter.

The Islam populated by these others of freedom comes to perform a limit to freedom, ostensibly providing freedom from imperial freedom. Banished in this construction are the questions: What precisely do neoliberalism, empire, indeed neoliberal Empire, offer by way of freedom to the racially marked immigrant, the incarcerated, the poor? What also do Guantánamo, rendition, or torture have to do with freedom? What does the virulent Islamophobia of Daniel Pipes, Pamela Geller, Bill Maher, a New Atheist such as Sam Harris, or the more diurnal and ubiquitous forms of it experienced by children in schools, veiled women on the streets, young men under surveillance, or by those put away for life in Guantánamo or Bagram have to do with freedom?[2] Why concede the word and its possibilities to neoconservatives, neoliberals, and the wardens of the great imperial network of domestic and international, visible and invisible, incarceration and "security"?

As capitalism devours the world, squeezing the poor into ever more restricted space, through land grabs, the creation of special economic zones in India, the privatization of coastlines across the planet, the "development" of land in high-end real estate projects from Dubai to New York, imposing on every place the aesthetic of the mall, the (same) beach resort, the homogenized storefront, the word that springs to mind to bring together varieties of incarceration and the constriction of the world for the few is an early modern one: *enclosure*. Enclosure is coincident with the rise of colonialism and the encirclement of the planet and hardly consonant with freedom, despite the liberal association of the word with the right to own property, which one might read as an extension of the practice of enclosure to concepts, indeed to language itself. What, except in the mesmerizingly surreal fictions of the advocates of neoliberalism and empire, does freedom have to do with late capitalism, and how does the emphasis on these figures enable an alternative?

In the first two chapters I address the thematic of freedom in the construction of this new Islam by reading an episode of the transatlantic television success, the British television show *Spooks* (released in the United States as *MI-5*) and the Hollywood movies *Hurt Locker* and *Zero Dark Thirty* to reveal the importance of the history of racial slavery and incarceration to current imaginings of Islamists in cultural production in the United Kingdom and the United States. The imagined power of Islamists functions to disappear the historical violence of Empire, as the continuity of practices that date to racial slavery and to the eradication of the Native Americans is erased. Practices fundamental to the making of colonial modernity are redeemed, their history effaced, by making them seem only products of the War on Terror. This is particularly evinced by the debate over torture, which proceeds as if it is a "new" American (or British) practice elicited by Islamists who have made the West lose its innocence by forcing it to act brutally.

A critique of the project of Black Britain launched by Tariq Modood and seconded by Talal Asad enables this imagination by defanging a project of a pan-ethnic antiracist radicalism. The current theoretical discourse regarding pious, devout, and orthodox Muslims into which this critique is enfolded enables such erasure. Indeed so far has the theoretical-anthropological equation of these figures with Islam *tout court* seeped into the left-liberal imagination that it can be fully normalized in a television episode such as "Who Guards the Guards?" (2003) from *Spooks/MI-5*.

Perhaps most intriguing, if unsurprising, is the pathologization of the author and of aesthetics, marking a turn away from the heroic author, the exemplary subject of Romanticism and the target of critiques and analyses of the death and dependency of the author, to the "good" militant. It is a substitution about which "Who Guards the Guards?" is remarkably explicit, and in which the figure of Salman Rushdie is writ large. Of course, the logic of this relationship repeats itself in a variety of contexts and imaginaries. So, in chapter 2, "The Echo Chamber of Freedom: The Muslim Woman and the Pretext of Agency," I show how, in contemporary discourse, the good militant of the show's imagining is supplemented by the pious and apolitical Muslim woman. The function performed by the literary author in "Who Guards the Guards?" and in critiques of aesthetics and liberal attitudes regarding literature in the work of Asad and Mahmood, poised on the death of Black Britain as conceived by Stuart Hall, is performed by the disappeared "secular," "progressive" Muslim feminist in contemporary discussions of Muslim women. The secular Muslim woman, now inconceivable as Muslim outside an economy of collaboration and treachery, disappears; and the pious woman who ostensibly desires her own enslavement, thus freeing herself from "Western" freedom, is hypervisibilized. The chapter examines the work this displacement performs in the fiction of John Le Carre, the theory of Alain Badiou, the scholarship on the veil in France by Joan Scott, and indeed in Mahmood's conception of the Muslim woman and how it is entangled with aporias regarding the history of the subject and the limits of modernity.

The function of all these figures, and the discourses, critiques, and valorizations that have come to encrust them, is metonymic. They stand in for "good" and "bad" Islam, depending upon who is perceiving them and when. Even as their goodness or badness depends on rapidly mutating political necessities, the seesaw of good and bad Muslim seems inescapable.[3] At the same time, the binary simplicity of the discourse of good and bad Muslim, the ease of the assimilation of the language of good and bad in relation to Muslims, marks the ethical vacuity into which this historical moment continues to conscript us. In the third chapter, we see that the function of the preferred Muslim, now the anti-Rushdie, pious Muslim author, is performed by Leila Aboulela, whose novels I read as manifesting, even advocating, this new Islam. In a collapse that is a function of this new Islam and also one of its latest turns, the increasingly outmoded liberal desire for the heroic author and the more recent one for the pious, Muslim woman who can certify liberal noblesse converges in the pious Muslim woman as celebrated author.[4]

Yet perhaps most intriguing is the relation between religion and secularism in Aboulela's novels. For what this Islam, and its most intellectual proponents, also seek to inhabit is the privileged space of the critique of secularism in its colonial and ostensibly most Protestant guises. But what precisely constitutes religion or secularism in the novel is a question that enables a meditation on the very possibility of a surgical demarcation between religion and secularism, and, equally, between Protestantism and postcolonial Islam. I approach these concerns by posing the heuristic question, "Can there be a religious novel?," which takes me back to the history of the novel, the genealogy of the marriage plot, and the importance of the Protestant project of social reform to narratives of female virtue and piety. This exploration of the possibilities of the religious novel begins to approach the issue of blasphemy, which is taken up in chapter 4, "How Injury Travels."

If, as is well known, there is no precise equivalent to blasphemy in classical Islam, why has it come to play so central a role in the representation and (self-presentation) of Muslims, who are repeatedly figured as constituted by injury, which, in turn, slides quickly into blasphemy? This question takes us all the way back to colonial law in India and, even before that, to Warren Hastings's commitment to "conciliating" native sentiments by producing and stabilizing religious knowledge and religionized subjects.[5] It takes us also to the laws' exacerbation under Zia-ul-Haq, that great friend of Margaret Thatcher and Ronald Reagan and special beneficiary of the neoliberal dispensation, and then back to the present and the plight of the Christians, Hindus, Ahmadis, and Shias in Pakistan. For injury, in London and Denmark, is fundamentally linked to colonialism and processes of decolonization, state formation, and citizenship in South Asia. The postcolonial nation cannot easily be disentangled from the colonial bureaucratization of religion and the metropolitan management of immigrant populations. How are we to think the figure of the minority injured by free speech once we have followed the genealogy laid out in this chapter?

I concur with Saba Mahmood that the stakes, of what is presented as "blasphemy" in confrontations in Europe, are clustered around issues of iconography, more specifically, around the question of devotion to the Prophet of Islam. In Pakistan, the postcolonial state's management of icons, and of attachment to the Prophet, turns out to be crucial to the state's policing of the boundaries of Islam and in the process securing its own *conceptual* borders. Nations, postcolonialists hardly need reminding, are also narrations, and this narration involves a complexly deployed iconography. At the same time, as the very concept of the nation makes clear, both narratives and iconographies travel. The centrality of the management and narrativization of what constitutes the proper icons to the Pakistani state might prove to have been an inspiration to the attempts to introduce blasphemy laws in Tunisia and Egypt, suggesting that we need a reconsideration of what we mean by "local" or "global" practices.

Since tracking the relation between blasphemy and religious injury returns us to the colonial management of populations in South Asia, and its postcolonial and Cold War aftermath, it is perhaps unsurprising that powerful, theologically intricate, and iconographically complex reformulations of and responses to the state's capture of an iconography of Islam—and to the globalization of this capture—are to be found in the work of artists and writers from Pakistan and the Pakistani diaspora. In the two concluding chapters, I read the work of two Anglophone novelists, Mohammed Hanif and Nadeem Aslam—both of whom draw on the work of Urdu writers such as Saadat Hasan Manto, Faiz Ahmed Faiz, and Qurratulain Hyder, which is profoundly shaped by Partition—and the painter Komail Aijazuddin, who uses Christic iconologies from Byzantine, Renaissance, and Baroque painting to interrogate the status of religious minorities while making a claim for their devotional practices and for their capacity to make meaning through the use of iconographies opaque and inimical to the state.

I gather the work of these figures together under the rubric Cold War Baroque. Cold War Baroque is a profoundly poetic (imbued with Sufi poetics in the case of Aslam) and occasionally ironic (especially in the case of Hanif, who is a fine satirist) set of aesthetic imaginings of icons and iconographies poised against the cultivation of iconoclastic and (sometimes iconically) antiaesthetic branches of Islam by the U.S. and Saudi governments and third world nationalist and praetorian regimes. Close attention to their novels and paintings, and to the forms of critique present in their work makes available the link between mutually informing and constitutive *connection*, implying a set of global relations, and *flux* in connection, changing and indicative of shifting alliances.

Even as such performances extend the possibilities of thinking with and through literature and art, they produce complex understandings of the rapidity of changing events "on the ground," in the "War on Terror," and of the historical imbrications between the new enemies of empire and empire itself. Nowhere is this imbrication more evident than in the atrociously named "Af-Pak," where the historical intimacy between the Americans, the Pakistani secret service, and jihadi groups is now reconfigured as a war on the terrorists. The amnesia, as I argue at some length in the first chapter, is far too exculpatory. What would happen if we were to think of this as intimate and secretive friends—as the Saudis, Americans, and Pakistanis are indeed presented in, for instance, Hanif's *A Case of Exploding Mangoes*— turning on each other with a particular virulence? What is gained by forgetting the intimacy? By whom? A critical epistemology interested in these questions requires the capacity to address the chronotopic challenge of remembering histories in the midst of movement. Such an epistemology is enabled by the work of these figures.

If I take the impetus for my critical practice from descriptions and readings of art and literature, it is because the most intricate narrations, reformulations, and even contestations of this imbricated and *late* history are coming from artists and writers. The lateness is significant because at stake is a structure of infolding and exacerbation, of entangled skeins of discourses, laws, and political decisions. How to address such entanglement is an epistemological challenge that requires at least an attempt to address the connections in such a way that the intrication of parts is not lost. Whether I have come close to achieving such address is for readers to judge.

CHAPTER ONE

The Maintenance of Innocence

CLEANSING EMPIRE

The sun pours down over Lord's. A black man ushers one of Bollywood's most amiably round-faced actors out from a dark corridor onto the unconfined open field. The men embrace. The stalls are empty, but ball and bat are found. The black man—athletic but young, sweet, and unthreatening—bowls; the South Asian bats and hits what could be a boundary or a winning stroke. He raises his bat, acknowledging the applause of the absent audience in a gesture straight from Bollywood and bearing all the marks of its sentimentality and melodrama. Both are transfigured by joy. It could almost be a scene scripted by an acolyte of C. L. R. James.[1]

What the audience knows as we watch this vision from "Who Guards the Guards?" (2004), an episode from the popular British television show *Spooks/MI-5,* is that the scene is a moment of joy engineered for a former colonial subject by a defunct empire at war with itself. Danny (David Oyelo) is a junior spy for the MI-5, Harakat (Anupam Kher) is a Pakistani ex-militant under the protection, now, of MI-5 and under imminent threat of assassination by MI-6, because the head of the agency, unbeknownst to the team at MI-5, has made a deal with the head of the organization (Path of Light) to which Harakat belonged before he was turned by the British. The scene, offered as a kind of sports-pastoral, enacts a momentary restitution of Empire through a celebration of its gifts to its darker subjects: here the joy of cricket. This vision is far indeed from C. L. R. James: the comity between former imperial subject and declined Empire is poised on the erasure of the violence of imperial history not in any way upon its recognition.

The strategies of the erasure are carefully choreographed, in many ways clumsily obvious, and yet rather mesmerizing. They hinge on two figures, Danny, the abject black spy—yearning for the uninterested blonde, Zoe (Keeley Hawes)—and Zuli, an author based on Rushdie trying get a fatwa calling for his murder removed, played with devilish unamiability by the bald, round-faced Simon De Selva (whose features register as the evil double of Kher's). Of course, both Kher and De Selva resemble Rushdie. The show justifies Zuli's ejection from the story within the first ten minutes by transforming it into a self-ejection. As Zuli stalks off into the arms of his new ex-CIA guards, we are to see only his treachery.

The conceit that the MI-5 team is guarding the wrong man, the author, is introduced in the second scene and enables its delineation of a very particular world of Islam. Zuli meets Harakat, his friend, a bookseller, in order to get the fatwa removed. Danny is present to guard the author; there is an assassination attempt in which Danny rolls on top of Zuli in order to protect him. Harakat is a little wounded. As it transpires the assassination attempt was aimed at Harakat, not Zuli. The good British spies were protecting the wrong Muslim all along. Although one spy appears to be a critic, for as he surveils the meeting, before it is violently disrupted, he remarks with what is meant to pass as wit and comes across as the cringe-making labor evinced when the British national commitment to wit makes a citizen try too hard: "There's only one thing that worries me. The last thing we want is to keep Zuli alive long enough for him to inflict another one of his novels on us" (*WGG*). That critical wisdom is ratified when Zuli, furious at the attempt, and thinking that he was the target, threatens to call the Home Secretary and rejects the British spies in favor of retired American ones. Yet Harakat, disposable like all Muslims in the show, is murdered right after his treat at Lord's.

The world of Islam the episode delineates is a marvel of flat simplicity: a good (because turned and hence moderate) cricket-playing Islamist; a bad Islamist making deals with the evil head of MI-6 in (bizarrely) Hebron. A bad apostate author, indulged by the British government because of his uppity friendship with the Home Secretary, who does not have the grace to be grateful to his guards and opts instead for the ex-CIA protectors, thus securing his expulsion from the community of decency and morality into which the show attempts to claw its way. Bombs in Karachi and Peshawar. There are no women in this vision. No engagement with the world of Muslims outside bombs and fatwas, inconvenient (apostate) Muslims, good and bad Islamists, who, although they are Pakistani in this episode, could be in Karachi, Peshawar, or Hebron.

The episode is a significant marker of the refraction into the British and (global) imaginary of the "Islam" that is the subject of this book. An erasure of imperial history that mirrors fully the erasure of its colonial genealogy in this constitution of Islam is achieved through the episode's arrangement of the tokens of this Islam's symbolic economy—Islamists, authors, bombs, fatwas—and through its deployment of a favorite trope of postwar British spy fiction: the foregrounding of the ignorant, even thuggish moral unredeemability of the CIA. The concluding exchange between the heads of the two agencies reveals the moral necessity of the narrative of U.S. excess to the ongoing project of British self-exculpation, and to the fortification of postimperial "historical amnesia."[2] The show's recurrent critique of the special relationship, into which the contempt for the CIA is folded, is part of the renewal of British innocence. It continues into the Blair era what Stuart Hall identified as Thatcherism's forging of "new discursive articulations between the liberal discourses of the 'free market' and economic man and the organic theme of conservative themes of tradition, family and nation, respectability, patriarchalism and order."[3] Even as the episode in particular and the show in general attempt to expel the moral contamination of American power, aligning it with the corporations, they position Muslims within these new discursive articulations by attempting to reimagine Englishness as a morally agonized, helpless, and noncorporate counterpoint to American force in relation to Muslims. As such the show returns to what Hall has called "the unresolved psychic trauma of the "end of empire" by imaging English benevolence: "[Thatcherism's] reworking of these different repertoires of 'Englishness' constantly repositions both individual subjects and 'the people' as a whole—their needs, experiences, aspirations, pleasures and desires—contesting space in terms of shifting national identity and culture precipitated by the unresolved psychic trauma of the 'end of empire.'"[4]

In "Who Guards the Guards?" the special relationship is the instrument of the British renewal of innocence, which is, in turn, an attempt to overcome the trauma of the end of empire. It is an innocence asserted in a move that relies on an imperial history it simultaneously expunges. British intellectual superiority relies on knowledge of the world that lies beyond its own borders:

Oliver Mace (MI-6): If you're asking me is there at present anything we shouldn't do to achieve our ends? Then frankly I don't know. Post 9/11 we made a decision that nothing, nobody was off-limits anymore. Look around at what's been happening since Iraq. We're up against it. We can't say any more: this we do not do. In the long term we will be proved right as a strategy.

Harry Pearce (MI-5): Whose long term are we talking about?

Oliver: Before you get on your hobbyhorse, Harry, think about this: Do you think we did this alone, without help from Langley?

Harry: And that justifies it? Part of the reason for all this trouble is that most Americans think anything east of the Hudson is like those blank spaces on medieval maps where they drew in a monster and wrote 'here be dragons.' (*WGG*)

Harry Pearce's dismissal of American ignorance is, of course, an insidiously brilliant rearticulation of imperial history, for it hides the relationship of the reach of British cartographic knowledge to British colonialism. That knowledge is presented now as a token of British responsibility and offered as a corrective to the imperatives of ignorance underpinning the violence of American world domination.

Zuli's relationship with his ex-CIA guards can then reinforce this cleansing. His dramatic and unattractive exit into the protection of his ex-CIA guards allows good, benevolent Englishness—here imagined as a loosely liberal critique of Blairite collusion in the war—to secure itself by learning to love the right sort of Islamist. His treachery is fully mirrored by Harakat's gratitude. In the scene that is an important precursor to the scene at Lord's, Harakat gives Danny a Wisden 1913:

Harakat: I'm sorry for what Zuli said to you in that meeting, but he was certainly not speaking on my behalf. And gratitude is not one of his things.

Danny: Clearly. (*WGG*)

The emptiness of the confining room in which this exchange takes place reinforces the intimacy of the scene. Harakat is revealed as the true lover of books as he props the few he has been able to bring on a table to give the room a momentary sense of home. Within the confines of this shelter, which Harakat has tried to turn into an impromptu home, Danny's growing care for Harakat allows Harakat's gentleness to become visible to the viewers. That he remembers Danny looking at a row of Wisdens in his bookshop is an invitation to the reader to shift her perception and see the Islamist through his capacity for quiet attention. The reminder of the small, if affectively important, detail from the scene leading to the assassination attempt pulls the reader into an interpretive circle in which the tutelage of the Islamist is to make her aware of the limitations of her own ability to see—and read. Once added to the order of his attention, Harakat's love for cricket provides implicit testimony of the decency and redeemability that turn him into the right sort of British subject.

Danny's loyalty to England, combined with his yearning for the very white, unavailable colleague who is being kind to him to help him through a bad phase, makes him the racial subject who justifies the nation. His receipt of Harakat's gratitude and his anger at Zuli's ingratitude give cover to the show's imperial fantasy. The black man who represents the state shows it to be inclusive, just, and worthy of gratitude for its present multiracial and multireligious benevolence and for its past largesse—a historical benevolence that allows someone like Danny to be in England in the first place. At the end of the season, in the episode where he will sacrifice himself to save another spy from Iraqis bent on revenge in London, he tells the gun-waving man (who has already declared, "We are all Al-Qaeda now"): "You will never win. If I'd been born somewhere else, it might have been me holding the gun now. If you'd been born somewhere else, you might be sitting where I am. For all your talk about choices we don't get to choose those things. But I guess you were just unlucky because somehow you have lost humanity and now have no kindness or pity left in you."[5] Danny's presence ensures the eradication of any viable radicalism on the part of England's nonwhite subjects. The show sets up a choice between Al-Qaeda, the CIA lovey, or the grateful colored subject, who realizes that being in Britain is morally providential. Born elsewhere, he could, on the show's terms, have been a damaged, moral monster.

Abject and sacrificial, Danny is the cohesive element in a representation that domesticates James, offering an anodyne reconciliation between nation and racial subject, in order to imagine solutions to a series of problems in political thought, imperial history, and the management of populations in the former and current metropolises of Empire. Perhaps most significant is the solution the episode appears to offer to Euro-America's ongoing inability to bring its much-stated commitment to freedom in line with the dependence of its ascendancy in the world upon the conquest and enslavement of much of the planet. This ostensibly irreconcilable antinomy is to be worked out, not through a serious engagement with the rest of the planet, but by being brought in line with an internal game of state multiculturalism—in this case, facilitated by putting forward black subjects patronized by the state who are to manage other populations by ensuring their gratitude.

It is a vision that seems fundamentally opposed to the radical notion of politics and culture that was part of the project and conception of Black Britain, at least as envisaged by Hall, and a quick contrast with *My Beautiful Laundrette* is useful, for historical as well as conceptual clarification. The politics of representation in "Who Guards the Guards?" are far indeed from the critical epistemology that underlay Hall's notion of Black Britain and that allowed him to write: "*My Beautiful Laundrette* is one of the most riveting and important films produced by a black writer in recent years and precisely for the reason that made it so controversial: its refusal to represent the black experience in Britain as monolithic, self-contained, sexually stabilized and always 'right-on'—in a word, always and only 'positive.'"[6] "Who Guards the Guards?" presents an equivalence between the nonwhite characters of the show and yet disarticulates them as Muslim and black, flattening them through a sentimentalized relationship with Englishness while mediating their relationship through the state, whose Englishness is based on a whiteness that dispenses occasional inclusion. The nonwhite subjects can only petition for belonging and can have no relations with each other outside the state's mediation.

This vision is at a significant distance from that in *My Beautiful Laundrette*, in which British identity is presented as fractious and contested. Its response to Thatcherism's reorganization of Englishness is not merely to present British subjects as engaged in a dance of petitioning the state for inclusion, but instead to show the complexities and organization of Britons who already belong even if that belonging is not recognized by racists, who seek to shatter it through repeated and systematic acts of violence. In Kureishi's vision, there is no sentimental attachment to the virtue of any one of the subjects, no attempt to put on display a morality that will earn the generosity of the state or even the nation. This lack of sentimentality is evinced in the refusal to equate victimhood with virtue, in the refusal to produce racial violence as the alternative to virtue or to make the freedom from racial violence something that has to be earned.

Even the somewhat surreally rendered landscape of the scene—in which Omar encounters his friend turned temporary fascist, Johnny, after a long time, as he drives his affluent cousin, Saleem, and Saleem's wife, Cherry, home—is an antidote to any conception of an English pastoral. As the car stops, Johnny's band of racist punk friends surround the car and appear to crawl over it. One man moons the passengers, pressing his buttocks against the window. Johnny watches at a distance. Inside the car, Saleem is drunk and Cherry is annoyed.[7] When the racists surround the car she is also terrified. The scene is already darkly surreal, the frames claustrophobic; and then Omar, who has been looking bored and, as always, a little impervious, gets out of the car as he spots Johnny watching at a distance and goes to shake his hand. Matching visual disorientation with racial violence without erasing the aggression within the internal sphere, the film remains attentive to what Gayatri Spivak calls "the double bind." I take Spivak's notion to refer to the (impossible) necessity of inhabiting intimate incommensurables that govern being and social life.[8] In *An Aesthetic Education in the Era of Globalizalition*, Spivak lists a series of double binds. Here are some: between body and mind, "the uselessness of human life (planetarity) and the push to be useful (worldliness)" and, perhaps most pertinent in the context of this book, "between metropolitan minority and postcolonial majority perspectives" and those generated around gender, of which most tellingly she writes, "figure out the double binds there, simple and forbidding."[9]

The scene blurs the line between the "public" metropolitan sphere and the "private" one of immigrant domestic life—thus refusing to be determined by the double bind that invites the immigrant to hide any aggression within domestic life for fear of feeding the racism lurking outside the door. Omar's getting out of the car to talk to Johnny is a reminder of the porousness of the division between the two spheres (*MBL*, scene 4): he went to school with these boys; Johnny was once a friend and will become a lover. The force of this blurring lies in its claim that Omar no less than Johnny is English and the racial violence, fascism, and Thatcherism will have to be fought as citizens who belong, without letting the fact of racism abject those who are considered incompletely English. At the same time, as Gayatri Gopinath has argued in her fine reading of *My Beautiful Laundrette*, even as queer desire "re-orients the traditionally backward-looking glance" of diaspora, that desire allows Omar to remember the "barely submerged histories of colonialism and racism that erupt into the present."[10] Moreover, if Johnny's desire for Omar includes the desire to erase his own racist past, that desire also allows Omar to abject Johnny, as when he yells at him to come back to work (*MBL*, scene 12). Functioning through their mutual desire, the reversal of Johnny's relation of power to Omar is further enabled by Omar's participation in the new aspirational economy of Thatcherism.

My Beautiful Laundrette's response to the racism and to the Thatcherite project is to produce a structure of representation that simply denies any redemptive racial or sexual binary. As Gopinath points out, the world the film delineates has no space for Tania, or for a queer *female* subjectivity. In other words, queer male desire cannot function as a substitute for the restructuring of relations of patriarchy and heteronormativity that make queer female desire invisible, and the film is aware of this.

Within the Thatcherite political economy, the enterprising Pakistani businessman can hire an ex-skinhead to eject a Rastafari from the property where he is squatting. The scene is darkly comic and historically symbolic, particularly since the movie has given us a figure of the defeated leftist in Omar's broken and alcoholic father—a socialist journalist from India and Pakistan who used to counsel Omar's school friends to do something meaningful with their lives before the possibility of a left working together was taken away by Thatcherism. The room in which the Rastafari has been living has a long wall painted with a mural, a little reminiscent of a Diego Rivera mural, with hammers, sickles, and a large clenched fist raised in a Black Power salute. Against the backdrop of this wall, Nasser (Saeed Jaffery) tosses the Rastafari's things out of the window; and it is left to Johnny to ask: "Doesn't look good does it? Pakis doing this kind of thing?" (*MBL*, scene 9). If Johnny's question shows his own blend of confused racism (he can't get away from the term *Pakis*, yet is a little befuddled because he expects Pakistanis to be better to other marginalized racial groups than he has been), the exchange that follows is no less revealing of Nasser's opportunism and its aspirational relationship to Thatcherism:

Nasser: Why not?

Johnny: What would your enemies have to say about this? Ain't
           exactly integration, is it?

Nasser: I'm a professional businessman, not a professional Paki-
           stani. And there is no question of race in the new enter-
           prise culture. (*MBL*, scene 9)

In contrast to *My Beautiful Laundrette*, the visual world of "Who
Guards the Guards?" is simple: an open field signifying a liberation
whose English provenance is secured by cricket, a confined and anon-
ymously empty room of refuge, some rather obvious play on the ubiquitous surveillance cameras, an office space that is presented in the
hues of London's fashionable modern bars, and—across the series—
opening credits with much Bond-aspirational strutting presented in
spliced frames that are meant to make spies sexy and contemporary.
The list of the actors—Matthew McFadden, Richard Armitage, and
Rupert Penry Jones—who play the show's active leading spies makes
the importance to it of the sexual machismo of the Bond films all the
more evident.

The stylish formal flatness is reinforced by the flatness of the
political vision of "Who Guards the Guards?," which represents
the normalization of a conception of people with Muslim names
and of South Asian descent as always caught within the representational grid of this new Islam. Indeed the episode not only marks
the normalization of this construct but also puts on display its genealogy, precisely through its replacement of Zuli with Harakat—of
the apostate with the Islamist. Harakat's role as the good doppel-
ganger is achieved through the similarity of the actors' physiogno-
mies to each other and to Salman Rushdie, enabling a larger historical replacement of the literary author with the Islamist as the
preferred subject of left-liberal identification. That the Bollywood
actor, Kher, who plays the sweet Islamist, has connections to Hin-
dutva reveals yet another aspect of the flattening circuitry of globalization, in which Bollywood can stand in for the other world of
dark people, and that very citation is meant to display the cultural
noblesse of the metropole, even as the complexities of the internal
politics within "other" groups are rendered invisible through slip-
pages ensured through a system of racial identification that does not
permit political differentiation; both solidarity and tension are then
absent any political or historical content.

How we get from the representational politics of *My Beautiful Laundrette* to those of "Who Guards the Guards?" is perhaps best understood by turning to a striking paragraph Talal Asad wrote, ratifying and expanding a point made by the British intellectual Tariq Modood during the Rushdie affair:

> The term black, signifying all nonwhite immigrants and their offspring (West Indian as well as South Asian), is used equally by the left and the right in Britain. While for the right it implies a racial or cultural unassimilability, for the left it underlines the experience of racial discrimination and the determination to organize politically against it through a radically reconstructed cultural identity. But South Asians have begun to argue that in using it this way, both right and left share the assumption that South Asian traditions and identities cannot become part of modern Britain. "The drawback with 'black' used as a descriptive term," one South Asian writer observed recently, "is that it defines people not in terms of their own identity but by the treatment [of them] by others; the aspirational use [of black], on the other hand, overcomes this deficiency but at a price of making British Asians have to define themselves in a framework historically and nationally developed by people in search of African roots" (Madood [*sic*], 1988). This viewpoint does not reject the call for alliances in the face of British racism, but only the assumption that Asians must elaborate their identities in Britain along the same lines as do immigrants from the West Indies.[11]

Modood's rejection of the term *black,* even in its variant as naming a political aspiration, and its promulgation by Asad, raise a number of questions. It is not at all clear why Modood and Asad equate the Asian "elaboration" of their identities with an African "search" for roots. Why, in any case, is a "search" for roots attributed to the project of Black Britain? Why is a South Asian belonging in Britain taken to necessitate an elaboration of South Asian identities? And perhaps most pressing, since this is a position articulated around Islam and its presence in Europe, why is South Asian associated with Muslim?[12]

There is, of course, a larger contradiction in Asad's passage, predicated on the way he uses Modood's troubling dismissal of blacks as a group in search of African roots, locating as it does an absence at the origin of blackness in contrast to the generative source and civilization that South Asians can then elaborate, suggesting that Modood's resistance to the term is based on the simple desire not to be called "black." Asad's passage, however, makes clear that the project of Black Britain involved a "radically reconstructed cultural identity"—thus, as Asad seems to know, not a search for roots at all.

Moreover, Hall, for instance, insists on the importance of ethnic differentiations and specificities within the idea of Black Britain: "If the black subject and black experience are not stabilized by Nature or by some other essential guarantee, then it must be the case that they are constructed historically, culturally, politically—and the concept which refers to this is ethnicity. The term ethnicity acknowledges the place of history, language, and culture and identity, as well as the fact that all discourse is placed, positioned, situated, and all knowledge is contextual."[13]

At the same time, Hall recognizes the genealogical contributions of diverse aesthetic traditions in the new politics of representation: "the experience is certainly profoundly fed and nourished by, for example, the emergence of Third World cinema; by the African experience; the connection with Afro-Caribbean experience; and the deep inheritance of complex systems of representation and aesthetic traditions from Asian and African culture. But, in spite of these rich cultural 'roots', the new cultural politics is operating on a new and quite distinct ground—specifically, contestation of what it means to be 'British.'"[14] I have quoted Hall at length because of the way in which his conception of the project of Black Britain shows the diversity possible under the rubric. Equally telling are his ambivalent quotation marks around roots. Hall's is not a vision of recovery or quest for roots; neither for that matter is Paul Gilroy's position in *There Ain't No Black in the Union Jack*, the book Asad engages relatively extensively. That Asad is aware of this makes his presentation of Modood's position without qualification all the more significant, suggesting that the act of anthropological representation is here also performing a ventriloquial function.

Later in the book, reading a character in *The Satanic Verses*, Asad associates radicalism with being English and thus, on the terms he has established, damningly with inauthenticity and cultural betrayal: "But Mishal, born and bred in England, is already in a crucial sense English—in her manner of speaking, her attitude towards her mother, her sexual behavior, her dress, and her *radical politics*" (my italics).[15] This suspicion of radicalism is coupled with a rejection of literature and aesthetic practice, which Asad seems to associate, through the specter of liberalism, with inauthenticity. As interesting as the premise of Englishness as presumptively politically radical is the alternate view that South Asia, which is where Mishal's family is from, is, a priori, *not*. On this view, figures such as Ismat Chughtai, Saadat Hassan Manto, Sajjad Zaheer, Faiz Ahmed Faiz, and Josh Malihabadi, to pick only Muslim names from the modern Urdu South Asian literary tradition, did not exist, or were simply traitors. This does not even begin to address the question of the arrangement of attitudes—such as fluid sexual practices, questioning of gender inequities, rejections of the authority of the ulema, social defiance in general—that are now taken to fall under the rubric of radicalism in regional languages and in periods prior to the twentieth century. What would one do with a figure such as the seventeeth-century Punjabi Sufi poet, Bulleh Shah?

Asad continues to develop and expand and make ever more explicit his opposition to literary modes and aesthetic practices. The dismissal works through the performance of a suspicion about the development of literature as a concept in the eighteenth century. The very notion of the concept and its articulation in the West in the moment of Enlightenment thus gives it a suspect genealogy that allows a skepticism about literature to perform an allegorical rejection of Empire. In a later essay the value of Asad's skepticism about literature and aesthetic practice is secured by producing aesthetic practice as fallen through its association with industrial capitalism. Thus by 2011, relying on the assimilation of Foucault's "What Is an Author?" into literary criticism's autocritique in the 1980s and 1990s, Asad is able to take the antipathy to literature he had begun to develop in *Genealogies of Religion*, in response to the Rushdie affair, and draw a line from the development of the concept of the author and of the literary work to Modernist aesthetics' relationship with paranoia, which is also for Asad the pathology of Islamophobia. By the end of the essay, Modernist aesthetics, standing in for aesthetics in general, is shown to give us Islamophobia.[16]

The moves are quick, the argument gestural, but what remains unclear is what the relationship of the modern concept of literature is to (say) the historical Arabic or even Urdu notions of *Adab*, Arabic and Persianate poetic practices that precede colonialism, mimetic and poetic practices that intersect with Islamic religious practices in South Asia such as (say) the *marsiya* (a long poem commemorating the martyrdom of Hussain at Karbala often inaugurating the Shia *majlis*, a gathering of Shias mourning the death of Husain), *nauḥa* (a shorter poem commemorating the martyrdom to which South Asian Shias may flagellate themselves), or even *naat* (a poem celebrating the Prophet often recited at the *milad*, a gathering commemorating his birth).[17] The complex relationship of these poetic performances to practices of everyday sociality invites attention. The different mimetic registers to be found in them are rich and textured, and allow for a more planetary conception of the relationship between *poiesis* and life practices.

In the case of the *naat* at stake is a notion of mimesis in which the description of the qualities of the Prophet, the desire for proximity to him, and the believer's desire perhaps even to mimic him intersect with Sunnah. Yet even such practice is considered *shirk* (idolatry—more precisely the sharing out of God's attributes with others) by Wahhabis. I have encountered members of Sunni *dawa* movements who express their rejection of these practices precisely because they are perceived as instances of *shirk*. Such rejections are increasingly part of neo-orthodox attacks on customary religious practices. Asad's preference for the juridical forms of Muslim practice allows little room to think the relation between Sunnah and *poeisis* in a form such as the *naat*. Equally important to the question of the connection between *poeisis* and life practices is the challenge a form such as the *marsiya*, with its chronicle-like attention to the martyrological story, poses regarding the relationship between mimesis, repetition, and notions of truth in devotional forms, especially when those forms seek to relate a history.[18]

Asad's dismissal of literature and aesthetics is further fortified by Saba Mahmood, who aligns the antipathy of "progressive secular intellectuals toward those forms of religious authority glossed as traditionalist" with a "certain commitment to the poetic resources of the Judeo-Christian tradition—evident in a literary and aesthetic sensibility."[19] Forgetting the Western constructedness of the idea of the "Judeo-Christian," Mahmood assumes a stable separation between "Judeo-Christian" and Muslim traditions, which are then produced as constitutively antithetical to "a literary and aesthetic sensibility." Moroever, she argues that the precedents to this antipathy include Marx, and the universalist vision such aversion represents needs to be recognized for its "paucity and parochialism," especially as it is "currently cavorting with one of the most ambitious imperial projects in history."[20] The argument itself is hard to take seriously, both because of its historical elisions and because the intellectuals she implicates in the "cavorting" without bothering to engage or even name their arguments are Gayatri Spivak, Aamir Mufti, R. A. Judy, Emily Apter, Stathis Gourgouris, and, of course, (posthumously) Edward Said, some of the contributors to *Critical Secularism*, 31.2 (2004), the *boundary* 2 special volume, the only example Mahmood cites of a set of essays displaying the antipathy she frames.[21]

Yet the exorbitance of the argument is interesting for the way it connects literature, radicalism, Judeo-Christianity, and, in its earliest articulation in Asad and Modood's work, the willingness to accept the term *black* in an act of solidarity. Such a repudiation of the use of "black" in an aspiration to solidarity leaves little room for a rejection of the divide and rule pretense of disarticulation on display in "Who Guards the Guards?," which is absent any political differentiation and cannot imagine any *ethically* fractious contestation of identity from within. What we have is perhaps more properly understood as divide, rule, and *reaggreagate*. In the show's version of this pattern, dark people are divided as Islamist and black but then gathered back together as collectively other to whiteness; the purpose of the divide is thus to defang any united political opposition to the structures of inequity underpinning this reaggregation.

What is so striking about "Who Guards the Guards?," then, is how it takes the attack on radicalism and the antipathy to literature in this position and puts them to use in the project of the maintenance of imperial innocence, all the while displaying the crucial role it has come to play in the project of left-liberal metropolitan self-exculpation. In this conception, the author's books are replaced by the author as the more offensive target, the body substituting as all threatening dark bodies must for any thing the mind might produce; and the expulsion of the author can help Empire absolve itself as it continues its quest for a more quiescent dark subject, extending habits of colonial management while seeming through a complex historical alchemy to redress them.

Given Asad's implicit reliance on Foucault's "What Is an Author?," it is perhaps unsurprising that what seems to be at play is a new and inverted form of "the author function." The name of the author is now to disqualify the work of the author and instead certify the authority of the Islamist who is opposed to authorial excess and to the name of the author on the work itself—as Harakat says, equivocally, to Zuli in the one Urdu sentence in the show: "Agar āp un kitābon se apna nām hatā do ho saktā hai āp ke ūpar se shāyad fatwā hat jā'e" (If you remove your name from those books it could happen that maybe the fatwa is removed from your head) (*WGG*).[22]

ONLY LIBERALS DON'T LIKE SLAVERY

The figure of the slave is fundamental to Asad's and Mahmood's representations of orthodox (Asad) and pious (Mahmood) Muslims. Yet Asad's attempt to set up a binary in which Muslims can be seen as liberalism's other reveals a fundamental confusion about liberalism, most visible in his recurrent references to the slave. In *Genealogies of Religion*, elaborating on a relationship between God and the Muslim believer in which the believer is figured as a slave, he writes a rather remarkable sentence: "For liberals, a slave is primarily someone who occupies the most despised status, and therefore the institution of slavery is utterly immoral (conversely, to be considered fully human, creatures must own themselves)."[23] Much is collapsed here, but I shall point to what I find the most puzzling move: the equation of a Muslim as God's slave—which is the view Asad is advocating—with the *institution* of slavery. Why is the metaphor of theological slavery collapsed into the historical institution?

Asad's rather complicated position on slaves can perhaps be explored better by looking at an exchange between him and Abdullahi An-Naim, archived on the *Immanent Frame* website. One of the more striking passages is the following, in which Asad seems to think that slaves having some rights by which the masters had to abide in Sharia, as he conceives it, is something that ought to be explored, and developed:

> Nevertheless, there is also something about the *Sharia* which might be further explored—and I don't know whether you would agree— and that is that beyond the question of *musawa*, the question of equality, there is the recognition of a legal capacity, which in an important sense all persons, according to the *Sharia*, have. This is truly a universal principle, if you like. And that is that everybody, even those who are unequal, even men and women who have conventionally and traditionally been unequal, nevertheless have a certain legal capacity and certain, if you like, inalienable rights. They may not be equal rights, in the way in which human rights thinks of them, but nevertheless, they are inalienable rights. Even slaves had certain rights, and the master had to abide by those rights. And I think this is something that we could develop.[24]

It seems hard to countenance the thought that Asad is suggesting a development of a conception of unequal inalienable rights by which "a master" might abide in order to resist the (imperial) universality of human rights discourse, but that is what he appears to be advocating here. On offer appear to be inalienable rights with inequality. Does this, then, make inequality inalienable? What kind of law and what sort of state would a juridical structure based on developing the rights—or the legal capacity—of the slave produce? How would one conceive of a social ontology based on the development of an acceptance of slavery? Is one meant to exit imperialist uses, or developments, of human rights discourses by aligning oneself with a form of inequality fundamental to the formation of Western imperialism and capitalist modernity?

In the service of exploring Anglo-American liberal philosophy's ostensible commitment to freedom, Saba Mahmood, too, turns to the figure of the slave. At stake for Mahmood is liberalism's "unique contribution," which is the linking of "the notion of self-realization with individual autonomy, wherein the process of realizing oneself is equated with the ability to realize the desires of one's 'true will.'"[25] Mahmood's turn to the figure seems influenced by Asad but is framed within the terms of a more elaborate discussion of liberal notions of positive and negative freedom, both of which share for Mahmood the concept of individual autonomy, and come twinned with ideas of coercion and consent. Within the "topography of freedom" so delineated, in order for an individual to be free, her actions must be the consequence of her "own will rather than of custom, tradition, or social coercion." But within this topography even "illiberal actions can arguably be tolerated if it is determined that they are undertaken by a freely consenting individual who is acting of her own accord." It is within this discussion, then, that Mahmood invokes the figure of the slave by picking up on the analytic philosopher John Christman's discussion of the "happy slave."[26] As Mahmood puts it, Christman "considers the interesting situation wherein a slave chooses to continue being a slave even when external constraints are removed."[27] The servitude in Christman's discussion is to illumine the behavior of a woman who does not want to be free. The figure of the slave it turns out is conceptually fundamental to Mahmood's account of the pious woman who does not want freedom and in so doing challenges feminist notions of subjectivity.

I am reminded here of Mahmood's defense of her alignment of Nasir Abu Zayd and Abdulkarim Soroush with the Rand Corporation in response to Gourgouris: "My object of analysis, however, is not their motives or intentions but the discursive assumptions (about knowledge, truth, language) that underpin their methods and programs of reform. Might people be politically opposed and share a set of episte-mological and conceptual truths? Could one analyze this convergence *critically* without being accused of 'belittling' the heroes of our sto-ries?" (Mahmood's italics).[28] If Soroush and Abu Zayd do not share the politics of the Rand Corporation but do apparently share an epis-temology of secularism and politics, *and* if epistemology and politics can be separated in this way, why in the same essay are a number of intellectuals accused of "cavorting" with empire through their habita-tion of the hermeneutic of secularism? It is indeed the designation of this hermeneutic that allows Mahmood to clump together a literary and aesthetic sensibility, the Rand Corporation, Muslim reformers, "one of the most ambitious imperial projects in history," and eventu-ally even Spivak, Said, Judy, Gourgouris, Mufti, Apter. What dance is this that, though one may be politically opposed to empire, makes one cavort with it so; and how does one decline? Well, might one ask then: What does it mean for Asad and Mahmood to share—as I will go on to show in more detail—the discursive assumptions that under-pinned slavery and its attendant racial discourses?

What I want to focus on, in these invocations of the slave—to set up an ostensibly irreconcilable antinomy between liberalism and slav-ery by Asad and a partially reconcilable one by Mahmood—are the concessions to the terms of a liberalism that quite cheerfully erases a history of racial slavery from its own self-presentation. Slavery and liberalism, as is well known, were well entwined.[29] It is simply not clear what purpose such an erasure of racial slavery from an account of freedom serves. The metaphorical turn here both calls upon one of the most fundamental aspects of colonial modernity and effaces it in the service of producing a very particular and, it must be said, trun-cated account of the relation between liberalism and Muslims.

Let me put this another way, relying on Asad's formulation: Is it only for liberals that slavery is utterly immoral? If liberals do indeed dislike it, is slavery somehow redeemed? Or, to turn to Mahmood: What about the slave who does want to be free? What about the social collectivities that are formed to fight for freedom? Why per-petuate the discourse of the slave who does not want to be free, upon which the institution of slavery relied, without acknowledging the his-torical violences that attended it? Why, in other words, participate in philosophy's historical deracinations?[30]

It is well known that slavery relied on the narrative of the slave who did not want to be free, yet equally significant is that abolitionists, frightened of the Haitian Revolution and the figure of the rebellious free black, produced consoling narratives about the piety and gratitude of "Negroes" who did not want to be free.[31] Moira Ferguson has written powerfully of the effect of San Domingo on the work of Hannah More, whose "A True Account of the Pious Negro" tied up piousness with the desire not to be free. Ferguson's account is economical and helpful:

> The "Pious Negro" is a slave who is never freed. An "English Gentleman" who meets the slave in North America discusses slavery with him, only to discover that the Negro's Quaker Master is so kind that this unnamed slave does not desire freedom. Reading the Bible avidly has taught him what a "very great sinner" he is. After questioning the bondsman closely, the "gentleman" finds him "perfectly" charming, a man with a "heavenly disposed mind." In the course of this intimate dialogue, they grow mutually attached, the slave weeping because of God's mercy.[32]

The story manages moreover to justify Protestantism through a quick dismissal of "works." The Englishman quizzes the slave on his "notions of sin," the "nature and power of God's grace," and the "insufficiency of His works alone."[33] The slave's joy in discoursing with the Englishman about matters of faith becomes an occasion both for a bid for Protestant theology by slipping in the case for *sola fide* and for a Providentialism presented subtly through the use of "new world" as a metaphor: "he seemed like a man thrown into a new world, and at length had found company" (34).[34] Given the Christian nature of the company, the very presence in this new world allows for a narrative of tribulation ecstatically redeemed by the fellowship of Englishman and Christian Negro, which would not have been possible without the institution of slavery.

Another and somewhat similar attitude toward abolition can be found in Maria Edgeworth's "The Grateful Negro," which advocated the gradual phasing out of slavery. The grateful Negro of the title was the one who saved the whites from the murderous slaves, who, inspired by Obeah, seek to murder every white on the island. In Edgeworth's story the incapacity for gratitude marks the inferiority of human beings; in other words the ungrateful slave would justify slavery by demonstrating the inferiority of the black as a "species." The bad slave owner "considered the negroes as an inferior species, incapable of gratitude, disposed to treachery, and to be roused from their natural indolence only by force."[35] By contrast, the good master, the reluctant slave owner, who is good to his slaves, who repay that kindness with gratitude, "wished that there was no such thing as slavery in the world; but he was convinced, by the arguments of those who have the best means of obtaining information that the sudden emancipation of the negroes would rather increase than diminish their miseries."[36] Recognizing the inescapability of the institution of slavery and the protection it offered the slaves by contrast to sudden or excessive freedom, "he adopted those plans for the amelioration of the state of the slaves which appeared to him the most like to succeed without producing any violent agitation or revolution."[37] The capacity for gratitude is that which ensures that kindness (without equality or freedom) will elicit the self-induced annihilation of revolution. Gratitude is the antinomy of revolution.

According to Alan Richardson one of the aims of these stories was to make it clear to British laborers that "violent rebellion is associated with African savagery."[38] In Edgeworth's story this is evident in the defense of partial remuneration for slaves who are paid for extra hours they put in, in order to encourage them to work, a practice that is clearly meant to enable a defense of wage labor and simultaneously showcase to British laborers the desirability of their own condition. More strikingly, the fear of the black revolutionary locates the end of slavery in the self-overcoming of the white woman and man. There is something therapeutic in such an account of the slave who does not want to be free, or who is too grateful to hurt the white master, who can thus be enabled to overcome fear and (eventually) set the slaves free. Slavery will end, thus, when whites understand that the black slave need not be feared. Gratitude and piety make it possible for the master to overcome that terror. Perhaps most chilling today is the lingering presence of these codes and tropes within cultural and political discourse, as is so strikingly on view in the *Spooks* episode, "Who Guards the Guards?," and in the philosophical example Mahmood so casually uses.

The limitations and contradictions of historical liberalism cannot foreclose questions of emancipation, or the burden of reimagining possibilities of freedom beyond the limits of narrow construals of rights and property ownership. Following Robin Blackburn's account in *American Crucible: Slavery, Emancipation and Human Rights*, one might also consider the radicalization of Enlightenment thought in its popular manifestations in discourses of abolition, emancipation, and most powerfully the Haitian Revolution, arguably the primary event in radical anticolonialism, the influence of this thought on figures such as W. E. B. DuBois, C. L. R. James, Paul Robeson, and Frantz Fanon, to name just a few, and the attempts at producing a just decolonized order in "the Bandung conference of 1956, the Cuban Revolution and the emergence of the Non-Aligned movement."[39] For Blackburn, the development of civil rights and the (often abused and manipulated) idea of human rights are part of this frequently interrupted arc. Asad's equation (and *advocacy*) of the acceptance of the relations that underpin slavery with a rejection of "imperialist" human rights ironically confirms the aptness of the trajectory Blackburn lays out. One might well argue for the inadequacy of contemporary notions of human rights, their inability to address the larger structures of capitalist inequality and their instrumentalization by the imperial war machine, but responding to liberal philosophy's conception of freedom by resuscitating the figure of slavery as an ostensibly anti-imperialist alternative seems like a rather odd way of resisting imperialism. What might one call a hermeneutic that demands such resurrection?

The frameworks regarding religion within which these positions are embedded have acquired greater currency since September 11, 2001. Nonetheless, such an erasure of slavery as I describe is important not only because it reveals the recurrent elisions of imperial history and violence in recent discourse, but also because it forecloses a full recognition of the continuity of violence in the American order. That order and its continuing desire and project to remake the world require a recognition of the relations of American force, and the particularities of its historical relation to modernity and to the world. R.A. Judy has argued that: "America is both the realization of perpetual change and the preemption of change."[40] This contradictory attitude can be found explicitly in the Bush administration's foreign policy snuck in under the cover of the War on Terror. The change that cannot be permitted is, of course, the end to American planetary power; the change that is not only permitted but also necessary is the "annihilation of all organizations of life that escape or deny the ubiquity of the market."[41] Its annihilating energies are fundamentally antipathetic to the mind. Reckoning with that order and its economies of force requires an account of a longer *duree* in which the means by which it attempts to consolidate itself are attended to carefully. Such a reckoning requires, moreover, recognition of how its disregard of the mind is manifested, and of how the extinguishing force of that disregard has been repeatedly circumvented.

Figures such as Anthony Bogues, Hazel Carby, Colin Dayan, and Robert Perkinson have argued for the continuities between the practices in Abu Ghraib, Guantánamo, and Bagram and the historical practices of violence such as lynching, the horrific brutality of plantation slavery, the large-scale incarceration of America's population, the recurrence of practices from slavery via the transformation of the penitentiary into the prison system, the cultivation of practices of torture in Latin America.[42] Equally significant has been the engagement with French attitudes of counterinsurgency in Algeria, including the showing to soldiers of Pontecorvo's *Battle of Algiers* after September 11, 2001.[43]

If British national self-understanding requires an externalization of the violence of slavery and the erasure of its centrality to the development of the modern British nation and modern capitalism, if it requires a bifurcation of the historical reality of colonial modernity (slavery is what occurs elsewhere, and what the English gave their colonies was civilization, trains, and economic development), the American imperial project separates itself from that earlier history of colonialism by repudiating the British imperial masters. American Empire is anticolonialist! The erasure of the history of the Americas is achieved by the continuing production of new threats that can then be used to normalize practices of violence that have their genealogy in racial slavery and the attempted eradication of the Native Americans, who figure even less in such narratives, as if the Atlantic world, fundamental to the making of modernity, can be so easily cleaved.

Accounts of imperial attempts to remake the world require a serious engagement with these continuities and equally with the practices that seek to make these continuities invisible. The image-making that attempts to remake the world in its own image comes with elaborate, albeit frequently surreptitious, mechanisms and strategies of erasure. That these strategies come most often in the visual forms of film and television makes their grip on representation seem all the more insurmountable, playing as visual media so often do with the illusion that what we see is what there is. It is to the employment of such strategies in two films from the American cultural context that I shall now turn.

TECHNIQUES OF INNOCENCE

I would like to begin this section with a hypothetical question: What if Kathryn Bigelow and Mark Boal's *The Hurt Locker* had presented its vision of embattled alienation and boredom within a visual landscape of monuments and sites of cultural activity, with the bomb squad extracting and defusing bombs near or around Mutanabbi street (the famed street of booksellers), the Abbasid palace, the National Museum of Iraq, or the National Library?[44] The question I am asking goes against the grain of what has allowed the film to be seen as a "critical success": its almost complete absence of history and context, formally manifested in bare frames that present a stark and minimal visual field. The film's "realism," which seems to be comprised of a certain minimalism of action and visual density, combined with the documentary quality, reinforces the ennui that pervades it, punctuated with the sudden eruption of violent movement in the form of an explosion.[45] It offers boredom and its attendant alienation, tense and numbing expectation of the next explosion, and every now and then the explosion itself.

The Hurt Locker presents a vision of the grinding routinization of the encounter with death, and within this stark landscape Sergeant James, the maverick soldier, is an archetypal figure, who quietly brings an American past into this present. The man at the frontier getting on with the work of conquest is reimagined as just getting on with the job. His difference, which might in an earlier incarnation have made him turn against the system, go native, become a renegade of sorts, is brought in line with the compulsion, unstoppable and resistant to his peers, to work. The repetition, determination, and sheer stubborn talent turn the soldier into an exemplary worker— ostensibly devoid of ideology but gamely going about his work in a way that even his recklessness becomes an aid to it. The maverick is the remarkable soldier adapted now to the moment of a new perpetual warfare. Neoliberal warfare turns the technician into a hero, or requires the transformation of the hero into a technician. The tension between maverick as hero and worker as hero suggests that the self-regulation of the technician, the mastery of *technē* is the fundamental characteristic of the worker-soldier-hero. The qualities of the maverick can then be channeled into the conflict with the peers who cannot do their work because though rule-bound they do not understand its actual imperatives.

It is an extraordinary brew of alienation and work. Indeed, it is work that redeems war even if there is in the limited world of the movie nothing to gain, no prize at the end. What prize could there be? The landscape is either desert or urban dump and invites the suggestion that there is nothing to ruin here and no ruins to indicate a civilization or even an aerial attack. There was no bombing of Iraq, no sanctions, no slow destructive attrition of a population. Moreover, the urban landscape the film presents suggests that there was little to destroy to begin with. This absence, combined with the numbing routine of waiting and explosion, reinforces the impossibility of any engagement with the Iraqis. In Bigelow's own words: "You're in an environment I would call a '360-degree threat'—the guy on the third-floor balcony could be hanging out his laundry or planning a sniper strike, and you won't know until it reveals itself. I tried to capture that extremely random and chaotic sense."[46] This environment of a "360-degree threat" provides, of course, the formal pretext for not giving us any adult Iraqi with whom there can be the possibility of an equal engagement; yet James gets to show his virtue by befriending a little boy who sells DVDs, dubbed "Beckham"—for who else could he want to be?

But even that friendship reveals the impossibility of any true connection because of what Iraqis are doing to their own kind. Sergeant James's attachment to the little boy must end, for Beckham too might end up with a bomb stitched into his stomach. The fate of the other young boy Sergeant James confuses with Beckham, disfigured and murdered, with a bomb placed in his stomach, makes clear that Iraqis have only themselves to blame for their plight. The allegory is not subtle: Americans cannot *afford* to care for Iraqis. And yet American soldiers are being asked to live the terrible anomie and fearful danger of this war to protect these people. At the end of the film, as James returns for yet another interminable tour of duty, trudging out of the plane like a spaceman having to stomp his way across an alien terrain, we are to feel only the misery of that repetition.[47]

The Hurt Locker does not seem to be interested in history. Yet it matches an absence of the Iraqi past with a surreptitious resuscitation from the frontier: the refurbished maverick represents an updated version of the cowboy and reveals an abstraction of the history of the colonization of America, overlaying the threatening frontier—both the space of the attempted eradication of the Native American and of the imagination of a perpetual threat from those being targeted for conquest and extinction—with the desert. The domesticated maverick—now a good soldier—can restore the innocence of that past by being, quite literally, the defuser of violence, not its agent. The film extends that abstraction into a more general abstraction of time, which in turn facilitates an abstraction of war into work. The critical acclaim the film garnered has everything to do with its ostensible contrast with most Hollywood films with aspirations to action, for if those provide constant stimulus *The Hurt Locker* presents its very opposite: there is no visual clutter here, no abundance of action either. Those absences reiterate the absence of history, which the film manages to transform into nothingness through its rendering of the experience of time as vacant and endless. The emptiness of space and time are the open parameters of soldierly alienation, which could manifest itself anywhere. Iraq need not exist.

At stake in this abstraction of time is the maintenance of American innocence. Even as Empire renews itself it must seem always exceptional and always new, as we see in *Zero Dark Thirty*, the film that develops and elaborates Bigelow and Boal's vision. *Zero Dark Thirty* is a story of a loss of innocence, and in that very fiction lies its elaborate mechanism for the *assertion* of American innocence. The story's focus on and focalization through another compulsive, brave, maverick figure allows the figuration of American selfhood as exceptional, relentlessly individual, and in that very individualism never connected to the historical past of the nation of whose mythos it is nonetheless an exemplum. The twist in that exemplum is significant; for in the moral economy delineated by neoliberal warfare the model worker is also the hero(ine). The company woman is maverick. In this representation is revealed the paradox of this self, for it is an individualism without interiority. It is also an individualism that masters itself through the *technē* of work in order to produce results, and in the possibility of the achievement of such results lies the reproduction of such selfhood.

Jostling uneasily this driven emptiness and yet crucial to it is the narrative of the loss of innocence, which is presented but never explicitly named through Maya's story. We see it largely in the film's framing of her facial expressions and the haggard and stressed mien she acquires over time, but also in the fact that she was recruited out of high school and has only had one mission: to search for Bin Laden. The hunt for Bin Laden is presented very much as her thankless journey into a life inhabited by her search, despite the recalcitrance of most of her CIA superiors and the general bafflement of colleagues. The most striking sign of this loss is her induction into torture.

The introduction to torture in the film makes clear that the story of her loss is also an allegory of the state of the nation's innocence.

Perhaps the most striking claim made by the opening shot is that there is no continuity between life before and after September 11, 2001. The screen is a black blankness bearing the legend, "September 11, 2001," accompanied only by tragic and harrowing recordings of actual calls from some of the victims. The blankness obviates the possibility of any past other than the attack, which becomes the originary event of history—quite literally the "fall" from innocence and prelapsarian purity.[48]

The next shot bears the legend "2 years later," again on a black screen, and then we see a wooden ceiling, with a ray of sun coming through a small hole on which are superimposed the words, "The Saudi group." The camera tracks down to show an agent walking to the room to address a man with a cut and bruised face, abjection in his posture and in the angle of his hanging head. The transition from blank screen to a scene of torture signals a fundamental rupture in time. At the same time there is an association implied between the cries and the torture (*ZDT*, scene 1). The shot with the cries invites a moment of vengeful relief at the cruelty that follows, as it suggests that the suffering will not go unpunished. That the suspect, Ammar al-Baluchi, already looks broken, although his torture is not over and will go on for some excruciating cinematic time, is meant to give the audience some satisfaction.

In the beginning of the film Maya is seen to overcome gradually her aversion to witnessing the actual torture. She repeatedly struggles with the instinct to look away, as Dan inducts her into the process at her request. The film presents that request as an ethical and *feminist*—ethical *because* feminist—decision to confront the dirty necessities of her job and not leave them to the men. The film attempts to position the audience in the same ethical space: like Maya, the audience, too, has to learn not to look away. In fact, as the audience, in order to follow the narrative and the action, the viewer has to keep looking and thus become habituated to what is being shown. The film is teaching the audience the necessity of enduring the ability to *inflict* pain and degradation. We are to understand that the true victim is the torturer, made so by the historical viciousness of the tortured. The film's justification for the cruelty is on the surface a result-oriented one. It yields information. But the subtler justification is present in the equation between the cries and the subsequent infliction of pain.

The scenes of torture participate in a series of erasures that are central to the theme of innocence. In one scene al-Baluchi has a dog collar placed around in his neck. In another moment he is stripped naked in front of Maya. After Dan has just stripped off al-Baluchi's *shalwar,* so Maya can see his genitals, he leaves the room. She responds to the pleading man with the moral certainty of a nun: "You can help yourself by being truthful," echoing the moral economy of the torturer's refrain, "When you lie to me I hurt you" (*ZDT*, scene 3). Maya's relationship to torture is to ensure the replacement in the public imagination of Lyndie England. What is at stake is the rescue of white (albeit untypical) femininity, and even white feminism, from the taint of the Abu Ghraib photographs. Maya's education is to both explain England and replace her in the public memory. Dog collars and sexually humiliated men are now to be associated with the averted and austerely dutiful features of Jessica Chastain. At the same time, by being in any way associated with feminism, this attempted recuperation of a very particular and exceptionally privileged, if morally bankrupt, white feminism deals a blow to less solipsistic and entitled global feminisms.

The larger erasure is present in the wider debate about torture in which this film has become enfolded and which replicates the resetting gesture of the first shot of the film. The film's narrative of the loss of innocence is predicated on a deep forgetting of imperial history. Nowhere is that crafted amnesia more evident than in the transition of the first shot to the first scene. By being linked to September 11, 2001, the use of cruelty is presented as a cathartic memorial. The film's insistence that torture yields information instrumentalizes it, and at the same time its connection to September 11, 2001, gives that instrumentalization a powerfully affective moral cover, contributing to its normalization. Yet the most striking thing about the first scene is that the first thing Dan says to al-Baluchi is, "I own you Ammar. You belong to me." As he slaps him around the head, he continues: "Look at me. If you don't look at me when I talk to you, I hurt you. You step off this mat, I hurt you. If you lie to me, I'm going to hurt you. Now, now look at me." After a little more abuse and humiliation al-Baluchi is dragged and suspended, his arms pulled up and to the side (*ZDT*, scene 1).

The phrase, "I own you," which is, of course, a fairly standard one in contemporary American idiom, itself asks for philology attentive to the history of slavery. How did the phrase become so ordinary? What kind of a dead metaphor is it? What sort of death does the deadness of the metaphor signal? But here the metaphor is not dead; it is in fact resurrected although stripped of its original racial component and now abstracted in such a way that it can be redirected. Even if Dan does not own al-Baluchi, the government he works for does. For the audience learns that he will never be free. As if the film were engaged in some complex psychic acceptance of the argument, "When we abolished slavery, we did not abolish it unconditionally, but with the Thirteenth Amendment qualification that slavery is okay for prisoners: 'Neither slavery nor involuntary servitude, except as a punishment for crime whereof the party shall have been duly convicted.'"[49]

The important point is that after September 11, 2001, the techniques of torture practiced on slaves and then resurfacing in prisons can be cleansed of their historical shame by being repositioned within the ostensible necessity—moral and bellicose—of the War on Terror. Such repositioning can then facilitate the ongoing management of American innocence. The bid to legalize torture may have had its initial superficial, though nonetheless real, prompt in the need to protect and fortify the presidency and to shore up the doctrine of preemption, but an equally significant stake seems to have been in the production of the fantasy for a new generation of Americans that Americans do not "do" torture, even when we do. Cruel and unusual, may not, as Dayan has argued powerfully, be unusual or even considered cruel, but the fiction of the temporally unusual—of the rupture—allows for the moral normalization of cruelty which is thus no longer cruel. The concentration on the techniques of torture, Rumsfeld's attention to its details, was an attempt to transform it into work and facilitated that normalization to which, of course, the fiction of the moment of historical exception was crucial. The importance of September 11, 2001, as an originary event lies in its facilitation of the narrative of a loss of innocence, which narrative is more important for its *production* of an innocence that it suggests was there to be lost in the first place.

Within this framework Muslims are important to the extent that they can fortify this narrative in their imagined role as powerful opponents and attackers on whom these techniques can be justifiably applied. At the same time, that framework masks the dispensability of Muslims as a group, for if it were not that group, it would be (as it so often has been) another one. In other words, American power and exceptionalism depend on fictions of the specific iniquity of the group being targeted and at the same time function through techniques and habits of force and management that rely on the interchangeability of all targeted groups.

The film attempts to disarticulate the attack from Muslims, for the only person one sees praying is a senior CIA man. There are "good" Muslims to be found in the CIA. It transfers the antipathy needed to motivate the tension in the film on to Pakistan and the ISI. Pakistan, Maya says, is "kind of fucked up." Yet the film cannot resist marking Pakistan as unpleasantly Islamic, for in a remarkable (because subtle) scene we see Maya's sleep unpleasantly disrupted by the Azaan as she scowls, mutters in her sleep, and turns (*ZDT*, scene 2). The Pakistanis are called "Paks" in what is presented as the hip and efficient (it takes too *long* to say "Pakistanis") argot of the CIA bureaucracy, providing a bizarre twist on the derogatory British "Pakis" (*ZDT*, scene 2). The ISI, too, comes in for jabs at its recalcitrance, and yet nowhere is the CIA's former intimacy with Bin Laden or the ISI mentioned. It takes a rather stunning feat of denial to make a two-and-a-half-hour film about the search for Bin Laden, set in Pakistan, critical of the ISI, and mention Peshawar—or rather "Pesh"—several times without a serious engagement with the history that had Peshawar host a huge concentration of Western spies and that had the CIA work intimately with, and immeasurably strengthen, the ISI and, of course, fortify Bin Laden's fantasy of toppling the American imperium and governments in a number of Muslim-majority states. As I will show in the two concluding chapters of this book, it is left to writers like Mohammed Hanif and Nadeem Aslam, in novels such as *A Case of Exploding Mangoes* and *The Wasted Vigil,* to redress this historical imbalance, produce a double historical critique, and disrupt the exculpatory binaries produced in films like *Zero Dark Thirty.*

So impermeable appears the polarity between "us" and "them" set up in *Zero Dark Thirty* that any serious response seems inadequate, maybe even a little obscene. It is perhaps fitting that two Pakistani columnists, Fayes T. Kantawala and Nadeem Paracha, responded by dropping into an adolescent argot mocking the inaccuracies, stereotypes, and ignorance of the film—Arabic being spoken in the streets, camels in the setting sun, an incomprehension of how fortified the U.S. embassy is, the film's ignorance about the possibilities of luxury available in Pakistan. In a column titled "Zero IQ Thirty," Paracha, no fan of Islamism or of the use of religion by the state, responded by annotating pictures of scenes from the United States and from Pakistan with balloons, mocking the stereotypes the citizenry in each country has of the other.[50] Kantawala (the nom de plume of the painter Komail Aijazuddin, whose paintings I discuss in chapter 5), also a critic of the state and of the religionizing of the nation, dropped, as he periodically does, into teenage tabloid talk. That this tone is a choice is demonstrated by the fact that, a week later, Kantawala would go on to write a powerful and moving piece on the assassination of a Shia doctor and his eleven-year-old son in Lahore, demonstrating a capacity for a solemn register when so required. About *Zero Dark Thirty*, Kantawala wrote:

> "You don't understand Pakistan!" White Chick screams at her supervisor at one point. And you do, Carrot-top? I wanted to ask. You, who just said "shukran" at a "bar" at the Marriot Hotel after you were served wine in a margarita glass? You? The moment the Marriot Hotel scene came on I knew they'd blow it up. It seemed inevitable that White Chick would be in the one big hotel bombing there was. Don't worry, she glides out of the back door while stepping over screaming hijabans (what they are doing in the bar at the Marriot I don't even want to ask).[51]

The contemptuous and deliberately absurd responses of these columnists suggest that there is nothing one could seriously say to mitigate a vision that is so utterly predicated on the rightness of the powerful (who are conceived in the film exclusively as American) or perhaps on the power that is always right. Yet located elsewhere the writers see the willed (and willful) ignorance of the filmmakers as pernicious in its (for want of a more profound word) *stupidity*. It is a stupidity predicated on, indeed enabled by, the innocence allowed the powerful, who do not need to know anything about those whose lives they trample and whose worlds they destroy and who refuse to understand that such ignorance can be consequential.

So deep is the film's commitment to the rightness of the powerful that it offers a remarkable justification of the doctrine of preemption, through a transformation of the mission to capture Bin Laden into an ex post facto justification for the invasion of *Iraq*. In a scene when the decision is being made to get Bin Laden the conversation becomes about the role of certainty in political decision making. Maya is impatient with the conversation but says, "Hundred percent he's there. Okay. Fine. Ninety-five percent, since I know certainty freaks you out." Earlier on the following exchange has occurred between the emissary from Obama's office and an advocate for the mission:

White House Man: This is pure risk, based on deductive reasoning, inference, supposition; and the only human reporting you have is six years old from detainees who were questioned under duress. The political move here is to tell you to go fuck yourself and remind you that I was in the room when your old boss pitched WMD Iraq. At least, there you guys brought photographs.

CIA Staffer: You know you're right. I agree with everything you just said. What I meant was a man in your position—how do you evaluate the risk of not doing something. Hmm. The risk of potentially letting Bin Laden slip through your fingers. (*ZDT*, scene 11)

The film's commitment to American power transforms the decimation of countries into a problem from game theory. At the same time, the film consistently presents the "correct" choice as moral because it is associated with the embattled and thus somehow feminist austerity of Maya's commitment to the enterprise. It is ethical to destroy countries based on a possibility that a suspicion regarding them *may* be true, *and* the rightness of the decision in the case of Bin Laden reveals Iraq to have been a risk worth taking. In the alchemical moral world of power: they *could* have been right and thus were. A woman's centrality to the process merely helps catalyze the transformation.

The performance of the moral rightness of absolute American power is linked to one of the most intriguing things about the film: the need to make vivid the ongoing threat from those who can only be encountered in any extended cinematic way as subjugated. To confront so total a vision by "humanizing" Muslims, understanding neo-orthodox Islam, trying to explain Muslim thinking and reasoning seems thoroughly inadequate or even absurd. The world is divided into friend and foe, and the right sort of Muslim can be assimilated. That rightness is, in turn, mutable and dependent upon the instrumentalities of any given moment.[52]

Yet even the very notion of the foe is limited, for there is a mutability to that relation as well. The wrong kind of Muslim was once a declared ally: Bin Laden was a friend; the ISI and the CIA

were, shall we say, tight. The metaphor attributed to the Pakistani
military of the "used condom" to describe the U.S. disengagement
from the Pakistani state after the end of the Cold War illustrates
the sense of betrayal and abandonment that underpins the current
mutual antagonism.[53] The soured intimacy that underpins those
relationships requires a different way of conceiving of the current
state of global relations. *Zero Dark Thirty* suggests that forgetting that intimacy merely facilitates the perpetuation of American
force.

WHAT'S ISLAM GOT TO DO WITH IT?

In a review of Reza Aslan's *No god but God*, Tariq Ali—angry at
Aslan for calling the war in Iraq a "liberation"—goes after Shi'ism:
"The Shia sects and some of their more esoteric beliefs have little
to do with Islamic theology."[54] It is not clear why Ali feels the need
to define Islam in this way, but what is hard to dispute is that it is a
position motivated by a need to defend the insurgency. One might be
prompted to ask, is there no way to oppose the war short of redefin-
ing who gets to be Muslim?

Since September 11, 2001, the multiplication of the divisions of the
world into "us" and "them," in which the "them" is usually populated
with some kind of Muslim, has come from unexpected quarters in a
number of rather unusual forms. Judith Butler's circulation of the position that women deciding not to wear the burka in Afghanistan after
the Americans removed the Taliban is tantamount to a "decimation"
of "Islamic culture," too, participates in such a stabilization of Islam,
which is now only to be construed as an other to the United States:

> The fear of the speaker was that the destruction of the burka, as if it
> were a sign of repression, backwardness, or, indeed, a resistance to
> cultural modernity itself would result in a significant decimation of
> Islamic culture and the extension of US cultural assumptions about
> how sexuality and agency ought to be organized and represented.
> According to the triumphalist photos that dominated the front page
> of the *New York Times*, these young women bared their faces as
> an act of liberation, an act of gratitude to the US military, and an
> expression of pleasure that had become suddenly and ecstatically
> permissible.[55]

Yet again "Islamic culture" and Islam are being defined in opposition
to the United States, and—even less conducive to historical or social

nuance—the American media. Islam, Islamic culture is that which is not the United States. The solution to the ideological manipulation of feminism in the war is to turn the burqa-clad Muslim woman into a World Heritage Site. As I suggest in the next chapter's discussion of the current construal of agency and history in relation to Muslim women, women veil for all sorts of reasons, and the practice is enormously contested and diverse, so producing Islam through the veil or the very specific burqa is to (re)conceive Islam only in reaction to the West's current conception of itself, in this case regarding attitudes toward sexuality and agency.

But perhaps more important than the conception of "them" is the formulation of "us" or "we." In an admirable attempt to oppose pro-war American nationalism Butler writes:

> Perhaps we can hear, in a limited way, about the way in which the al-Qaeda group makes use of Islamic doctrine, and we want to know to shore up our liberal framework, that they do not represent the religion of Islam, and that the vast majority of Muslims do not condone them. Al-Qaeda can be "the subject," but do we ask where this comes from? Isolating the individuals involved absolves us of the necessity of coming up with a broader explanation for events. Though we are perhaps perplexed, by why there is not a greater public repudiation by Muslim leaders (though many organizations have done that), we cannot quite understand why it might be difficult for Muslim leaders to join publicly with the United States on this issue even as they condemn quite clearly the acts of violence.[56]

Perhaps the most striking thing about this passage is recurrence of the "we." Who are those it calls into its ambit? Who does it exclude? Is it the "we" of the nation, or of the liberals? If the "we" is the United States and its citizens, where do Muslims fit in that continuum? What, one might ask, is a liberal Muslim: a friend, a traitor, or simply an ontological impossibility? In this passage Butler is very much writing in the tone of someone persuading interlocutors who are part of the same fellowship, but the exclusion of Muslims from this fellowship, their absence from the "we," raises in turn some questions about the constitution of the nation and the imperatives of belonging. There have been Muslims in North America since before the Republic. To name just a few groups: there were Muslims among the African slaves, and one of the earliest slave narratives was in Arabic by a Muslim slave; the African American Muslim community is large; South Asian and Arab Muslim immigration significantly predates September 11, 2001.[57]

In what sense are those populations not part of the "we"? In other words, who precisely is the "we" to which Muslims and Islam are to provide the other? That such a designation must be slippery is easily evident, because in the very next paragraph it is implied that the Northern Alliance is within this pronomial ambit, suggesting furthermore that to allow the lines drawn in the war to be the parameters of what constitutes Islam only leads to a giddily perpetual and perennially opportunistic metropolitan redefinition of Islam.

An engagement with the question of American force, and the imperial remaking of the world in the interest of change and the market, might well call into question a national "we" in which Muslims are the other and a historical "we" from which Islamist groups are excluded as foes despite the centrality of so many of them to the Cold War. Such an interrogation might then lead to a broader consideration of a less pronomially divided planet, in which the relations of force are thought in terms that do not elide third world realities to privilege first world dispensations; it might also require a more sustained understanding of the intimacy of the historical relations of force that have come to shape the structures of American power and their transformative effect on "local" realities across the world, including those parts of it in which Muslims are a majority. Maybe the questions are not what do Muslims think or why and how can "we" redeem "their" humanity but rather how did the planet come to be so? And then might one ask: How did its becoming so go unnoticed by "us"?

CHAPTER TWO

The Echo Chamber of Freedom

The Muslim Woman and the Pretext of Agency

For it is against the grain of this responsibility of the national in the international that we feminist internationalists strain. I am thinking now of the worldwide group called Women Living under Islamic Law, extending all the way from North Africa to Indonesia with members from immigrant communities in the First World. These feminist internationalists must keep up their precarious position within a divided loyalty: being a woman and being in the nation, without allowing the West to save them. Their project, menaced yet alive, takes me back to my beginning. It is in their example that I look at myself as a woman, at my history of womaning. Women can be ventriloquists, but they have an immense historical potential of not being (allowed to remain) nationalists; of knowing, in their gendering, that nation and identity are commodities in the strictest sense: something made for exchange. And that they are the medium of that exchange. When we mobilize that secret ontic intimate knowledge, we lose it, but I see no other way. We have never, to quote Glas, been virgin enough to be the Other. . . . Cultures are built violently on the enforced coercion that they are. War is its most extreme signature, and, like all signatures, patriarchal. Our lesson is to act in the fractures of identities in struggle.

GAYATRI SPIVAK, "Acting Bits/Identity Talk"

WE'RE ALL INDIVIDUALS

"You're all individuals," cries Brian, the not-quite Jesus, of Monty Python's *Life of Brian*. "We're all individuals," chant the followers, who want to turn him into their leader. "I'm not," someone from within the crowd insists. "Shshhh," says someone else.[1] This could be read as a punchy but slight comic identification of a paradox, but it turns out to be part of *The Life of Brian*'s larger exploration of the theme of how a life might acquire a transcendent shape, and of what makes a prophet singular. The prophet is, after all, a figure who is chosen and who uses this status to give him a transcendent autonomy from extant norms. The prophet is also the figure who alters those norms—one might think of Jesus in the Temple or Muhammad smashing the idols in Mecca: antinomian, iconoclastic, and yet apparently acting with transcendental authorization. *The Life of Brian*'s governing conceit, that Brian is not Jesus but could well be, folds into an unexpectedly serious meditation on individual lives and the way they get caught in the mesh of history. Like the individual who does not want to be one and thus becomes one (if only in a moment that is both joke and paradox), Brian, too, is invited over, by circumstance and by those who would impose a shape upon it, to become singular, a prophet, at the end of the film: a martyr. As he hangs upon the cross, crying out that his crucifixion is the result of a terrible case of mistaken identity, he is claimed as a martyr by one of the Judean fronts, and the followers he has not sought, but who have attached themselves to him, sing hosannas, finding transcendent meaning in his imminent death.

The Life of Brian is a reflection on human pain. Brian's proximity to Jesus, and his simultaneous exclusion from prophethood, makes his crucifixion a judgment on Providence itself. For most people, including those who would have been on the crosses next to Jesus, life is painful happenstance, mishap, and inglorious accident. The final scene has all of those on the crosses singing "always look on the bright side of life." Brian's death is not a resurrection into a happier eternity, even if the scene of torture is read by witnesses, or by those who wish to transform his suffering into martyrdom, as a theodicean promise of hope. On the film's terms, Providence is a fiction that attempts to redeem human pain and the terrible violence of history; and the very fiction enables further violence. The song's changing refrain charts the ease of that slide: from "always look on the bright side of life" to "always look on the bright side of death."

Brian cannot refuse his suffering even if he is not a prophet. Perhaps the point becomes clearer when one thinks about the implications of the thought of what Jesus's death would signify if there were no claim of resurrection underpinning the theology of the passion. There is no Providence, and yet Brian is picked for crucifixion, and the only individual in the film is the one who refuses individualism. Suffering does not produce prophets, and individualism (the very "ism" implies a norm, something external to the person) does not produce individuals. The film strikes at a cherished ancient and a favored modern narrative of redemption. What links the two narratives is the presumption of singularity (of prophet and of modern person) under-lying both of them. The film's meditation on the figure of the prophet (on that which Brian is not) is resolutely anti-Romantic, indifferent to Enlightenment reason (what shape of history, what rationale, could possibly justify this?), and yet profoundly secular: the prophet is dis-placed in the film not by a secular Romantic poet figure but rather by an ordinary man. The film compresses a historical allegory into a joke-paradox: the man mistaken for prophet, collectively designat-ing a host of people individuals, who then assent in chanting unison, could well signify the modern age's slow banalization of the idea of the subject: from "true" prophet to Romantic poet- prophet to every-one is an individual. The moment refuses every historical step of this notion of the subject.

The Life of Brian showcases, in the odd abstraction of farce, cen-tral tensions in modernity and the paradoxes that come to mark the limit of the subject: Who gets to be an individual in the age of indi-vidualism? Is emancipation a necessity, and if so, how can one choose it? Indeed, how does one free oneself from freedom? These paradoxes are globally ubiquitous and consequent. In debates about religion, they have come to acquire a particular resonance, especially in the current encounter between Islamicate cultures and Muslim-major-ity societies and the West. Cultural works are increasingly anxious to stage their political implications. So, in a very different context, they erupt into the fury of the lead Islamist in *Snow*, Orhan Pamuk's political novel about the battles surrounding religion in contemporary Turkey. In the novel, Blue, the charismatic Islamist, cries, "There's a word Europhiles very commonly use when they denigrate our people: to be a true Westerner, a person must first become an individual, and then they go on to say that in Turkey, there are no individuals! Well, that's how I see my execution. I'm standing up against the Western-ers as an individual; it's because I am an individual that I refuse to imitate them."[2]

Blue articulates the problem relatively explicitly: imitation of Western norms lands one in the kind of group Western individual-ism seems to eschew on principle. But in *Snow*, the paradoxes are most evident in the decision of young women to wear the headscarf against state law, in the character Teslime's decision to commit sui-cide in order to claim the right to wear it and to claim thus the right to be freed from the "emancipation" from the veil, which the Turkish state has forced upon women.[3] The Islamists in the novel are the ones most determined to refuse the Kemalist state's Europhilic manipulation of the notion of secularism, but the male Islamists are also happy to manipulate the women's choice to wear the veil.

The historical situation to which *Snow* speaks so well is one in which the Turkish state has cast itself as Westward- looking in its project of brutal top-down and statist secularization. This has in turn helped coalesce a pan-Islamist reaction to secularism, freedom, and individualism and their ostensibly inherent connection with Western modernity. Of course, the discourse of individualism has always been entangled with the rhetoric of emancipation and freedom; and in the wake of September 11, 2001, it is virtually impossible to hear the word "freedom" without an entire colonial history, and the consequences of the encounter between Muslim societies and the West, being summoned. It is not news that the forcible imposition of a much-touted and entirely denied emancipation has frequently been an ideological justification for Western colonialism. Individualism and freedom can sometimes seem like the discursive struts upon which the entire edifice of contemporary imperialism rests. In the current encounter between the West and a range of varieties of Muslim practice and life, these notions have acquired an additional layer. They are the rhetorical sticks with which the West beats Muslims and calls into question the civilization of all Islamicate cultures; they have been pressed into service to "liberate" Muslim women, secularize Muslim culture, "save" the "Muslim world." In turn, the War on Terror has simply calcified an Islamist imaginary in which the lost power of the Ottoman Empire and betrayal by the subsequent Kemalist project loom large. If secularization and individualism have a negative face in a variety of Muslim contexts, it is because they are associated with Muslim imperial decline, Western imperial success, and Kemalist brutality.[4]

But Pamuk layers the choice to embrace conservative Islam within contemporary Turkey through differences of gender. The women's decision to veil very quickly gets manipulated by everyone. State-sponsored secularists, seeking to further consolidate their sponsorship by the state, and antistate male Islamists are both happy to use the women, and within their clash the choice to veil inhabits a precarious place. One of the young women seems to choose suicide as a kind of deliberate pride—no one can have the woman's body unless on her own terms. The explanation gets slowly more complicated through the many interpretations of those still living, but it appears that the female suicides attempt to subvert capture by all ideological sides and, sometimes, their families by refusing the world.

Self-extinction emerges as a refusal to surrender to extinction by someone else, as a tragically ironic form of self-assertion. What *Snow* suggests is something that we increasingly see elsewhere as well: notions of the subject, individualism, freedom, agency, change, and history (in other words, the ideas that are used to mark the boundaries of the West and that generate the most sensitized aporias of modernity) have come to cluster around the figure of the Muslim woman for whom the metonym is increasingly the veil. The Muslim woman is object of imperial rescue, justification for imperial warfare, Orientalist cipher, target of jihadist violence, and, increasingly, the discursive site on which the central preoccupation of our time—how do you free yourself from freedom?—is worked out.[5]

THE WOUND AND THE VEIL

Within the academic turn to religion, and the postsecularist theoretical machinery that has led this turn, the Islamic resurgence is the most sensitized node. Muslim women are perhaps the most visible emblems of this resurgence. In classic fashion, they have come to be seen by both Muslims and non- Muslims as bearers of Muslim identity. The veil, in turn, has become metonymic of Muslim women and of Islam. The "problem" of the veiled woman in Europe and America has generated a series of theoretical responses whose fascination lies primarily in their sinuous, creative, usually more philic than phobic attempts to deal with the anxiety generated by the veil and by the Islam it is taken to signify.

When Alain Badiou turns to Saint Paul in his attempt to find a personage in history who can satisfy the requirements of the search for a "new militant figure," he interprets Paul as a "subjective figure of primary importance," someone who can bring forth the "entirely human connection between the general idea of a rupture, an overturning and that of a thought practice that is this rupture's subjective materiality."[6] Badiou's aim is, in his own words, "to refound a theory of the Subject that subordinates its existence to the aleatory dimension of the event as well as to the pure contingency of multiple being without sacrificing the theme of freedom" (*SP*, 4).

Badiou's work is part of a larger project of left self-questioning fueling the theoretical turn to religion and reveals that one impetus for this turn is the desire to find precedents for successful change in history. The historical moment is ripe for a series of elisions. The Left's ideological crisis after 1989 is exacerbated by a paralysis in the face of the culturalist and identitarian challenge to left universalism, which, in Badiou's context, acquires a particular charge because of the confrontation between immigrants from France's former colonies and the French state.[7] The challenge to French identity—to *laïcité* and the asserted if not always honored ideal of republican universalism—posed by the counterassertion of a Muslim-identified politics in the form of the *affaire du foulard* spirals into a threat to the very possibility of a universalist politics.

Badiou's answer to these difficulties is to configure the French law banning the headscarf as a contribution to the Pétainization of the state: the law is an identitarian phenomenon that refuses the singularity of cultural difference even as it falsely universalizes its own identitarian proclivities. The "sorry affair" of the foulard reveals that the law is valid only for the French. The demand to integrate demonstrates that what is being produced is the "communitarianization of the public sphere, the renunciation of the law's transcendent neutrality" (*SP*, 9). The creeping Pétainization of the state recalls protocols that were once used to define the "Jew as the prototype of the non-French" (*SP*, 9). Within this configuration, the veiled woman is a challenge to the law. And this conceptual stretch is truly elastic: Paul's stand against the law both mirrors the situation of the veiled Muslim woman and supersedes it by offering a universal vision that absorbs difference even as it appears to preserve it. For Badiou, the Muslim woman and Paul turn out to be interchangeably antinomian, and Paul is, at the same time, a salve to the anxiety generated by the veiled woman in the European midst. Such communitarian categories as veiled Muslims must be subsumed upward into a more universal cancellation of the law, and for that Badiou's figure is Paul (*SP*, 8–9). The figure of Pétainization equates the Muslim woman with Jews in Europe, and Paul functions as the universal Jew who both represents the Jew and breaks the barrier of his identity: "How clearly Paul's statement rings out under these conditions! A genuinely stupefying statement when one knows the rules of the ancient world: 'There is neither Jew nor Greek, there is neither slave nor free, there is neither male nor female' (Gal. 3.28)!" (*SP*, 9). Paul is the solution to a historical, a conceptual, and a national crisis, catalyzed by the anxiety generated by the sensitized knot of culture, identity, the memory of Cold

War atrocity, and left failure, which the Islamic resurgence represents in the renewed age of empire. The happy secular use of a religious figure, such as Paul, as a solution to the culturalist problem ends up offering a diagnostic of a contemporary political anxiety.

Joan Scott's critique of the French law banning the headscarf takes her in a different direction. *The Politics of the Veil* offers a critique of French racism and links the outrage over the headscarf to a history in which the veil represents resistance to French colonialism. To the extent that Scott describes and analyzes a history of the French attitudes toward the veil, the critique is powerful enough. But Scott is not only interested in the secular French view of the veil, although this is indeed what she claims; she also has views about how Islam should be represented by those who have lived under Muslim regimes or who are Muslim themselves. An Iranian feminist is described as giving "sensationalist" accounts of life in Iran; others who support the law are said to have lived under Islamist regimes and thus to not understand the French context.[8] Significantly, their lives under Islamist regimes do not give them any access to knowledge; their experience only implicates them in a web of interest, which works to their discredit. As Scott represents the matter, in this French context, those who oppose the law and are ardent in their commitment to orthodox Islam assert their agency as they choose to wear the scarf. They get more space, their personal testimony is treated with far more respect, their experience and choice are valorized; they are the agents who get to represent Islam.

Scott is eager to minimize the possibility that there might be any coercion involved in girls younger than eighteen wearing the headscarf. Reporting on a study by François Gaspard and Farhad Khosrokhavar, she mentions the example of the "adolescents whose families demanded it as a sign of modesty, a way of controlling sexuality. This was a way of reworking tradition, a way of dealing with the chaos of urban life, and it allowed girls from orthodox families to gain access to public schools—schools, for example, or jobsites—otherwise forbidden them" (*POV*, 137). Here, when she does acknowledge coercion as a reason some young girls don the headscarf, that coercion is represented as a reworking of tradition, as a cultural therapeutic meant to mitigate the chaos of urban life, as if this somehow explains the issue away. One of the political effects of this manner of casting the matter is that when she says that honor killings are not, in fact, sanctioned by Islam, the position seems indefensible (*POV*,

66). Once coercion has been cast as a reworking of tradition, and tradition implicitly cast as Muslim in this hurriedly exculpatory way, there is no way of arguing that a practice that claims the sanction of a tradition associated with Islam is not, in fact, authorized by religion. It is hard to see how the transformation of religion into culture (implied here by tradition) can be superseded by a recourse to doctrine. As I understand it, there is no doctrinal basis for honor killings, but how is one to argue this in a discursive context such as the one provided? Which tradition, which cultural practice, gets to prevail? Whose interpretation of Islam is relevant in such a context? Who gets to decide between competing claims?

Scott acknowledges that there is, in fact, patriarchy in Muslim contexts as well. She is frequently quick to remind us, however, that this is no worse than the French case. At the level of the sentence, one can see the anxieties pervading her work in the following case from her report on Gaspard and Khosrokhavar. Another reason for the turn to the headscarf is that it is "chosen by young women as a form of self-protection, or as an expression of identity—a way they found to assert themselves in environments that endangered and discriminated against them" (*POV*, 137). The need to instantly equate self-protection with assertions of identity reveals that Scott cannot bring herself to write about what kind of danger would make the veil a form of protection on a French street. The reference to a threat from men who think women who do not veil are inviting trouble has to be quickly made equivalent with the threat of discrimination in a book that is already focused mostly on racism. Does the first kind of danger not even require a sentence of its own? Who is served by such haste?

But perhaps the most stunning moment of what ought to be called "the politics of no worse than" occurs when Scott claims that Islamic jurists who use the concept of *fitna* (the threat of female sexuality as a cause of disorder in the public sphere) have conceived a politics of recognition of the power of sexuality, unlike the French, who have a politics and culture based on the denial of the disorder brought on by female sexuality. A regressive concept in Islamic jurisprudence is rehabilitated because it is claimed to be no worse than French patriarchal norms. There is a sophisticated Orientalism here: the case of the Islamic jurist is used to show the limitations of the French case. The lives of Muslims are there to help make an ironic point about the West. I would like to borrow Achille Mbembe's language about the function of Africa in the Western imagination, not just because it is apt, but because it helps to register the ubiquity of such moves. What Mbembe says about Africa is still apt about Islam, more than twenty-five years after the publication of Edward Said's *Orientalism*: "Africa is the mediation that enables the West to accede to its own subconscious and give a public account of its subjectivity."[9] There is not much new about this practice, or even in my critique here, but what is so intriguing about the current discussion of Muslim women is how familiar it seems, even if the rhetorical garb is occasionally dusted and refreshed with some new theoretical ribbons. Perhaps *fitna* is additionally interesting to Scott because it offers a principle of sexual regulation appealing to a feminism suspicious of the manipulation of female sexuality. But if we think of the "positive" aspect of *fitna*, as conceived by Scott, we should also be able to consider its contemptuous and coercive force. Khaled Abou El Fadl, who has the honor of having been called a "stealth Islamist" by Daniel Pipes, points out that the concept of *fitna* is often at the heart of arguments that insist on the necessity of the veil and that discourses that exclude women from public life have "an obsessive reliance" on the idea.[10] El Fadl argues that it is not uncommon to find language of the following sort in classical commentaries that rely on such notions: "Since God has made men desire women, and desire looking at them, and enjoying them, women are like the devil in that they seduce men towards the commission of evil, while making evil look attractive [to men]. We deduct from this that women should not go out in the midst of men except for a necessity, and that men should not look at their cloth and should stay away from women altogether."[11]

This, then, is what a politics of the recognition of the power of sexuality can sound like. There are arguments to be made for the right of women to veil, but why filter them through a recuperation of *fitna*? El Fadl, it is worth pointing out, argues that the application of *fitna* to women emanates from a juridical tradition that is at odds with Islamic principles, early Islamic history, and the Qur'an. It is an argument that is often made. Whether one agrees with this or not, the fact remains that there are less regressive interpretations available than the ones Scott chooses to emphasize. The veil in the context El Fadl describes becomes the only thing mediating between (deserved) affront and safety. If this is a form of recognition, then what it recognizes, or perhaps more accurately *institutes*, is a notion of "uncovered" femininity as a magnet for evil, whose (inescapable) invitation is a source of disorder and must be contained.

We might say that Scott's reading of *fitna* is just an anodyne apology prompted by a panic about the fight about the veil. But, repeatedly, the very haste of Scott's apology in the book begins to smack of condescension. Does Islam really need that much help? Are arguments between Muslims simply irrelevant? Can coercive practices of subordinating women that seek Islamic authority ever be critiqued when they take place in contexts where Muslims face discrimination and where there is the backdrop of a brutal and long colonial history? Are secular or reformist Muslim feminists allowed to talk about patriarchal structures that draw upon Islam, or are they always to be subjected to disciplining by the metropolitan gaze, which, in Scott's case, exercises an Archimedean privilege derived from an American position external to France and to Muslim communities across the globe?[12] In other words, are Muslims always to remain caught between the distortions, misrepresentations, and bigotries of the media-empire-neocon complex and the high-minded apologias of this configuration's left-liberal critics?[13]

In an ironic inversion of the neoconservative hierarchy, the priority given to metropolitan concern, and postcolonial guilt, means metropolitan intellectuals get to anoint good Muslims and tar bad ones. They get to choose between those who raise acceptable concerns, and thus get to retain their Muslim status, and those who do not. A more counterintuitive consequence is that Islam and Muslims both become an undifferentiated block, despite the numbingly familiar and yet increasingly meaningless assertion that Islam is not a monolith—within the postsecularist universe, there can be no secular or anti-Islamist Muslims or Muslim reformers.[14] There is, in other words, a recurrent invocation of the plurality of Islamicate cultures and yet a continuous subsumption of most Muslims to the most orthodox kinds.

**

The desire to accommodate Muslims in Europe and make restitution for America's conduct in the War on Terror permeates John le Carré's *A Most Wanted Man* (2008). At the end of the novel, the left-liberal German lawyer, who works for Sanctuary North (a vaguely Christian organization that provides legal help to refugees and illegal immigrants), tries desperately to intervene as American spooks crash into an operation staged by German spies and violently rendition two

Muslim men. The men are a cleric and former Muslim Brother, Faisal Abdullah, who is (rightly, it turns out) suspected of aiding a militant organization outside Europe, and a young Chechen-Russian Islamist, Issa Karpov. The agencies know that Issa is innocent. After they have been driven away, the lawyer, Annabel Richter, stands on the empty street with a banker, who has also been duped into trapping the two men, and the good German spy who had hoped to turn Abdullah. In a final gesture of futility, Annabel places the scarf she is wearing back on her head: "Her scarf had fallen round her neck. Absently she lifted it over her head and retied it under her throat."[15]

The politics of *A Most Wanted Man* are impeccably European and left-liberal. The novel is indignant about America's handling of the War on Terror, of Britain's complicity in post–Cold War atrocity, and is sympathetic to the Chechen plight. Nonetheless, the real interest of the novel lies not in its rather European critique of the War on Terror but instead in how the plot becomes a vehicle for another kind of encounter, for which rendition is the negative frame. In this other encounter, the scarf that Annabel reties around her head in an ultimate gesture of failure is central.

Annabel is presented as a beautiful woman who disguises her beauty in masculine and deliberately desexualizing clothes. That she hides her body and has refused to make social capital out of her sexuality makes the veil she later puts on for Issa merely an extension of an implicit distaste for Western norms of sexual objectification. Early in the novel, she has donned the scarf out of "respect" for Issa, who gives her periodic lectures on her sex life and tells her that when they are married she will stay at home and have children while he undertakes her education. Issa seems arrogant, but she has the key to the apartment where he is hiding from the authorities while she tries to get him legal permission to stay in Germany. Annabel is from a very well connected German family, is, of course, legal, and thus, crudely put, has more power.

This is how le Carré has her explain her decision to wear the scarf in response to the banker's questions:

[*Annabel:*] "He's a Muslim. That's number one. Devout. So it's tough for him when he's got to deal with a woman lawyer." "But tougher for you, surely?"

"He asks me to wear a headscarf. I wear one. He asks me to respect his traditions. I respect them."[16]

Issa (the name is significant: he is as brutalized as the tortured Jesus, whose Muslim name he has taken) is presented as wounded, destroyed, and otherworldly—a child-man:

> Issa was lying on his mattress in his underpants, drenched in sweat and hunched on his side. . . . [H]e seemed unaware of Melik's presence. . . . Issa's upper body was a slough of crisscross blue and orange bruises. Some appeared to be whiplashes, others bludgeon marks. On the soles of his feet—the same feet that had pounded the Hamburg pavements—Melik made out suppurating holes the size of cigarette burns. Locking his arms round Issa, and binding a blanket round his waist for propriety, Melik lifted him tenderly and lowered the passive Issa through the attic trap and into Leyla's waiting arms.[17]

The novel contrasts the brutalized male, tortured in a network of prisons across Eurasia, deprived of his virility by a childlike frailty (Issa and, briefly, at the end of the novel, Abdullah), with the masculinized liberal European woman. Yet it also unites them in a strange equivalence. She may be more socially powerful and less likely to be arrested but is nonetheless helpless: she cannot prevent her government from colluding in this terrible war. In response to her own helplessness, the liberal woman can only don the headscarf as a gesture of "respect" for the innocent Islamist who is arrogant but yet powerless. In fact, his arrogance is presented merely as an effect of his brutalized helplessness. The novel allegorically recasts a sexually regressive Islamist ideology as merely a form of politically desperate bravado.

In order for this machinery to work fully, Muslim women, too, have to be imagined differently. The Muslim women in the story are either veiled like Leyla (the simple, devout Turkish woman who takes Issa in and is fierce in his defense) and Abdullah's ambitious graceful daughter (on her way to the London School of Economics) or raped and dead but still traditional, like Issa's mother, whose specter haunts the novel and, the implication is, modern history. Issa's very conception is an allegory for the birth of Chechen Islamism. He is the son of a Russian officer who subsequently falls in love with the young girl he has raped. Unable to have her (she is killed by her brothers for having been violated), he takes his son to Russia with him. Issa is simply a wounded son making restitution for the raped mother he has not known.

The women themselves either freely choose their empowering and comforting Islam or, in Issa's mother's case, are the absent victims of Cold War atrocity. At the end of the novel, Leyla, too, ends up in a Turkish prison, but we do not see her frail and destroyed. The wounded masculinity of the Muslim male is the spectacle that requisitions the veil into service as an emblem of respect. This "respect" is the name of the sentiment that tries to compensate for the helplessness of liberal opposition to torture and the War on Terror at the same time that it seeks to absorb the torment of women who are brutalized by the war, who have to see the men of their communities detained, renditioned, and tortured, and who may also have to endure their misogyny.

If le Carré cannot imagine any other Muslim woman, it is because he is channeling left-liberalism's intense anxiety about doing right by Muslims. This liberalism matches its own helplessness by focusing on the defeatedness of the Islamist. But that vision of defeat also displaces the contempt for women in Issa's version of Islamism. The white woman donning the headscarf in this way works as an erasure of struggles over patriarchy and misogyny in Muslim contexts. The symbolic elevation of that gesture in *A Most Wanted Man* is the cultural trace of that erasure.

**

The spectacle of humiliation and pain offered by Guantánamo and Abu Ghraib, to speak only of those visions of atrocity that are (partially) visually available to us (Bagram, renditions, and so much more seem more mythic because they are less present to the eye), is central to the way Muslim masculinity is now conceived.[18] The discussion of torture, its defense, its ostensible newness within American political practice, is part of the discourse of this war. In fact, as I suggested in the previous chapter, if there is anything that marks out the war, it is the attempt to legalize and justify torture—as if it is an aberration within U.S. state practice, as if it were not already a normalized part of the prison-industrial complex, had no genealogies in America's Cold War history (although one has only to think of the School of the Americas), and did not have a ready lineage available in practices from racial slavery.[19]

In *Terrorist Assemblages: Homonationalism in Queer Times*, her generally apt critique of the role of homonationalism in the War on Terror, Jasbir Puar remarks this history and its continuities with the current abuse of prisoners in Abu Ghraib.[20] Alongside Badiou and Scott, Puar's work showcases the growing importance of the claims of Muslim minorities in the West upon the global discourse about Islam, and, equally, of the merging of the concerns of these minorities with the discursive apparatus that has grown around the War on Terror. But what interests me is the way that Puar configures Muslim women, Muslim feminism, and anyone critical of conservative brands of Islam in her account. In her discussion of the Abu Ghraib photographs, she mentions the fact that photographs of women being tortured have not been circulated, perhaps, she suggests, because the exposure of the abuse of women would completely discredit the pretense that the United States is attempting to save Muslim women from oppression in its current wars (*TA*, 98). But, in a powerful and disturbing paper on the connections between lynching postcards and the Abu Ghraib photos, Hiram Perez has also raised the question of why critics of the U.S. government have tended to remain silent on this issue.[21]

I would like to suggest that the silence of the critics speaks to the way in which the vision of a wounded and destroyed Muslim masculinity is necessary as much to the administration as to its critics, not least because, within critical discourse, Muslim female suffering is too equated with a theoretically discredited rhetoric of female passivity. This has, of course, a general theoretical provenance and also a specific political one. In the political context, even describing Muslim female suffering at the hands of the torturers seems, counterintuitively, to feed on the ideological zeal of interventionist wars. More troublingly, the silence seems to emanate from a kind of discourse fatigue: the media talks about Muslim women suffering so much, the critics are just bored. Ironically, although women can no longer be seen as victims, and that prohibition fuels much of the theoretical critique of liberal feminism, Muslim men can. Although Puar points out the way in which the discourse around the images has worked to create a vision of Muslim masculinity as both flaccid and pathologically virile, and though she mentions the absence of Muslim women in these accounts, she reproduces some of these tendencies by (1) taking a characteristically vigorous and rhetorically fierce stand against all secular positions (which are usually also twinned with liberal as epithet) while absenting all Islamist ideology or Muslim historical complexity from her discussion, thus reducing the position of the Muslim male to only a tortured brown body (*TA*, 55, 60, 85–87); (2) using the critique by the Revolutionary Association of the Women of Afghanistan (RAWA) of the Feminist Majority's role in the war but then pointing out its complicity in a middle-class privilege that erases working-class Afghan women without offering any account of these displaced women (*TA*, 6); (3) speaking of Muslim feminists, who apparently refute what she reports as Barbara Ehrenreich's claims that "gender-segregated spaces are the product of Islamic fundamentalist misogyny," but then being unable to account for this work at all (*TA*, 59); and (4) asserting and then disavowing analogies between the turbaned Sikh body and the veiled woman in a long chapter on the Sikh male turban. The effect of this is to displace the veiled woman, who is, as we shall see, simultaneously turned into all Muslim women (*TA*, 181, 182, 200).

The sum of all this is to produce a vision of a striking absence of any contestation within Islam—in a range of Muslim diasporas or Muslim-majority societies—and, at the same time, a bizarre tendency to adjudicate between Muslims. The mandate is sheer, but it seems as if Islam exists only to reveal the fallenness of secular-liberal assumptions. Puar spends more time on the religious symbolics of wearing the turban than she does on any Muslim practice but is happy to make all sorts of assertions about Muslims.

Perhaps the problem can be rendered visible if we look more carefully at the terms in which she dismisses Ehrenreich, "who otherwise rightly suggests that linkages among misogyny, masculinity, and terrorism need further probing" (*TA*, 59): "Ehrenreich's assessment that gender segregated spaces are the product of Islamic fundamentalist misogyny (veiling is usually cited as the most egregious example of oppression by liberal feminists) ignores decades (centuries even, per Fatima Mernissi's work) of Muslim feminists arguing the contrary. As Saba Mahmood argues, this myopia is due to the inability of liberal feminism to conceptualize the agency of religious women unless it appears as a resistance to the nonsecular" (*TA*, 59).

It is a bit hard to unpack this, but it is important to do so. What is the myopia in question? Do Muslim feminists argue that gender segregation has nothing to do with Islam, or that it has nothing to do with fundamentalism, or that the veil has nothing to do with gender segregation, or that the veil does not necessitate segregation, or that Islam does not require the veil? This is not mere quibbling; the question is an object of some considerable debate. All these, and more, positions are possible. Many quite devout Muslim women do not veil, even though they are religious, and some veil for other social reasons. Many male Islamists in a variety of contexts do try to impose the veil, and a number of religious women do not like that. Mahmood's book, which is made to speak for all religious women, is about a particular group of neo-orthodox women.

This passage, however, affords an opportunity to open into a different history. The one article Puar cites in the footnote, by Lila Abu-Lughod, defends the burqa in Taliban-controlled Afghanistan as a "customary" Pashtun garment, thus attempting to delink it from Islam flatly construed.[22] On this view, the belief or religiosity of the wearer is irrelevant. So too is any enforcement of it by Taliban forces or the Northern Alliance—it is all just custom.[23] Abu-Lughod does not cite any of Valentine Moghadam's work on the role the Mujahideen played in the persecution of women refugees in Peshawar (the murder of the founder of RAWA, the poisoning of the wells of girls' schools) or the complicity of the CIA and the Pakistani ISI in sustaining disciplinary misogynistic regimes of gender segregation.[24] Neither Abu- Lughod nor Puar shows any awareness of the consequences of the role that the Pakistani state played in the cultivation of the "religiosity" of Pashtun Afghans.[25] For instance, in order to receive aid from the Pakistani government, refugees had to register with one of the Islamic parties. What does it mean to talk of custom in the face of such massive and brutal (multi)state-sponsored social engineering?

Puar's reference to Mernissi is particularly interesting. Presumably, she means to refer to *The Veil and the Male Elite*—Mernissi's attempt to reinterpret the Muslim tradition regarding the veil—to argue against the continued necessity of veiling and of gender segregation. But it is equally possible to read that book as a response to the orthodox aspects of the Islamic resurgence, especially when one recalls that Mernissi also wrote a pamphlet titled *The Fundamentalist Obsession with Women*. In this context, it is worth recalling that, in 1990, the group Women Living under Muslim Laws held a conference engaging with reinterpretations of the Qur'an, with the feminist theologian Riffat Hassan (who is happy to speak as a practicing Muslim but does not veil) as the keynote speaker, as a response to growing state religiosity in many Muslim-majority countries after 1979, the year of the Iranian Revolution.[26]

Is there a claim about Islam and feminism here, or is there not? Practicing and devout Muslims take many attitudes to the veil, and many of them, in fact, do not veil. Moreover, the discussion about the veil simply forgets other forms of covering that have been customary. One might think of the South Asian *dupatta*, which is worn over the shoulders but can be, and often is, used to cover the head. The most visible form of head covering current in the West (and grow-ing elsewhere), the contemporary hijab, has circulated rapidly in the era of neoliberalism and globalization. The homogenization it repre-sents is itself an effect of the forces associated with late capitalism. To reconstitute Islam only through such a position on the veil, or indeed through the veil at all, even when responding to a critic who seems to be doing that, seems puzzling. Muslims who do not practice are also known to refuse the veil. Secular Muslims (not all of whom are elite—there is a history of vigorous Marxism in many Muslim coun-tries) also do not veil. Abu Ghraib, it must be said, holds many secular Iraqis as well, given that there are many former Baathists there. Nor do cluster bombs, depleted uranium, and daisy cutters discriminate between the devout, the orthodox, the heterodox, the apostate, or, for that matter, non- Muslims, who also live in Muslim-majority coun-tries. (This is usually forgotten in most media and theoretical discus-sions.) A person from any of these groups might collaborate. The sec-ular/religious divide does not mean much in this context.

Puar's argument about the turban must be read within the frame of her discussion of Muslim women. She discusses the turban as an object that evokes hate and violence, marks Sikh men as bearers of communal identity in a reversal of the more common view that women are bearers of tradition, and leads to hate attacks that involve their feminizing subjugation. This reading works to displace the veil as the focus of attention. Queerness, as an optic, provides a discourse of alterity that consolidates the disappearance of Muslim women and replaces them with male Muslim and Sikh bodies, which are linked together by the figure of terrorism.[27] Puar's is a discourse in which an analysis of homophobic and racist ascriptions of sexual perversity to the "faggot" terrorist Muslim male can be made to recuperate the veil—by substitutive way of the turban—as the redemptive token of violated male bodies (*TA*, 87). Puar's way of queering the brown male body takes attention away from the obsessive imperial focus on the brown female body as an object of rescue, but that deflection, though somewhat welcome, reveals a disabling anxiety about succumbing to that imperial fixation. The project of producing (or preserving) a sub-stantive concomitant critique of misogyny and patriarchy becomes a casualty of an anti-imperialist anxiety. Empire and racism, pretty much as usual, get to call the shots.

Racist murder compounds imperial war, and death comes to have complete priority. In this death- and torture-determined world, misogyny and patriarchy can be recognized, but one is not to attend to them. The problem seems deferrable, not terribly urgent. There are greater violences to face, more suffering to contend with, more visions of pain to fight and banish. The telos (and there is a telos here) is always of afterward: after imperialism, after racism, after the end of pain, of death, perhaps when we are restored to some prelapsarian future.[28] Then, we are to imagine, other injustices and violences, more diurnal, less exceptional inequities, will be dealt with.

Returning to Badiou is clarifying. Another way to understand Badiou's celebration of Paul as the figure who reduces Christianity to a single principle ("Jesus is resurrected" [*SP*, 4]) is to see it as an attempt to resolve the crisis induced by the tortured body, to find a way to redeem suffering within a *telos* that appears to defeat death even as it, with devastating and, one can only hope, inadvertent irony, ends up enshrining it. For to the atheist (Badiou, though not Paul), resurrection can only be a metaphor, an idea, an emblem of utopia— and here utopia is not only literally no place but also now no time, a neverwhere of political symbolism. To read resurrection from within a universe accepted as godless (Badiou's) is to read it as consolation, not as hope, is to produce, at the same time, a devastating hollowing out of the object of hope, and to enable its reduction to something emptily therapeutic even if psychically sustaining. Worse: it is to produce it as mystification, as that which obscures the world. Resurrection is, at the same time, the cover for the death- and torture-induced paralysis of our present crisis, a figure of justice and of its permanent deferral, as if Badiou is trying to imagine a time after torture, after crucifixion at the hands of the imperial army. Paul is the figure who can make that time (of very long waiting) into an idea of hope, of grace, and of the cancellation of the law. He is the one who can transform the very instrument of torture into its own permanent cancellation and yet install it eternally. Can you resurrect those who are not dead? Should you resurrect those who were not tortured? This is both a deferral of ostensibly smaller injustices and a way of coping with intolerable suffering, a way of finding meaning in death, of unearthing moral consolation so that we can achieve a way to deal with the unbearable suffering of those who are now beyond our redress. For the battered body, the battered heart, or the mind quietly battling a thousand daily inequities, is no competition. We are left not just with an ethic but also an affect of crisis and of permanent postponement.

AGENCY, PIETY, HISTORY

When confronted with discomfiting parts of Islamist ideology, especially in relation to questions of patriarchy and misogyny, postsecularists tend to reach reflexively for "agency." Indeed, the term gets adduced with metronomic reliability whenever Muslim women, or the very possibility of religious injustice, are the object of discussion. For instance, in a hedged, yet revealing, sentence, Scott presents the gesture of donning the headscarf while contrasting agency and subordination: "Far from representing the subordination of women, these gestures demonstrated a desire for, if not the actual achievement of, agency" (*POV*, 139). Another instance: as part of a critique of the "activities" of a British-based queer group OutRage! Puar responds to one of its members, who posted "No Islamic State No *Shari'a* Law": "This latter conviction reflects queer secularity; it is inconceivable that women or queers could negotiate or have agency within an Islamic state" (*TA*, 17). Since Puar is speaking of law (Sharia) and of the relationship between agency and the law, it might be worth pausing here to supply the missing term: *rights*—that is, what the law allows or forbids. Is agency, perhaps, a substitute for rights? Does it mean giving up on changing the law? Agency, in this context, becomes the name of that which is exceptional, which exists in the crevices and interstices of the law. It is the law, which is always already (and apparently forever) given.

Both Scott and Puar draw on *Politics of Piety: The Islamic Revival and the Feminist Subject*, Mahmood's influential study of women involved in the *dawa* movement in Egypt. In this she seeks a more thorough understanding of the way neo-orthodox Muslim women inhabit trajectories of Muslim thought. But Mahmood (as is her ethnographic mandate) is more rigorous and thorough in her analysis of the reflexive registers, discursive engagements, and ethical practices of her anthropological subjects.

Although the ambit of the study is narrow, the theoretical apparatus of the work has proven its greatest draw, perhaps, because it is more universalizable and because parts of it are more familiar. By "theoretical apparatus," I mean Mahmood's familiar and frequent iteration of the importance of context, her commitment to being sensitive to difference, and her invocation of the local. The less familiar, and more interesting, part of this apparatus is Mahmood's treatment of the question of women choosing their own subordination and, in turn, being produced as agents by it. Mahmood has given us an account of this apparent paradox embedded in a non-Western culture, using poststructuralist and postmodern theories of subjectivity, embodiment, and agency.[29]

This theoretical apparatus is also part of Mahmood's attempt to face the conceptual challenge of writing analytically about Muslim women in a global situation in which they are repeatedly cast as victims of Islam requiring rescue by the West.[30] There are four crucial thematic struts of Mahmood's attempt to confront this situation: (1) a frequently iterated emphasis on the local, the specific, and on the importance of attention to context; (2) a suggestion that the analytical and prescriptive projects are merged in feminism and that they need to be uncoupled; (3) assertions now and then that Islamism and secular liberalism are imbricated; and (4) a rethinking of agency and subject formation. The last is, of course, the most theoretically weighty, and it is around this that the other emphases are made to revolve.

Mahmood is largely critical of the equation of agency with resistance in the liberal imagination. In order to execute her critique, she turns to thinkers who are more or less influenced by Foucauldian notions of power. She quotes at relative length from an essay in which Abu-Lughod criticizes her own earlier preoccupation with "explaining resistance and finding resisters."[31] The example of resistance Mahmood cites from Abu-Lughod is of young Bedouin women who wear alluring lingerie to challenge social norms. According to Abu-Lughod, such actions reveal that these women call upon alternate forms of power drawn from "capitalist consumerism and urban bourgeois values and aesthetics" (*PP*, 9).[32] To understand such acts, one needs to locate them within shifting and intersecting fields of power. Equally important to Mahmood is the question of whether the abstract valuing of acts of resistance such as these "impose[s] a teleology of progressive politics on the analytics of power" (*PP*, 9).

The figure most theoretically central to Mahmood, however, is Judith Butler. Butler's use of Foucault allows Mahmood to set the stage for her own position. She finds most useful two well-known insights from Foucault as processed by Butler: (1) that power ought to be understood as a "strategic relation of force," which saturates life and in turn produces "desires, objects, relations, and discourses" (*PP*, 17); and (2) that the subject does not precede but is instead produced by these relations, which are then necessary conditions of its possibility (*PP*, 17). This paradox of "subjectivation" is centrally important. The language is crucial: "the very processes and conditions that secure a subject's subordination are also the means by which she becomes a self-conscious identity and agent" (*PP*, 17). The understanding this enables is that a subject's forms of agency do not exist prior to or outside operations of power but are instead their very product.

Once such an understanding is in play, we can see that agency is not simply another name for resistance to domination but instead the "capacity for action that specific relations of subordination create and enable" (*PP*, 18). Mahmood emphasizes that processes of exclusion and Lacanian notions such as "abjection" and "foreclosure" are central to subject formation as understood by Butler. Butler's greatest virtue, then, is the challenge she offers to liberal feminists who privilege autonomy and the separation of the individual from the social. She offers instead the prospect of subordination—of something that might be the very antithesis of autonomy, and that has nothing to do with resistance—producing the subject. By critiquing and destabilizing the sex/gender division that had underpinned feminist thinking since the 1940s, she has also made it possible to destabilize the very notion of female desire of the nonsexual kind as somehow autonomous. At least, this is implicit in Mahmood's discussion. But as Mahmood sees the matter, although Butler's critique of humanist notions of agency and the subject is powerful, it is not antihumanist enough. For Mahmood, ultimately Butler, too, is too caught up in finding resignifications and subversions of norms as sources of agency. Her theory of the subject, and of agency, relies too heavily on an agonistic conception of norms. Butler's framework depends on an untenable dualism in which norms are assumed to be entities that are done and undone, made and resisted, instead of inhabited, lived, and practiced (*PP*, 23). Such a framework makes it impossible to understand how different groups of Muslims can agree—assenting to a norm broadly construed—that female modesty is a virtue but nonetheless argue about, say, the status of the veil. Mahmood's own awareness does not lead to an account of these various groups; instead, the people who interest Mahmood are the ones who argue for the veil. The reason for this is apparently theoretical: their embrace of the veil allows for a refinement of theories of the subject. The women she chooses to focus on interest her particularly because their use of the veil shows that it both creates and expresses modesty. They can demonstrate, in other words, the subject-producing capacity of the veil (*PP*, 23).

It is evident that Mahmood is aligning herself with a Butlerian tradition that is inspired by the sections in Foucault where he insists that the presence of interdiction and prohibition has been overstated in Western traditions of sexuality, and that, as a result, it is a mistake to think that freedom and resistance are necessary for the production of subjectivity.[33] But if Butler and Foucault are both committed to overturning any notion that interdiction might be limiting of the production of agency, that it might even be a huge discursive ruse, and if Butler wants to call into question notions that emancipation and resistance are necessary to the production of agents, to pose, indeed, such a conception as misguided liberal feminist fantasy, Mahmood is able to do Foucault and Butler one better and show instead that Butler, too, is too implicitly committed to the idea of emancipation. Butler's notions of agency, gender, and embodiment are simply not theoretically austere enough, and to understand this one has to turn to the instantiation of the Islamic resurgence that can be found in the mosque movement she studies in Egypt.

In addition, Butler's draw is that she offers a critique of liberal feminism in the manner of Chandra Mohanty, Abu-Lughod, and Marnia Lazreg (figures Mahmood claims as important precursors), but her version provides a theoretical update of these figures by adding a queer analytic.[34] Mahmood relies on the queer critique of feminism and of liberal feminism's normative reliance on the idea of "woman" and of its consequent inability to recognize the constructedness of gender. Her project, then, is to mount a claim for Islamist female agency from within a queer critique of liberal feminism by framing the issue in a way that interrogates how gender norms are constructed, inhabited, and perpetuated.

But this relies on a peculiar process of doubling and alienation evident in Mahmood's ostensibly contrapuntal discussion of Butler's understanding of the drag queen's relation to norms. Mahmood argues that, unlike the drag queen, whose success in approximating heterosexual norms of femininity poses a challenge to those norms, the mosque movement participants' "excellence at piety" (*PP*, 164), which is performative, behavioral, and yet creative of subjectivity, in fact consolidates those norms.

Moreover, the effort drag queens pour into improving their performance nonetheless requires a disjuncture between what is "socially performed and what is biologically attributed," and is, indeed, "necessary to the very structure of that performance" (*PP*, 164). On the other hand, for

the mosque participants, the "relevant disjuncture" is between "a religious norm (or ideal) and its actual performance: their actions are aimed
at precisely overcoming this disjuncture" (*PP*, 165). Mahmood goes on to
discuss these contrasts within the framework of explicating and discussing Butler's theory of embodied performativity that is so central to her
own project. This longish discussion is meant to elucidate

> the range of productive questions that are generated through an
> encounter between philosophical "generality" and ethnographic
> "particularity"—an encounter that makes clear the constitutive role
> "examples" play in the formulation of theoretical concepts. More-
> over, an analysis of the historical and cultural particularity of the
> process of subjectivation reveals not only distinct understanding of
> the performative subject but also the perspectival shifts one needs to
> take into account when talking about the politics of resistance and
> subversion. (*PP*, 167)

It is not at all clear why the politics of resistance and subversion across
different cultures are made to be at stake in this discussion. Mahmood has chosen to talk about drag queens in the West versus Islamist
women and not drag queens from Egypt versus those in Butler's discussion. The claim about cultural particularity affecting theoretical
concepts seems strange. Why stack the question of whether a performative subject can work to consolidate norms by introducing historical and cultural difference? The contrast has little to do with culture
or history and everything to do with different spheres of action within
a culture: orthodox, revivalist women, on the one hand; drag queens,
on the other. Mahmood sets up the contrast this way because she
needs (1) a notion of culture as stable and different (despite numerous
disavowals; the occasional references to the imbrication of Islamism
and secular liberalism that do not seem to get developed are part of
this practice of disavowal); and (2) the queerness of the drag queen to
transfer onto the mosque participants. In the process, she erases the
Egyptian drag queen completely.

Mahmood's is a complex procedure. The mosque participant is
surreptitiously queer because, like the drag queen, she is distant
from Western norms of heterosexual femininity. At the same time,
she is an emblem of cultural stasis because she is irreducibly culturally different from the drag queen and the consolidator of norms of
an inherited discourse. Although Mahmood says that she wishes
to refine theoretical concepts, presumably by putting some pressure
on the kinds of examples used, by choosing to talk about alterity

through the figure of the mosque participants, and not Egyptian drag queens, she actually exacerbates the difference, sacrifices an understanding of fault lines within cultures, and thus makes the culture seem monolithic. She could, for instance, compare drag queens across cultural divides and religious women involved in church groups committed to heterosexual norms of femininity with the mosque participants. Those comparisons then could be placed against each other. By comparing consolidators and destabilizers across cultures, we could have a different understanding of those who transgress and those who consolidate norms within a culture and thus have a more nuanced account of cultural particularity. To put this another way, we would achieve a better understanding of what is particular about cultural particularity.[35]

The way that culture can become the mediating term in this discussion shows that the spatial distance and claim of difference are crucial. The women of the mosque movement can be antinormative by being alternatives to Western norms and entirely, comfortably, consolidating of "Other" norms. They serve the appetite for antinormativity by being agents of another normativity. They destabilize notions, assumed to be Western, of freedom, resistance, and emancipation by demonstrating an alternative relation to norms, by ontologically resisting and challenging Western conceptions of agency, that is, just by being who they are. The very fact of their alterity frees them from Western conceptions of freedom.

As it stands, Mahmood's procedure can satisfy the demands of a poststructuralist-inspired queer theory (by appearing to correct it from within) and a more intellectually mainstream, multiculturally inclined liberal Anglo-American political and moral philosophy (by seeking to correct it from within). Mahmood's discussion can thus elicit the following quite stunning blurb on the back cover from Charles Taylor: "Mahmood carefully unpacks the distortions that common modes of liberalism and feminism impose on the Muslim world. She combines richness of description with theoretical sophistication to provide insight into the struggle of some Muslim women to live their faith in the face of not only Western liberal influences but also Arab nationalism and political Islamism." For Taylor, these women are both entirely exceptional (victims of common modes of liberalism and feminism, Arab nationalism, political Islamism, and Western liberal influences) and completely emblematic (in seeing what is being done to them, you can see what is being done to the "Muslim world"). It is worth pausing here to ask: What are the acceptably uncommon modes of liberalism and feminism Taylor has in mind? Is the "Muslim world" in this imaginary immune to history, where the "influence" of ideas can be so easily externalized? That is: Was it always Muslim? All of it? Is Islam more indigenous to, say, Africa (parts of which overlap, after all, with the Muslim parts of the world) than Christianity? What is the relation between philosophical indigeneity and time?

On the question of culture, the tensions in Mahmood's work run deep. This is perhaps most interestingly evident in the manner in which Mahmood adjudicates between two different responses to what she calls the "compulsory norm" of heterosexual marriage in Egypt (*PP*, 168). She presents the example of Nadia, a woman from the mosque movement, advising a fellow participant to consider a proposal from a married man to become his second wife. Mahmood presents Nadia's explanation that there are tremendous pressures on single women within the culture. So, although Nadia does not much like polygamy, it does offer a solution to an asphyxiating social norm. By way of contrast, Mahmood offers the example of a self-declared secular woman, Sana, who is also single but who has chosen to seek "self-esteem" and solace in her work.

This comparison then becomes an opportunity to explain that the practice of *sabr*, roughly meaning "to persevere in the face of difficulty without complaint" (PP, 171), does not signal passivity as the secular subject, Sana, might think but is instead "integral to a constructive project: it is a site of considerable investment, struggle and achievement" (*PP*, 174). As Nadia has already presented the matter, Job, known as Ayub to Muslims, is the example to cultivate, not because he tried to "rise above" his pain, but because of the way he "lived" affliction and hardship (*PP*, 173). Mahmood concludes this segment by arguing:

> Neither Sana nor Nadia could pursue the project of reforming the oppressive situation they were forced to inhabit. The practice of *sabr* did not hinder Nadia from embarking on a project of social reform any more than the practice of self-esteem enabled Sana to do so. One should not, therefore, draw unwarranted correlations between a secular orientation and the ability to transform conditions of social injustice. Further, it is important to point out that to analyze people's actions in terms of realized or frustrated attempts at social transformation is necessarily to reduce the heterogeneity of life to the rather flat narrative of succumbing to or resisting relations of dominance (*PP*, 174).

This account seems to take the unchangeability of social expectations of marriage for granted. The inevitability of the humiliation, disenfranchisement, and loneliness is assumed. Polygamy is one panacea; work, simply another. Sana's solution and the language of self-esteem are clearly meant to link her to the West. The problem with finding resistance or talking about succumbing to domination is, moreover, *aesthetic*: the narrative it produces is flat.[36]

Now it seems from this account that Mahmood is merely adhering to her commitment to uncouple the analytical and the political. What she has shown, with the detachment she is also asking her readers to cultivate, is that neither a religious nor a secular orientation can guarantee social reform—or so it seems. But one has to look to an article by Mahmood, "Secularism, Hermeneutics, and Empire: The Politics of the Islamic Reformation," which I discuss at some length in the previous chapter, to see that her larger project does not just entail asserting an equivalence between the religious disposition of the mosque participants and a secular orientation; it is, instead, to discredit secular and reformist Muslims altogether.

Mahmood attempts this in the article by showing that "secularism" and "reform" are part of a "hermeneutic" advocated by George Bush and the Rand Corporation.[37] As a result, Muslims who advocate reform from within a religious (Abdolkarim Soroush is one example she gives) or secular (Nawal El Saadawi) framework are complicit with U.S. imperialism. The attempt to discredit these thinkers is almost subtle, as it comes in a bit of theoretical wrapping: Bush, Soroush, and El Saadawi are to be yoked together by a shared hermeneutic. It seems not to matter that El Saadawi might have had the commitment long before the U.S. government (once a devoted cultivator of right-wing Islamism), or that Soroush was once a fervent supporter of the theocratic Iranian Revolution and that he continues to work from within a religious framework. But what the example of El Saadawi reveals is that Mahmood's project is not just to promote a better understanding (as is her frequently iterated contention) of the agency of the members of the *dawa* movement; it is to undo the project of any kind of secular feminism as an agent of social reform in Muslim contexts and at the same time to mount a defense of the most conservative varieties of Islamism by mounting a critique of reformist Muslims.[38] Given the long and vibrant history of feminism in Islamicate societies and the sheer number of Muslim reformers out there, this requires some serious footwork.

One could argue that this is simply diaspora trying to have the last word, or, on the other hand, trying to absolve itself of its guilt for its own complicity with the institutions of empire. After all, each one of us in the diaspora is catering to a Western audience. We are paid for this service, exist in institutions of unprecedented comfort for academics, have research grants, and speak to audiences that consume what we say with a relish that depends on the vagaries of metropolitan discursive fashion. But to acknowledge this complicity does not, I think, buy us an exemption from this privilege. Self-consciousness itself is merely one more swirl in the ever-tightening gyre of reflexive sophistication, enlisted for an exemption it cannot bestow. There is no escape from complicity. Deferring judgment, or displacing the (self-)accusation of our privilege onto those who have refused the status of émigré intellectuals, simply secures our own privilege, buys our pardon, at the expense of those elsewhere. At the same time, the way that discourses circulate, the context of creation, does not have to coincide with the ambit of reception. Arguments that seem to be responding to conditions "here" can have consequences and influence elsewhere.

There are many unexceptionable claims about, and even brilliant interpretations of, practices of piety in Mahmood's book. Agency can be produced out of subordination; choosing subordination can be an exercise of agency; agency is not just comprised of acts of resistance but can consist of modes of inhabiting norms. Female desire does not have to take emancipation from religion as its object. Practicing modesty by veiling can produce an interior experience of the trait. Mahmood's behaviorism is sophisticated and even persuasive. However, her project exceeds the ethnographic specificity, value, or accuracy of these claims. One might contrast it with Lara Deeb's fascinating and more specifically located study of Hezbollah women, *An Enchanted Modern: Gender and Public Piety in Shi'i Lebanon*.[39]

But perhaps the largest contradiction in Mahmood's work lies in the claim of uncoupling the political and the analytical. On the one hand, Mahmood describes the ethical emphasis of the mosque participants as political only because it has elicited the ire of the state and of some political Islamists—so it is largely apolitical but the way it is opposed by explicit political players imposes a politics upon it. Ironically, her vision of her subjects simply repeats a conception of the politically transformative effects of feminine domesticity that Nancy Armstrong has shown to be part of liberal feminism's version, or manipulation, of female virtue.[40] The mosque is the space that allows a personal ethics to flourish and yet stay personal, even as it appears to have a larger communal aspect to it. At the same time, Mahmood wants to protect this vision of self-subordinating piety on larger, more global, political terrain by claiming that any critique of Islamist views of women's roles in the order of things is dangerous in the world after September 11, 2001. The ease with which feminist critiques of the Taliban were used in the war means, moreover, that any critique of inequalities of the status of women in the Egyptian context is "recruitable" by empire.[41] The slide from Afghanistan to Egypt is odd, especially once one remembers the frequency with which Mahmood invokes specificity and local context.[42] There is, moreover, a certain Pollyannaish innocence about what defeats empires in this vision. Mahmood simply underestimates imperial opportunism. Obama's insistence in Cairo that America would defend the right of women to veil even though he has escalated the "Af-Pak war" shows that both religion and secularism, veiling and unveiling, reform and conformity, can be, indeed have been, recruited by empire. Trying to change one's position every time empires do leaves one tilting at very swiftly turning windmills. It also places an insultingly secular cast on a deeper religious question. Presumably, if one is indeed religious, one does things, or tries to, regardless of what expediency demands and because one is trying to live as God wills. This position is simply not sensitive to the piety of which Mahmood is otherwise such a powerful advocate.

What we see, then, is that Mahmood is not concerned so much with uncoupling the political and the analytical as she is with reframing the analytical in such a way that any position critical of conservative Islamist ideology appears as political because it is political in the wrong way. So that any criticism, whether from within (by secular, progressive, or reformist Muslims and feminists or non- Muslims in Islamicate societies) or from without (by internationalists expressing feminist solidarity), that does not bend to the more conservative claims of the Islamic resurgence becomes political because cast as interventionist.

A clue to this project lies in her claim that there is a problem with the imposition of a "teleology of progressive politics" upon analytics of power. Perhaps the claim Mahmood wants to make is that feminism ought not be progressive at all. Talal Asad, whose antisecularism underpins much of Mahmood's position, has written that he does not see what is intrinsically wrong with conservative projects.[43] If that is indeed the case, perhaps the real question Mahmood and Asad want to pose is whether we should be persuaded by a politics that is progressive. It is also not at all clear what teleology means in this context: is it a desired outcome or merely an inevitable one? What is the desired outcome attributed to progressive politics? What precisely does the word add other than a mild fog of disreputability?

It is not interesting to say that Mahmood's discussion of the participants in the *dawa* movement or her larger critique of secularism (which she tends to equate only with liberalism, as if there have never been Marxist or left manifestations) is relativist.[44] It seems to be, but, in these antifoundationalist times, most of us are relativist in the sense that we do not usually think that there are metaphysical grounds on which the superiority of ideas, cultures, or social practices rests. Neither is it academic habit to explicitly connect metaphysical concern with social observation. In Mahmood's case, what is more interesting is the way she elevates certain practices and discursive preferences within a culture to the status of "the culture" and the processes by which she attempts to secure these practices from critique.

REDEMPTIVE ANTITELEOLOGIES

Within the postsecularist universe, history is local. It is, as Dipesh Chakrabarty might put it, "History 2," which interrupts the "totalizing thrust" of a conception of history governed by teleology and necessity.[45] It is antiuniveralist, antiliberal, anti-Western, antinormative, fundamentally anti-Hegelian. One of the attractions of this antiteleological approach to history is that it refuses the idea that conquest, the destruction of lifeworlds, the eradication of peoples, untold human suffering, can be justified by a notion of progress. Crucially, the objection is not just epistemological—it is not merely to the notion of a rigid causality being imposed upon contingent events—it is ethical: it refuses a redemptive account of suffering and exploitation.

In the conversation I discuss, there has been a transfer effected from history onto agency. Increasingly, agency stands in for antiteleological history, and, at the same time, it is now the redemptive term. It sanctions the present and justifies suffering. Like most redemptive terms and practices, it absolves even as it redeems. It is the coin used to buy a way out of the irredeemability of human pain and worldly injustice, the term to which we turn when we want to be helped out of our sense of futility and absolved of our complicity in structures of privilege. Change in history is not needed; there is always, we can tell ourselves, agency.

Increasingly, in theoretical discussions about religion, Muslim women are the pretexts for working out a series of tensions in contemporary thought. They have become the site upon which a cluster of wrinkles in liberalism is ironed out. The current discussion rotates the conversation about freedom, seeming to eschew it, and makes the very notion seem like an imposition. Muslim female agency reveals the Western imposition of freedom to be manifestly enslaving, without ever needing to make a resistant move, or so the positions I have described seem to assume—all the while, as I argued in the previous chapter, relying on tropes from the history of slavery. The way Muslim women have been used to provide moral justification for the War on Terror has made it easier to yoke these concerns together. If the West uses the rhetoric of freedom as the bludgeon to "save" them from inequity, if Sarkozy wanted to ban the burqa, the inequality is either not there or it is trivial compared to other suffering. What Muslim women require most is to be freed from "our" freedom.

In a striking and possibly inadvertent concession to the Bush Doctrine, academic discourse seems to have fallen into the habit of treating September 11, 2001, as the inaugural of history. There is a tendency thus to see the structure of repetition and exacerbation that is the present as historically exceptional. There is a simultaneous tendency to see all coercion and injustice, across cultures and time, as commensurable—no worse than. We are asked to sign on to a theory of absolute commensurability (between coercions) and occasional differentiation (between coercions). I want to contrast the commensurating impulses I have been discussing with the very different sense of coercion in the lines I quote from Gayatri Spivak in my epigraph.[46] Part of their power lies in the gesture of solidarity with which Spivak ends this essay, produced around the time of the first Gulf War. Today, that gesture seems almost outmoded in its commitment to a (complicated) internationalist feminism. But these lines and that gesture also remind us that it is crucial not to succumb to the discourse fatigue that fuels the vanguardism of many (including queer) forms of antifeminism. For Spivak, no less than for many postsecularists, all cultures are coercive ("cultures are built violently on the enforced coercion that they are"), but for her this does not translate into a license to halt a critique of a culture because it is, has been, or is being colonized. Neither does it preclude the project of trying to attain and create the conditions to be able to achieve the possibility of "uncoercive rearrangements of desire."[47] White men may be trying to save brown women from brown men, but brown men may indeed oppress brown women, and brown women (elite and otherwise) may also collude in sustaining structures of misogyny. (One may try, among other variants, Muslim and non-Muslim in this sentence.) As these lines suggest, another way to approach the question of coercion is to strain, and always to register the costs of that straining, in a colonized world, against coercion within the culture colonized without exempting colonial culture or imperial institutions. The precarious, precious enterprise of double critique means, then, that feminist concern—within colonized, postcolonial, decolonized, reimperiled cultures, diasporas, societies, nations—cannot be postponed. The project of imagining change from within the double bind of identity under conditions of conquest and war is not new. The War on Terror has done much to complicate the enterprise and little to obviate its necessity.

The project remains as menaced as ever and . . . incomplete.

CHAPTER THREE

Religion and the Novel

A Case Study

LITERATURE OR RELIGION?

In current discussions, it sometimes seems as if conversations about religion can take place only as fights about literature. One need look no further for the reason than the Rushdie affair, which was central in the consolidation of the Muslim political presence in Europe and served as a vehicle for the expression of many of the disappointments of the (mostly South Asian) immigrant experience in Britain. The kind of protest that started with the burning of *The Satanic Verses* in Bradford, has become a template for expressions of militant Muslim anger elsewhere in Europe, in such controversies as the case of the Danish cartoons. The polemics, controversies, and apologetics that have followed these events have helped consolidate a notion of a transnational Muslim polity constituted by offense and injury.[1] Rushdie's positions subsequent to the fatwa have not helped matters at all.

If the publication of *The Satanic Verses* in 1988 was a catalyst in the political consolidation of Muslim militancy in Europe, it was also crucial to the renascence of academic discourse on religion. In his hugely influential *Genealogies of Religion: Discipline and Reasons of Power in Christianity and Islam* (published in 1993), Talal Asad devoted not one but two chapters, in the section "Polemics," to the Rushdie affair.[2] Of the critiques of Rushdie, and of secularism, generated at the time, it is Asad's that has proven most conceptually influential, possibly because of the theoretical register of his work.[3] He has emerged as one of the most important critics of secularism.

According to the religious turn initiated by Asad, literature has taken over the functions once performed by religion and, at the same time, has targeted religion for criticism, indeed, for insult and parody. Even as literature continues to perform this category-confusing, attack-and-mirror maneuver, it is misunderstood as stably secular. For Asad, *The Satanic Verses* provides a particularly stark example, for this slippery move is precisely what the novel executes: it claims an unassailable status, as a work of art, that is itself a version of sanctity and at the same time attacks the very notion of the sacred (*GR*, 285–91). As if that were not enough, the novel's British reception demonstrates the way this doubleness fuels an intense social and political hypocrisy; in the leap to defend Rushdie from Muslim outrage, critics, writers, and even politicians demanded a respectful secularism from politically weak immigrants even as they asserted the sanctity of literature (*GR*, 269–306). Immigrants were, and are, required to assent to this sacred status in what is nothing so much as a tacit pledge of allegiance, a social contract imposed by national aesthetic fiat (*GR*, 239–306).

Asad's recognition of the hypocrisy and sanctimoniousness in the British reception of *The Satanic Verses* is useful enough, but it is subordinate to his greater conceptual commitments: to the identity of something called modernity with liberalism, to the idea that the sanctity of literature is one of the joints of the modern and the liberal, and to the project of recuperating political religion. In Asad's argument, modernity, the West, anything secular, liberalism, literary culture, and even antinomianism, are made synonymous through a series of displacements. He presents those who are outraged by the book's blasphemy as non-Western and repeatedly designates the Muslims (secular and otherwise) who object to the protests and the threats of murder as Westernized (*GR*, 278–88). And for that designation one might, without too much trouble, substitute "collaborator." Britain's more conservative Muslims stand in as symbols of a host of non-Western lifeworlds, and literature emerges as the lifeworld-flattening juggernaut of a catastrophic colonial modernity. As I suggested in the first chapter, Saba Mahmood does not distinguish between literature and criticism, tracing them both to "the poetic resources of the Judaeo-Christian tradition," which are in turn just a disguise for a colonial secularism.[4] In her argument, anyone committed to any kind of secularism, or to reform, is in bed with the Bush administration's imperialism; the rhetoric has become so inflated that it leaves no way of distinguishing between Edward Said and Bush and Cheney.[5]

For the architects of the religious turn, the leeching of religion from life disenchants the world and in the colonized world is, to boot, quite inextricably a result of imperialism. Committed to a reenchanted world, they see secularism as damaging even its own adherents. Religion is the anti-imperialist elixir of lifeworld harmony; it alone heals the ruptures in the West's dissociated sensibility and preserves the radical alterity of Europe's Muslim migrants. Aamir R. Mufti powerfully makes the case that there is a "mood"in current scholarship and theory in which religion as "belief, ritual, institution, worldview, or identity" is seen as a means of healing the "shattered totality of life in [colonial] modernity."[6] It is a mood shared by thinkers as diverse as Ashis Nandy and Talal Asad. Of course, religion has equally often been an instrument of empire, and there is a complex forgetting of the role of religion in the colonial project in the set of positions Mufti critiques.

It seems easy enough to identify the author of the position regarding literature attacked by Asad. In *Culture and Anarchy*, when Matthew Arnold suggests that the way forward in the march toward human "perfection" lies in the cultivation of culture—loosely synonymous with literature—the thing to be surpassed is religion, which was once a source of moral improvement but provides, in the end, only lopsided development.[7] For Arnold, the new obsession with freedom means that anarchy lurks around each corner and haunts every corridor, deforming the spirit of humanity and holding it back from the true perfection of "sweetness and light," which is comprised of an Aristotelian combination of virtue ethics, a cultivated happiness, and an aestheticized vision of a common, balanced culture (*CA*, 33–57). The agents of this deformation are modernity's gallery of freaks and mutants—the inexorable army of machinery; middle-class, liberal, commercial, fanatical Protestants; other, antinomian, kinds of dissenters and nonconformists; and Jacobins (*CA*, 62). Arnold argues, "the English reliance on our religious organizations and on our ideas of human perfection just as they stand, is like our reliance on freedom, on muscular Christianity, on population, on coal, on wealth,— mere belief in machinery, and unfruitful." Moreover, "culture is the eternal opponent of the two things which are the very signal marks of Jacobinism," "its fierceness and its addiction to an abstract system" (*CA*, 424). Yet Arnold seems to exempt Anglicanism from religion that ought to be rejected. The Anglican Church is a moderate, encompassing thing: it split the difference between Catholicism and

Calvinism; but it has not worked. For Arnold, Anglicanism preserves the historic, millennium-long rapprochement between Aristotle and Christianity, but culture is better, for it is like the Anglican via media that might have taken hold had Elizabeth I managed to rein in the dissenters from the start: it is the better, the true middle way (*CA*, 20). And it will inherit the task of one version of religion (triumphing over other kinds), which is to provide a national culture from which no one will want to withdraw.

It will anchor and produce ethical life but without the inevitable conflict that accompanies religion. Arnold's focus on dissenting Protestantism, which stands in for all that can go wrong with religion, allows for a partial rescue of religion, of which nondissenting kinds are then to be preferred; but, exception notwithstanding, or perhaps precisely because such balance as Anglicanism ostensibly provides is ever only an exception, eventually religion ruptures social and cultural unity (*CA*, 37).

Arnold is not a liberal, even if large segments of the discursive culture that he helped spawn are. His Aristotelian commitments lead to the idea that humanity requires cultivation, that being human is something one has to get good at. Culture gives one a head start in a life worth living. This notion is very unlike the idea that all human life, even prior to work and cultivation, is worth living. There are forms of bare, unbuffed humanity that just are not worth it. In a move that is anything but liberal, Arnold sets up the state as the agent and guardian of culture: "The Sovereign, as his position raises him above many prejudices and littlenesses, and as he can always have at his disposal the best advice, has evident advantages over private founders in well planning and directing a school" (*CA*, 98). The State will farm a properly Aristotelian humanity.

Arnold's antiliberalism gives him unexpected friends. He thinks of dissenters, Jacobins, liberals, and the rank and file of a commercial culture as more or less the same thing—that is, like Asad after him, Arnold lumps commercial culture, liberals, and secular radicals into one damaging cluster. Asad and his allies might appear superficially to be at odds with Arnold, but the recent turn to religion turns out to share a great deal with Arnold, not least of which is a preoccupation with Aristotle.

The current proponents of religion are opposed to mechanization, the triumphalism of progress narratives, liberalism, and, in their most antiteleological guise, to Marxism (collapsed into liberalism through

Marxism's commitment to history—often taken to line up neatly with a redemptive account of the devastations of historical progress).[8] As a reaction to Western imperialism's brutal manipulation of the rhetoric of freedom, they are usually suspicious of the appeal to freedom; Asad, for instance, casts the controversy over *The Satanic Verses* as a fight against a modern, secular, liberal culture that privileges individual freedom but does not understand and cannot value "cultural unity" (even the phrasing is immaculately Arnoldian), the symbol and symptom of hale lifeworlds.[9]

What is finally at stake for both Asad and Arnold is a cluster of historical developments: liberalism, anarchy-producing commitments to freedom, techno-progressivism. But where Arnold offers literature as an alternative vehicle of perfection, in the current discussion, literature is the usurper of religion and itself an engine of the modern. The fight between Asad and Arnold is really about what can restore lifeworld harmony to those non—or perhaps just reluctant—moderns caught in the web of modernity: religion or literature? Asad takes himself to be opposing Arnoldian Britain, but the more important point for the rest of us is that this is very much a family fight. Arnold wants to combat liberalism through literature. Asad, it cannot be emphasized enough, does not want to cancel Arnold's argument; he merely wants to undo its final step. Perhaps it is the overlap between these projects that accounts for the intensity of Asad's opposition to literature.

Religion is, in this constellation, the truest form of anti-imperialism, sometimes because it is constitutively non-Western and antimodern and sometimes because it just happens, in its most non-Protestant guises, to be the entity that allows for the production of nonliberal subjectivities: this desire for varieties of anti-Protestant religion is, after all, one of the reasons why Asad is so fascinated by medieval Catholicism. But if religion is literature's Other in this fight, what are we to make of literature? The contest between the two, the question of whether religion can be reconciled with literature, raises a host of other questions: How can literature work once you have come out against it? What function does one assign to literature once one has rejected the basic assumptions of Arnold's account? Can one win literature a reprieve by subordinating it once again to religion?

If we are to put pressure on the relationship between religion and literature within the terms of the kind of critique of modernity that presents religion as the alternative to the wounds of colonialism,

and that takes literature as the usurper of religion, it seems right
to sharpen the focus. Let us focus, then, on the literary genre most
committed to psychological, sociological, and nonmythical forms of
explanation, the form most associated with cities, commercial life,
the middle class—in effect, the most modern genre, the novel—and
ask: Can there be a novel that is properly subordinate to religion? Can
there be a religious novel?[10]

HOW TO WRITE A RELIGIOUS NOVEL

The answer to the admittedly heuristic question, Can there be a religious novel?, seems easy enough. All one need do is write a novel
with religious protagonists, which observes their pieties with sympathy. Such contemporary novels are rare, outside Christian genre
fiction, and it is striking that the Sudanese British, avowedly didactic, Muslim writer Leila Aboulela has written not one but two such
novels. Formally cautious and convention-bound to their core, they
are still genuinely intriguing. The first one, *The Translator*, was published in 1999, at a moment when the Gulf War, the subsequent sanctions against Iraq, anti-Muslim feeling attendant upon the Rushdie
affair, the increasing visibility of Europe's Muslim migrants, and an
American rhetoric of a coming clash of civilizations were already con-
spiring to turn Islam, *tout court*, into an anti-imperial token. The
novel is clearly meant to be a response to these events. Set in Aberdeen, it charts the fraught and difficult romance between a recently
widowed, devout, and veiled Sudanese woman, Sammar, and a Scottish professor of Middle East studies, Rae Isles. The chief obstacle
to their union is that he is an infidel—vaguely a Calvinist—and so
cannot marry a Muslim woman. Sammar is the novel's eponymous
translator. She translates Arabic texts for Rae, and the novel implies
that she translates Islam into a properly felt system of beliefs for him.
Prior to this, he has been a leftist and has told her that as a matter of
professional and political principle he believes everything practicing
Muslims believe about the religion, but—exposing the paradoxical
noblesse oblige of cultural sensitivity—he is not a "believer."[11] The
novel's more striking suggestion is that he translates Islam back to
her, that she learns more about Islam from him than she did in Sudan.
The obstacle to the romance is resolved through Rae's conversion.

If religious characters are what are required to make a novel religious, *The Translator* already seems to fit the bill. But it is doing

more than that; it is calling up religious narrative forms that might be precursors to the novel—stories of conversion, confessions, the providential tale—such as the early modern captivity narrative that interprets the brutality of abduction and the travails of escape as part of God's design. The happy rescue or a fortuitous flight show that God rewards the faithful and punishes the wicked. Of course, conversions and confessions—themselves closely aligned—are usually testaments to Providence. While these forms might seem remote from the novel as a genre, the novel is perfectly capable of preserving these earlier forms—telling stories of conversion, staging confessions, clarifying the divine design at work in worldly affairs. In fact, that is precisely what *The Translator* does. In the novel, Sammar's progress follows the arc of confession, Rae's is the trajectory of conversion. When Sammar finally asks Rae to convert so they can marry, he says he is uncertain. She lashes out at him, returns to Sudan, and gradually comes to the realization that she was wrong. She should have wanted Rae to convert for his own salvation, not just so that they can marry. Miraculously, he does, and then comes to Sudan to fetch her. She thinks of the conversion as an honor and a reward, God's provision for the patient and faithful; Rae interprets the fact that, for the first time, he has had no trouble on a trip to Africa as a divine gift bestowed because his "intention is good" (*T*, 195). The romance is absorbed into a providential union (at least as the characters understand the matter), evident reward for their renunciatory patience and devotional labor. Their union is like the divine sleight of (an invisible) hand that replaces Ismail with a lamb because Abraham and Ismail had already consented to the imminent slaughter and accepted it as a duty. Romance, confession, conversion, and providence—neatly wrapped up.

Aboulela has said that she writes fiction that reflects "Islamic Logic" ("Author Statement").[12] She does not refer to any specific Muslim thinker on theodicy, but the novels suggest that Muslim logic is something like a providential understanding of the world with a Muslim accent, as opposed to, say, a Christian one, or with Allah instead of Yahweh as architect.[13] This intention seems to be the propulsive force of the narrative logic of her novels. The way to write a good religious novel may well be to make every aspect of it evidence of the workings of Allah, to make it body forth religion with each turn of the plot, every twist of character. What might such a novel do?

Again *The Translator* is intriguing. The novel's construction around a simple marriage plot obeys all sorts of narrative conventions: a man and a woman experience difficulty, some misunderstanding; the misunderstanding is overcome, the obstacle surmounted; and the culmination of the narrative is their union. The marriage plot offers opportunities for multiple reconciliations through a process that involves social negotiation (between classes and different groups), individual learning, some change, and a rearranged but still contained social order. One has only to think of *Pride and Prejudice* and *Persuasion*, or *Pamela*, or just about any Bollywood romance; the narratives are vehicles of social conflict, but they also offer up finely calibrated imaginings of socially ordered reconciliation.

Pamela, as Nancy Armstrong has argued brilliantly, offers the vision of female virtue conquering aristocratic excess, leading the way for the development of middle-class feminine goodness as a distinctive form of social power.[14] Even as the novel makes a Miltonic claim for the inviolability of the female body (one might think of the Lady in *Comus*), of its ability to transcend the assault of the aristocratic male, it contains that initially insurgent form of resistance in a round of domestic chores and conduct-book virtue. If the woman is not just her body and her lack of fortune she is no more than her carefully husbanded pantry and her morally managed, immaculately attended husband. Protestantism's growing commitment to "companionate" marriage—as distinctive a feature of the Reformation as *sola fide* or nails hammering theses to church doors—shapes the domestic novel's dependence on the marriage plot.

Even as *The Translator* shares a Richardsonian commitment to the transfiguring power of female virtue and the domestic novel's tendency to produce a middle-class ethos of ethically religious female behavior, it transposes these imperatives and possibilities upon a different kind of social and ideological difference and vaster geographical terrain. Marriage offers the possibility of a reconciliation between the hyperbolic clichéd oppositions of cable news punditry—"Islam and the West," "Western modernity" and "Eastern simplicity," "Western development" and "Eastern stasis"—which Aboulela nonetheless confirms in her fantasy of union. Aboulela's commitment to a version of companionate marriage serves to remind us that the tradition of Muslim reform out of which Aboulela's Islamism emerges is known for its reliance on Protestant thought. Paradoxically, this vision can then be grafted onto a companionate and consensual vision

of polygamy. The geopolitics upon which Aboulela draws serves ironically to occlude the relation between Protestantism and Islamism.[15]

One of the distinctive pleasures of detective fiction lies in the
moment when the reader learns how the detective solved the mystery.
Quickly switched pronouns, day-old cigar tobacco, snippets of conversation suddenly become clues, bristlingly alive with significance.
The detective's explanation satisfyingly slots the least important
seeming details into a tidy grid of cause and effect. Romance novels
have as their generic correlative the moment when love is recognized
as requited and the lovers retrace their steps to their now-achievable
union. Fear turns out to be misunderstanding; the absence in which
the lovers feel forgotten reveals itself as filled with emotional event
and a steady pull toward the beloved. All—each indifferent glare,
every look stolen at a suspected rival—is explained. What one gets
in both genres is a recapitulation of the narrative in brief, with the
pegs on which it has been woven clearly exposed. Perhaps one of the
most revealing exchanges in *The Translator* occurs at the end of precisely such a moment, when Sammar and Rae, after rehashing their
romantic travails and the path to their union, are discussing their
future. What seems only loosely, metaphorically providential in most
instances of the romance novel—and here I am thinking particularly
of *Mills and Boon* variants—is suddenly limned with a divine glow.
The happy ending is evidence of the truth of Islam, a confirmation of
its essential mystery and its generosity:

> She had been given the chance and she had not been able to substitute
> her country for him, anything for him.
>   "Ours isn't a religion of suffering," he said, "nor is it tied to a par-
> ticular place." His words made her feel close to him, pulled in, closer
> than any time before because it was "ours" now, not hers alone. And
> because he understood. Not a religion of pathos, not a religion of
> redemption through sacrifice. (*T*, 198)

Rae's claim that Islam is not tied to a particular place finds its resonances throughout the novel. Not only does Sammar learn more
about Islam from him than she did in Sudan; Islam is produced
as both properly global and anticolonial. Although Frantz Fanon,
the novel tells us, did not understand the religious feelings of the
Africans, the link between Islam and anticolonialism is great (*T*,
108–9). This anticolonialism is not nationalist and can be equated
with Islamic practice. Rae's Scottish nationalism, early socialism,
and anti-Orientalist anticolonialism can be swallowed by a placeless

Muslim universalism, an effect of globalization but eventually—and this too is providential—perhaps its gift. Marriage allows for the conversion that allows for the union of East and West. Earlier on, the novel has already showcased the thought that "marriage was half [a Muslim's] faith" (*T*, 108). The marriage plot is thus made to align neatly with the conversion, with faith properly observed, and with transnationalism—with what Olivier Roy has identified as a newly "deterritorialized" Islam.[16] Marriage is faith, destination, and reward: the marriage plot is divine (global) design. The history of the genre and its subsequent development make it particularly apt for Aboulela's purposes. The point cannot, I think, be overstated. The resources the novel as a genre offers (and these include the possibilities of the marriage plot) make Aboulela's resolution possible: its genealogical burden is also its gift. The novel provides a space where Protestantism, Salafism, and the fantasy of happily consensual ("companionate") marriage can merge. The Anglophone novel is itself a deterritorialized space that allows for these transformations and can call upon generic histories that exceed the ambit of various localized and customary Islams. And it is here that gender does some of the most intriguing cultural work. Since Islam is almost synonymous with misogyny in the West, Aboulela makes her heroine's desires consonant with the most conservative interpretation of Muslim injunction, no matter how inequitable. Any clash between the devout man and the devout woman, between female desire and divine command might confirm unsympathetic Western perceptions, which are often unsurprisingly ready to leap to self-flattering prejudice. Hence Sammar's desire for a man who will guide and instruct her and her desperate desire to be remarried, which leads even to her contemplation of polygamy.

Aboulela's novels' characterological interests have to lie in other frictions—hence the hostile mother-in-law, hence also Sammar's indifference to her son and her abandonment of him. The mother-in-law, who wants her to work and support her son instead of remarrying, becomes the symbol of a modernity hostile to the faith, her archetypal mother-in-law villainy submerged into the villainy of history—as if Aboulela's answer to the question, What do women want?, is "marriage," because that's what God wants, because God knows women want it. But the obstacle to the achievement of this desire, which is also a command, is modern men and women. Modernity itself is overcome in this imagining of marriage.[17]

The Translator taps deftly into the contemporary taste for the unlikable, complicit protagonist, an instant mark of narrative sophistication. (Think of the protagonists of Ian McEwan's *Atonement* and *The Innocent,* John Banville's *The Sea,* J. M. Coetzee's *Disgrace.*) The resentful, complaining, and fearful protagonist becomes a symbol of an inevitably flawed humanity, which is transformed by the march to converted salvation: the unlikable protagonist is a providential vehicle, an instrument of divine forgiveness. Islam is not a religion of suffering—by marked contrast to the "dour[ness]" of the Calvinism in which Rae was raised—and unlikability can be redeemed, always forgiven, as long as it is accompanied by a moment of renunciation (*T*, 102). In an essay Aboulela has rather strikingly written: "I wanted to point out that the secularism which the West championed and exported had, when it cancelled sin, cancelled with it forgiveness. And a life without forgiveness is a harsh and (paradoxically in a freedom loving society) a stunted, congealed life."[18] This is Augustine for readers of domestic fiction in literary London: the inevitably complicit, politically formed protagonist of leftist taste or the antiheroine of liberal preference, of an error-prone humanity muddling along, becomes the redeemable sinner of religious social psychology. The conceit and frame of conversion thus enable a cultural eschatology in which all literary forms, social formations, and historical developments can be providentially absorbed.

So it seems that one may comfortably argue that the way to make a novel formally, structurally religious is simply to resuscitate the theologico-formal imperatives of these earlier genres. In fact, we might best read Aboulela's writing as a series of variations on the idea of conversion. Her novels are not just about religious people, not just in touch with older, religious forms of narrative; they also convert specifically novelistic narrative modes to religious ends. Her most unusual talent is her knack for converting literary strategies of secular provenance to religious purposes. The marriage plot, the unlikable and complicit protagonist of late-twentieth-century taste, and the idea of globalization in a heavily migratory modernity—which is to say, a time in which both people and the idea of the modern itself migrate—are all subjected to conversion; and the formal correlative of conversion in novels, the explanation of cause and effect, might well be the logic of providence.

Let us add another way to write a religious novel to our list: produce an apologetics. Again, Aboulela obliges. She offers up visions of women who seek their own subjection and writes a romance that attempts to dramatize the conditions for what it casts as an ideal Muslim marriage, as if she had decided to model the Qur'anic declaration: "Men are in charge of women, because Allah hath made the one to excel the other, and because they spend of their property (for the support of women). So good women are the obedient, guarding in secret that which Allah hath guarded."[19] Sammar learns from Rae in a way that marks her subordination; she looks up to him; and she is potentially happy to accept the role of a second wife in a polygamous marriage. Add to Aboulela's ode to subordination allegories of the (happy) defeat of the Left, and we have a perfectly steeped apologetic brew. Rae's conversion is one such allegory; he used to be a leftist—hence his sympathy for Islam, a sympathy that starts as an honorable, anti-imperialist attempt to undo Orientalist violence—and the novel stages his conversion as the proper culmination of his gently leftist beliefs. He is, in fact, a proxy for the novel's intended audience, the readers whom the novel goes out of its way to address: leftists who should really be Muslim. Rae's conversion shows that the Left should have recognized all along that Islam provided superior forms of anticolonial redress.

For the metropolitan leftist—the one who would have read *The Wretched of the Earth* and *Culture and Imperialism*, two of the books on Rae's shelf, and who might have thought that capitalism is a global historical phenomenon, a phenomenon that is no respecter of religious boundaries—the novel stages a paragraph-long lecture. In his mode as instructor to Sammar, Rae says that one of the reasons he has always admired Islam is that capitalism did not "ultimately" develop in it (*T*,109). The "ultimately" carries a world of hedging. Rae presents a theory claiming that the way Muslim inheritance laws fragment wealth prevented the accumulation of capital. Through him, Aboulela manages to mount an argument against leftist historians who argue that a rhetoric claiming the authority of Islam was used by the emergent Sudanese middle class against older elites, that Muslim traders were crucial in incorporating Sudan into the global economy, and that one of the ways they did so was by plundering the south for slaves. The Turko-Egyptian colonization of southern Sudan in the nineteenth century, which was part of this process of incorporation, used a created distinction between Muslim and non-Muslim groups to authorize the enslavement of the latter.[20] Rae's lecture is clearly meant to counter this narrative and to stand in for Aboulela, who has said that she would like the book taught in postcolonial courses.[21]

The apologetic mix is even more strikingly evident in Aboulela's second novel, *Minaret*, published in 2005.[22] September 11, 2001, has come and gone, Anglo-American imperialism has blossomed, like a malign mushroom cloud, into a full-scale occupation of Iraq, and Muslim apologetics seem to be of snowballing urgency.

In this novel, the Westernized daughter of a corrupt political official in Sudan accepts her desire for spiritual peace over a period of time that includes her father's execution after a coup, her mother's fatal encounter with cancer, her brother's imprisonment in England in a drug-related attempted murder, and her rejection of her exiled, Marxist-atheist lover for being hostile to Islam and too critical of her father. She falls in love with a much younger Islamist man, for whose family she is now a maid, but gives him up, under pressure from his family, so that he is not estranged from his mother. Then, choosing conservative custom over Islamic precedent (as Muhammad's first wife was significantly older than he was), she accepts money from his family to leave him alone and decides to go on the Hajj with it.

Both *Minaret* and *The Translator* are allegories of the Left's defeat: they offer Marxists who are vanquished by Islam, Rae because he converts, Najwa's first lover because he is presented as obviously inferior to the younger Islamist and is replaced by him. Both novels are variations on romance plots. In both, a community of women at the mosque provides comfort and solace that are otherwise absent in the lonely West. Both make use of favored tropes of postcolonial literary arrival and are liberally littered with immigrant trauma, culture shock, and references to the inadequacy of English in rendering bicultural experience. In both, Islam provides comfort, community, and access to identity. Aboulela's is a vision that refracts Monica Ali through Syed Qutb, a vision that takes traditions of domestic multicultural romance and filters them through contemporary right-wing Islamism.

Both novels take the usual generic markers of domestic immigrant fiction—the problem of the accommodation of female desire in the face of the double challenge of Western hostility and the demands made by cultural codes of belonging; the management of allegiance and of accusations of cultural treason that are the staple of migrant fiction and of second-generation young immigrant life—and translate them into a context where the only operative category of belonging is Islam. They imagine solutions to the problem that the Muslim woman presents for left-liberal, anti-imperial discourse. What Aboulela offers up are reasonably deft visions of Muslim women who desire their own subordination, thus making resistance to imperial dreams of female rescue simpler, more clean. So if Laura Bush, mercifully oblivious to her own predicament, could offer the vision of female suffering under (say) the Taliban as a justification for war, the anti-imperialists can, if they choose, cite Islamist women who loathe the burdens of modernity and wish for different times, whose consent to subordination is really the muscle flex of "agency."[23] Of course, this false choice is one of the oldest predicaments of Empire, the ugly face of imperial blackmail.[24]

It is a choice that has frequently been refused by the indigenous Left and by many a Muslim feminist—and they too need to be neutralized. The fight that these novels stage with the Left, a fight that has been going on between leftists and right-wing Islamic militants in many a Muslim-majority society, and on many a Muslim-majority campus, bleeds into their apologetic function. To make the representation of gender do its work by showing consensually self-subordinating womanhood, Aboulela needs to produce narrowly focalized fictions, stories that are closely identified with the protagonist, where the social canvas is not too broad. Broader canvases, a wider range of sympathetic identifications, might necessitate representing men and women who resist religion—even as they resist colonialism—as more than just venal, petty, and inadequate. In *Minaret*, it is the exiled, indigenous Marxist who is too committed to progress and to change, even as he is aggressively hostile to the West; he is the one who has burned the American flag and is an opponent of the IMF (*M*, 156). The heroine—for whom Western culture and consumer goods are rarely an issue—can then stand in for an Islam that is able to make its peace with the West, in a way that the leftist will not. It is as if the problem in the current conflict were really Thomas Friedman's imagination. Friedman thinks that the confrontation between Islam and the West can be coded as a choice between the olive tree and a Lexus; Aboulela can resolve the entire problem by showing devout Muslims happily watching *Dallas*, being fascinated by John Travolta, and listening to Western music, weaving the Lexus through the olive grove. The problem can then be subtly displaced upon the indigenous Left. Rae, the Scottish leftist of the earlier novel, knows better and is able to see the resolution to the failures of Western modernity in Islam; conversion to Islam is the proper telos for the leftist. "Modernity" is one of the things that

Sammar lists as what is different about Britain, but over the course of the novel, it emerges, quite opportunistically, as a category that covers social and cultural radicalism (which needs to be eradicated) but from which imperial economic domination, consumerism, and capitalism can be rescued: modernity is reinterpreted (*T*, 44). This, of course, is a typical right-wing Islamist move. The fantasy reconciliation between Islam and the West is achieved at the expense of the secular Sudanese, in this case working-class, radical.

By writing these narrowly focalized fictions, Aboulela is able to engage in a strange political two-step. She can present authoritarian Sudanese positions as dissenting ones. One of the more startling moments in *Minaret*, a novel rife with astonishing moments, is when Najwa visits her brother in prison and wishes that the very first time he took drugs he could have been "punished according to the Shariah—one hundred lashes. I do wish it in a bitter, useless way because it would have put him off, protected him from himself" (*M*,193). Politically, this is key. One of the major points of contention in the second Sudanese civil war was the imposition of Sharia law upon the country.[25] By presenting the argument in defense of Sharia as the protagonist's purely personal response to her brother's failure to fulfill his filial and sibling responsibilities, and as a rankly behaviorist solution to his violent drug addiction, which at the same time is polemical in the British context because of Islam's status as the religion of a despised minority, Aboulela is able to mount the Sudanese government's political argument as a dissenting position.[26] It is important to be clear here: Aboulela attempts an empathetic gloss on the state's brutalizing policies, even as the representation seems completely removed from the sphere of the state. The virtuous authority of domesticity, which is simply the genre's inheritance, allows for the burial of the state's political brutality and immigrant Islam's besieged European context becomes an opportunity for a cunningly displaced political fight. A right-wing Islamist position is turned into a dissenting liberal one because it is held by protagonists oppressed by their otherness and produced by an author who is a member of a minority in the West. Waïl S. Hassan is right to identify Islamophobia as part of the context in which these novels have been produced.[27] In the manner of their response to this bigotry, the novels are able to reveal (almost despite themselves) the more brutal challenges of globalization in a world that is still battling imperialism—the metropolitan, sometimes diasporic, erasure of indigenous political radicalism.

Now, one could argue that the novel's title makes clear something that postcolonial fiction has always done—translate; and perhaps conversion and translation have been the same thing all along.[28] At least one aim of postcolonial literature has been to transform the metropole, to change its culture, to make it more equitable. The claim implicit in a great deal of postcolonial literature has always been that colonial history has given the formerly colonized a claim to global history and the imperial canon. In *Shame*, in a passage that is almost a manifesto for the branch of postcolonial studies most concerned with diaspora, migration, and hybridity, Salman Rushdie equates migration with translation itself: "I, too, am a translated man. I have been borne across. It is generally believed that something is always lost in translation; I cling to the notion . . . that something can also be gained."[29] The transformations and physical dislocations of migration find their correlative in a literary carrying across of linguistic habit and cultural trope. In this case, translation points to alternatives to revivalist versions of cultural nationalisms, takes the emphasis off historical purity or authenticity, keeps company with concepts such as transculturation, adaptation, indigenization. Aboulela is very much signaling—with her title and with the central character—that she inhabits the mainstream of the postcolonial literary project.

The cunning of the fiction lies in that Aboulela takes what was already committedly transformative about this literature and subjects it to a systematic series of further conversions. Though less structurally overt, the practice is akin to that of the Christian medieval and Renaissance poets who would take erotic—or what were known as "profane"—lyrics and, at the practice's baldest, change only the occasional word to redirect the lyrics to divine devotion, since, so the logic went, the proper object of all worldly activity and devotion is God. As many of these lyrics were already known, the tunes used for the profane poems could now be used for their sacred palimpsests. Parody was not burlesque but instead transformation.[30] Sacred parody, then, is the formal principle that governs Aboulela's fictional practice—the translations translated. The aim is not just the burbling mélange of hybridity, but a deep absorption into a different universalizing teleology, smuggled in under the cover of one of postcolonial theory's most popular concepts.

But even if they are not converting anyone, these novels seem to be working quite well as apologetics. *The Translator* elicited from the *Muslim News* the judgment that it is the "first halal [permitted by the religion] novel written in English" and from Coetzee that it is "a story of love and faith all the more moving for the restraint with which it is written."[31] The Sudanese ambassador in London described it as a "dialogue of civilizations" and contrasted it with Tayyib Salih's classic and edgily anticolonial Arabic rewriting of *Heart of Darkness*, *Season of Migration to the North*, which he said depicted "the clash of civilizations."[32] *Minaret* prompted a *Guardian* reviewer to describe it as "beautiful, daring, challenging," and to write that it explains why a fundamentalist politics emerged in the first place—presumably, although the reviewer doesn't spell it out, because Muslim women needed protective men.[33] Implying that the possibilities of emancipation can be articulated only in a "Western" idiom, an *Observer* commentator wrote that the novels show a very different picture of Muslim women than does Monica Ali's *Brick Lane*, that Aboulela's heroines do not desire "Western culture."[34]

The dichotomy between East and West—as separate systems of ideas regarding women—is precisely what Aboulela wants to calcify. In *Minaret*, when Najwa is wracked by guilt for having premarital sex, she has the following thought:

> Who would care if I became pregnant, who would be scandalized?
> Aunty Eva, Anwar's flatmates. Omar would never know unless I
> wrote to him. Uncle Saleh was across the world. A few years back,
> getting pregnant would have shocked Khartoum society, given my
> father a heart attack, dealt a blow to my mother's marriage, and
> mild, modern Omar, instead of beating me, would have called me a
> slut. And now nothing, no one. This empty space was called freedom.
> (*M*, 174–75)

As Aboulela casts it, the "West" offers loneliness and sexual freedom, the "East" discipline and claustrophobia mysteriously transmuted into happy collectivity—in fact, happy only because a collectivity. But since the protagonist is not happy outside the West and does not seem to like Sudanese sociality, marriage provides a whittled-down alternative to customary collectivities.

In the *Edinburgh Sunday Herald*, Ziauddin Sardar, a fairly prominent British Muslim cultural commentator of Indo-Pakistani extraction, who writes for the *New Statesman* as well, celebrated *The Translator* for its truly non-Western values, of which the heroine is an exemplar. The review makes clear that he loves the novel even more because it shows the proper way to honor Islam. We do not have to endorse Sardar's normative religious claims to see that he reads

Aboulela fascinatingly well: that is, perhaps because of their ideological affinity, he reads Aboulela without any attempt to bypass the novel's claims to didactic anthropology:

> Rae . . . is the good side of the West, but even at its best, and most learned, Aboulela seems to suggest, the West has little knowledge of other cultures. Sammar's request, for Rae to convert to Islam, is an invitation to true knowledge. Fascination and bookish knowledge is not enough, she seems to suggest, without real experience. . . . Sammar's principles finally have an effect on Rae. He realises the surface nature of his expertise; and comes to terms with the fact that he is not above those who he seeks to represent. Being alienated with Christianity is not the same thing as being estranged from all religions. Prayers can be accepted, and miracles can happen, even if people around you don't see them as such. He discovers his own route to Islam before returning to the object of his love. . . . Aboulela shows the rich possibilities of living in the West with different, non-Western, ways of knowing and thinking. In Sammar, the heroine of this reviewer's dreams, she has created a personification of Islam that is as genuine as it is complex.[35]

Conversion is, in these terms, the only form of genuine respect for Islam's constitutively non-Western values. But if Sammar's version of female virtue is what counts as "non-Western," and Muslim, we should finally recognize *Pamela* and *Clarissa* as part of the secret canon of non–Western Europe, the literary Knights Templar of Europe's veiled Muslim truth. Islam, in other words, cannot be parochialized in this way; and a larger affinity, a more global religious connection, becomes visible through the history of the marriage plot.

Together these responses point to the historical intrigue of Aboulela's novels, which lies in the way they simultaneously inhabit at least three moments in the history of Islam. It is hard to imagine the current role of an increasingly global and political Islam without Salafism, and Salafism, in turn, is hard to understand without the waves of reform—comprised of an emphasis on Qur'anic interpretation (*ijtihad*) and, paradoxically, on the revival of the purity of the earliest Muslim societies—which have periodically swept a range of Muslim contexts since the eighteenth century.[36] The increasingly restrictive project of Islamization in which the Sudanese government has been engaged since the 1980s is part of the longer *durée* of this brand of the religion. In the latest historical twist, this brand of Muslim identity is consolidated in the metropole by a Right committed to a clash of civilizations and a left-liberal anxiety about doing right by "other" cultures. A host of customary social forms are abstracted into the self-authorizing and stabilized notion of "tradition," a range of regional and national cultures turned into fodder for "Muslim identity" and non-Western tradition. The transnational context of migrants from Europe's former colonies helps obscure a long and complex global history.

HALAL FICTION

I would like to return now to my question about whether it is possible to write a religious novel. Aboulela's fiction, a fiction that is didactically religious, seems to suggest that such an enterprise is shot through with tensions and contradictions, and that it is not so easy to do so after all. So what happens to religion in her novels?

In *The Translator*, Aboulela has one of her more stridently anticolonial and Muslim female characters quote Marx with some hostility. The West's antipathy to Islam is an emanation from the aphorism that religion is the opiate of the people. This hostility—also named in Rae's diagnosis as part of what is wrong with Western modernity—is upheld by a fantasy that "mankind is self-sufficient" (*T*, 42). In both novels, the heroines' desire for masculine romantic tenderness becomes a partial allegory for what is also explicitly stated—a psychological need for social peace.

Nowhere is the mesh of displacements more evident than in the exchanges and passages in *Minaret* that explain what leads to Najwa's breakup with her Marxist lover. She wants comfort, and he offers hard, social analysis: "He knew facts and history but nothing he said gave me comfort or hope. The more he talked, the more confused I felt, groping for something simple, but he said nothing was simple, everything was complicated, everything was connected to history and economics" (*M*, 165). He is too critical, too hostile to the fundamentalists. He thinks it is regressive to have faith in anything supernatural. He argues that religion is not benign because it has political and social effects, but this is where Najwa says she "got lost":

> I did not want to look at these big things because they overwhelmed me. I wanted me, my feelings and dreams, my fear of illness, old age and ugliness, my guilt when I was with him. It wasn't fundamentalists who killed my father, it wasn't fundamentalists who gave my brother drugs. But I could never stand up to Anwar. I did not have the words, the education or the courage. I had given in to him but

> he had been wrong, the guilt never ever went away. Now I wanted
> a wash, a purge, a restoration of innocence. I yearned to go back to
> being safe with God. I yearned to see my parents again, be with them
> again like in my dreams. These men Anwar condemned as narrow-
> minded and bigoted, men like Ali, were tender and protective with
> their wives. Anwar was clever but he would never be tender and pro-
> tective. (*M*, 242)

What makes Najwa finally leave is that in order to confront her about
her growing religiosity, Anwar asks a theological question:

> And he knew how to hurt me. "If everything you hear in the mosque
> is correct, your beloved Aunty Eva will go to Hell because she's not
> a Muslim. How can you justify this, after all the good she's done for
> you?" I started to stammer, I burst into tears, whimpering into the
> receiver. He tried but he couldn't stop himself from laughing. (*M*,
> 244)

Aboulela's novels, when most committed to religion and to Islam,
reveal themselves as most in line with the idea that religion is a brand
of sociopsychic tranquilizer. On Aboulela's terms, the problem with
the Marxist-atheist is not that he misrecognizes religion as an opiate
but that he fails to administer it. The question of divine justice, of
salvational inequity reduces the properly devout heroine to whimper-
ing tears—tears that the Marxist atheist doesn't know how to mop. It
turns out that atheists are bad lovers because they ask pressing theological questions. It is, of course, important to remember here that for
every Marxist committed to women's emancipation there have been
several who have been all too happy to avail themselves of the pho-
tocopying and tea-brewing skills of their female counterparts. The
domestic and sexual labor of many a Marxist's wife has been forgotten. But, unlike Aboulela, the feminists who criticize such inequity do
so in the service of more emancipation, not less.

Aboulela's fictions avail themselves of the resources of the realist novel but subordinate social realism to psychic representation and
realism. Meanwhile, they thrust theology aside—as if the novel were
a vehicle for a degraded lyric subjectivity. The female heroine's desire
for peace and the restoration of innocence is presented as properly,
devoutly womanly, and the ostensible ability of religion—through the
vehicle of tender and protective men—to deliver this peace is cast
explicitly as an antidote to a world in social flux.

To clarify the point, we might think briefly about a novel that is
likewise realist but which has a much larger range of identifications

and presents a Muslim social network in a very different way. Nadeem Aslam's *Maps for Lost Lovers*, which I discuss at greater length in the concluding chapter, is a story of an honor killing within an enclosed, lower-middle- and working-class British Asian community.[37] In the breadth of the novel's social canvas—its charting of the effects of varieties of conservative Islam upon a range of people, and of the workings of asphyxiating codes of gender upon men and women both; its refusal to censor the internal violence of the community while representing the intense brutality of British racism, colonialism, and globalization—the novel concedes nothing to power. At the moment of greatest personal and metaphysical distress—having lost her husband, her children, and, perhaps most important, the moral certitude that has both prompted those losses and made them livable—Kaukab, the novel's fiercely realized, utterly devout protagonist questions how what has happened to her, her family, and just about everyone on the street can possibly be a fair reward for her quite genuine fidelity and for the decency of those killed in the name of communal honor. She ends up wondering how what "[God] does to humans can be called justice."[38] This questioning turns into a longer meditation on salvational justice, yet Kaukab stays faithful and ends by saying, "help."

In *Maps for Lost Lovers,* social realism opens into a theological challenge. Paradoxically, Aslam's progressive, but also sympathetic and immanent, critique of religion presents religion as the very antithesis of an opiate: instead, it emerges as a genuine cause for psychic and conceptual struggle. Faith requires hard, uncomfortable work, work that Aboulela chooses not to represent.

Aboulela's novels recode religion as social practice, as psychic comfort and focus, as providential design (which substitutes for a represented God). Providence can only be presented as an interpretation by the characters of worldly cause and effect, because heavy-handedly vocal, omniscient narrators—so outmoded they would annul didacticism by turning it into costume drama—are not part of contemporary fashion. The novels also relentlessly sideline justice, the one simultaneously worldly and theological concept that can pose a challenge to religion on its own terms. But in Aboulela's novels, exploring the more traumatic impact of religion on the world, even in its effects as a powerful discourse, is prohibited, because to broach these issues is a sin and, at the same time, a compromise with Empire. The attributes that allow the novels to be designated as Muslim and *halal* (permitted by Islamic law) are thoroughly secular, by which I mean that they have little to say about divinity and bracket theological questions and the more troubling effects of religion on the world. In their chaste and narrow romantic focus, they make religion private. Secularism, it turns out, is constitutive of their *halal* goodness.

There is a formal puzzle here. Aboulela's entirely obedient observation of the taboo against divine representation and of the more social taboo against any form of religious questioning means that she cannot really represent religion as anything but (in this case anodyne) social practice and psychic salve. Cosmological speculation, imaginings of creation or revelation, divine representation, and theological argument must be absent in order to earn them the imprimatur of the *halal*. Their theological safety, their closing off of aspects of religion—that is, their secularism—makes them good Muslim novels.

Narrowly focused and truncated in their realism, the novels reduce Islam to just another discourse, a set of beliefs held by some people, showcased by a sympathetic novelistic portrayal. Such a reduction may well be an inevitable feature of novels themselves; the leveling reduction of all systematic belief to one discourse among many—that might, in fact, be the Bakhtinian reading. Without some prior belief, how can one be sure that providential design is anything but simply another authorial illusion, unless one believes that God is the author of the novel?

According to Asad (or, more broadly, the prevailing position on religion), the very fact that I am talking about "belief" means that I am performing a rigidifying operation, that I am forgetting that religion is always social and ascribing to it some "essentialized" mode of being.[39] Asad's view seems to mean that the ascription of any belief at all is a form of essentialism. This is a more austere vision than an argument for variations of belief within and across groups or sects. T. S. Eliot's fantasy of a Pre- Reformation Catholic Church in which thought is as inseparable from feeling as sugar from well-brewed tea has mutated into the idea that Pre-Reformation, and thus premodern, religion offered a perfect blend of the social and the religious. As Asad would have it, religion as an entity necessitating belief is itself a modern invention. And since the modern is the West, so the argument goes, in the "non-West," religion is a fluid, collective, social, communal set of practices that it is mistaken to call religion in the same sense as we might in the West.

How, then, do we account for God? God is difficult to incorporate into the generic frame of the realist novel, so the form allows Aboulela to sidestep a larger reckoning with the presence, or absence, of God in the world. But by choosing the realist form, Aboulela commits herself to engagement with the world and religion's presence in it. So the narrowness of her novels' focus allows her to evade the examination of religion's social effects that a more expansive realism might yield. Nevertheless, the novels cannot close off the uncomfortable questions that they seek to contain. What is to prevent one from making the judgment that the subordination Aboulela models is silly, one deluded belief in a world teeming with deluded beliefs?

NARRATIVE AND DIVINE JUSTICE

What if we reformulate my initial question as, Is it possible to write a referentially serious religious novel, by which I mean one that does not void God? I am suggesting that we think of religion as a category that is more than simply filiative, more than just signaling an allegiance to a particular community. Such a novel might have to conceptualize accounts of God as describing something that exists and the metaphysical realm as if it were known, as even the monotheisms claim that at least some of it is, even as they make a case for an absent God, who is also inscrutable. It might have to represent God, which would involve making God into a character. It might have to imagine God as the monotheisms do, find a way to stage the inscrutability and the fictional correlative of an inconceivability that is also good, omnipotent, omniscient, merciful, and just. It might have to read Judeo-Christian-Muslim stories as history, not as myth—and represent them as novels represent history. Would this lead to a religious novel or just a theological one? Are they the same? This is where the problem of whether literature and religion can be reconciled fires up.

A novel that is referentially serious about religion, in the sense that it makes claims about God present in the monotheisms, would make God into a character and put the world and heaven in some kind of dialogue; it would have to world God and deal with the pull to anthropomorphism in language and representation. In such a case, representation would have to reconcile divine omnipotence and omniscience with the wretched state of the earth. In this process, it would have to push away the theological question of justice and yet observe the defiant blasphemy of all theology in its demand for intelligibility, which reveals that to ask for intelligibility from an omnipotent God is to demand accountability. But this very act would then cancel its other (nonblasphemous) religious status to make it anything but *halal*, anything but nonblasphemous. "Religious," when applied to novels, turns out to be a social and secular category, the name for a representational propriety—an iconoclasm—that removes heaven from scrutiny. To ask for heavenly scrutability is paradoxically to ask for a genuine worldliness that, at the same time, meets religion on its own conceptual turf. Such worldliness entails an ethical encounter with the divine. The demand for heavenly scrutability requires, in turn, that religion be more than a tranquilizing cultural practice, and identity more than merely a form of comfort. An ethical encounter conceived in such a way means that "religious pain" or "offense" cannot be designated as limits to questioning.

It is difficult to imagine a religious novel that is referentially serious about divinity, but a theological novel—one that interprets God by representing God—is more conceivable, if less reliably religious (one might think, say, of Naguib Mahfouz's *Children of Gebelawi*). Religious and secular as concepts become muddled within the very form of the novel. Like anthropology concerned with religion, religious novels make religion ontologically secular. The current defenders of religion need a notion of it that is as fuzzily adjectival as the dreadful, all-purpose "spiritual"—not religion, but religious, a free-floating category that lumps together all manner of antiliberal practices regardless of what any of its practitioners believe. This defense is sustained by a recourse to an ostensibly Marxist commitment to the collective and the social but without a concomitant sensitivity to the fact that not everything is social in the same way and that not all collectivities are politically redemptive. Those postsecularist anthropologists, critics, and now novelists, in the case of Aboulela, concerned with religion are working within a constellation that Matthew Arnold was one of the first to assemble, but they break with him because of his own break from religion in favor of culture. Yet we might call this group Arnoldian: they want to undo Arnold's surpassing of religion in favor of culture, but the only reason they continue to talk about religion is that they have already turned religion into culture.

Even if their construal is imprecise, conflating, as I suggest in the first chapter, all manner of literature and aesthetic practice, Asad and Mahmood are right to be suspicious of at least one kind: even when allegorical-theological and not conventionally realist novels are inimitably worldly. Novelistic cause and effect demands intelligibility, and representing God within them transforms scrutability into a formal imperative. Novels resist transcendence by making anything with claims to transcendence subject to representation. Representation is, of course, no less a challenge for narrative verse, as is famously the case with John Milton's *Paradise Lost*. But as *Paradise Lost* shows all too well, once such a representation is in play, the collision between justice, power, and world becomes hard to avert without a ruthless suppression of all questions of justice and a simultaneous banishment of the problem of power.

CHAPTER FOUR

How Injury Travels

But historical beginnings are lowly: not in the sense of modest or discreet—like the steps of a dove, but derisive and ironic, capable of undoing every infatuation.

MICHEL FOUCAULT, "Nietzsche, Genealogy, History"[1]

NATURALIZING MUSLIM PAIN

Why has injury come to govern so much of the contemporary academic discourse about Muslims? Why are pain and hurt the affective labels by which the outrage of some Muslims over disrespect for Islam are represented? Why is the response to what is loosely termed "blasphemy" used to constitute a Muslim polity by people who claim to represent "the Muslim community" and also, more surprisingly, by academic theorists? The quick answers that suggest themselves seem both obvious and inadequate: Hurt expresses the effects of the relentless racism and xenophobia faced by many Muslims in the West. It does not take much to see that after September 11, 2001, the word *injury*, even when conceived as discursive or "moral," implicitly summons connotations of the physical wounds inflicted by Western-led wars on a range of countries in which Muslims are a majority. Injury and pain are the conditions of Muslims in Iraq, Afghanistan, Somalia, and parts of Pakistan.

Moreover, in the academic context, in the age of identity, Muslims have to be identified by some act of affiliation. But since Muslims have now become the intellectual object against which practices assumed to be constitutive of the modern secular order are critiqued—perhaps even constituted—a mode of identification and (communitarian) subject production has to be found that cannot be coded as "choice." For "choice" is an umbrella word by which a cluster of modern fictions—individualism, neoliberal economics, the free market—that sustain the structure of a globalized, increasingly homogenized and fundamentally inequitable late capitalist modernity are now organized together. In what one might consider the philosophical slang of capitalism, one chooses to be poor, deprived, or politically oppressed. Capitalist modernity is like the abusive lover who beats his beloved, tears streaming down his face, claiming with every brutalizing blow, you make me do this and you can stop it any time. Academic anti-liberalism thus requires a way of coding Muslim affiliation in a form that cannot be read as choice; "injury" can do this work. "Injury" makes identity ontological, without being, as we shall see, precisely biological. The one word can encompass the spectrum of violence against Muslims and link that violence, discursive and physical, in a form that then speaks to the ontological status of Muslims. When adduced in response to what is sometimes called blasphemy, injury is able to connect the discursive and unbodied representational and semiotic acts that might be construed as attacks with the affective response of hurt, to enable a slide from discursive injury to embodied response.

The aim of this chapter is to think about the transnational, indeed planetary, effects of linking injury, blasphemy, religious pain, and Muslim identity together. One effect might already have become visible: Injury and pain are also the conditions of Christians, Hindus, and Jews in countries bombed by the coalition, but I have hidden the violence inflicted by Empire on non-Muslims (even the description *non-* produces them only through negation) in "Muslim" lands in the way I have begun this chapter. Daisy-cutters, depleted uranium, and cluster bombs are no respecters of religious difference; they do not inquire of bodies, before they tear them apart, whether they are atheist or Christian, or Bahai, or Muslim, whether they are secular, or "post," but in bringing together religious pain, identity, and empire in my framing of the problem, I have replicated a civilizational divide and erased the violence done to minorities in these lands.

Let me begin by looking closely at two academic representations of the varieties of Muslim hurt. One is a consideration of Muslim responses to the Rushdie affair and another to the controversy surrounding the Danish cartoons. Both are concerned with the specificity of Muslim pain in response to insults to the Prophet of Islam.

But, first, a caveat is in order: It is crucial to distinguish the two controversies, even as furor subsequent to the publication of the Danish cartoons followed patterns established in the Rushdie affair: the riots, death threats, assertions of the embattled, intrinsically European virtues of free speech, counter-assertions of the European blindness to Europe's own taboos (witness, the critics of the free speechers would say, the crushing oblivion meted out to Holocaust deniers), the travel of Islamists from Europe seeking solidarity in rage from Muslims elsewhere. The mockery in the cartoons is distinct from the use of a novel, by racists, to goad Muslims enraged by an "apostate" Muslim who had written a novel about apostasy and the destruction of a believer's mind upon thinking the unthinkable, by thinking, in other words, the prohibited thoughts that can lead to apostasy.

The first example I want to consider is Tariq Modood's discussion of Muslim pain in an essay first published in 1990 and reprinted in *Multicultural Politics: Racism, Ethnicity, and Muslims in Britain* (2005). Modood argues that those who make a case for the right of publication of *The Satanic Verses* on the grounds of the necessity of allowing free speech simply do not understand the nature of the violence experienced by Muslims when they encounter insults to their prophet.[2] Perhaps, more significantly, he wants to claim that the Rushdie affair cannot be addressed by speaking about racism:

> "Fight racism, not Rushdie": the stickers bearing this slogan were worn by many in 1989 who wanted to be on the same side as the Muslims. It was well-meant but betrayed a poverty of understanding. It is a strange idea that when somebody is shot in the leg one says, "Never mind, the pain in the elbow is surely worse." Why should reference to the real problem of racism lessen religious pain." (*MP*, 103)

The consequence of this claim for Modood is profound. He wants to reconceive the ways of thinking about how ethnic minorities inhabit Britain: "in their understanding of race, Muslims are wiser . . . than radical antiracists: in locating oneself in a hostile society one must begin with one's mode of being, not one's mode of oppression, for one's strength flows from one's mode of being" (*MP*, 107). Of course, for Modood, the mode of being is Muslim and should not be confused with racial or regional self-understanding. It could be said, then, that what is conceived as hostile is, in fact, produced by the mode of being. The specificity of the injury has to do with the specificity of Muslim self-constitution. Even more so it has to do with forms of devotion particularly strong among South Asian Muslims of rural, peasant background (*MP*, 106–7). Antiracists simply fail, then, when they demand other forms of political solidarity, or when they subsume Muslim pain to racist anger. Modood is insistent that this mode of veneration of Muhammad is quite distinct to South Asians. In addition, it is important, according to Modood, to remember that, aside from Teheran, the demonstrations were held in Johannesburg, Bradford, Bombay, and Islamabad (*MP*, 106).

At the same time the social conditions in Britain and India exacerbate the pain (he does not mention Pakistan here):

> It was not the exploration of the religious doubt but the lampooning of the Prophet that provoked the anger. This sensitivity has nothing to do with Qur'anic fundamentalism but with South Asian reverence of Muhammad (deemed by many Muslims, including fundamentalists, to be excessive) and cultural insecurity as experienced in Britain and even more profoundly in India. (*MP*, 106)

So social oppression is important, but it should not be coded in terms borrowed from the racists because of the distinctness of South Asian Muslim immigrant identity. My suggestion that injury is a useful term because of racism would not be quite right according to Modood because it misrecognizes the ontology—the mode of being—that is the source of this Muslim group's identity. Although Modood does not specify the group, presumably he means to refer to Barelvi attachment to the Prophet. To the extent that this group is denied rights and persecuted, the persecution feeds sensitivity that is already in place because of this very particular form of regionally identified reverence. More than fifteen years later, it is significant that in his response to the Danish cartoons Modood does not emphasize religious pain or a South Asian aspect of a particularly intense form of very personalized religious devotion. He does point out that arguments such as his have become normalized since the publication of *The Satanic Verses*, as evinced by the fact that many British papers did not reprint the cartoons. It is a normalization in which Modood has played an important role; and, for his contribution, he has been recognized by the British government with an MBE.

Saba Mahmood, too, talks about religious pain in her essay on the Danish political cartoons, although she does not cast the veneration Muslims feel for the Prophet as merely regional. Her discussion of religious pain is reprinted (from *Critical Inquiry*) in a volume called *Is Critique Secular? Blasphemy, Injury and Free Speech*, whose contributors include some of the most vociferous critics of secular liberalism on the theoretical scene: Judith Butler, Wendy Brown, and, of course, Talal Asad.[3]

As is to be expected, Mahmood's is a more theoretically inclined discussion than Modood's; it also has a different conceptual prompt. Mahmood was "compelled," she says, to write the essay because of the "immediate resort to juridical language" by all sides in the controversy (*RR*, 36). Both defenses of the cartoons and opposition to it "remained rooted in 'identity politics' (Western versus Islamic) that privileges the state and the law as the ultimate adjudicator of religious difference." Mahmood's project, then, is to "think critically about the ethical and political questions elided in the immediate resort to the law" (*RR*, 67). Mahmood is insistent that her aim is not to "provide a more authoritative model" for understanding Muslim anger over the cartoons since the motives for the protests were "notoriously heterogenous" and cannot be explained through a "single causal narrative" but instead to "push us to consider why such little thought has been given in academic and public debate to what constitutes moral injury in our secular world today" (*RR*, 70).

It might not be unfair to say, then, that the object of intellection in the essay is something called a "modern secular order." More interestingly, to the extent that all current law is modern, it is also secular and liberal. This is evident in Mahmood's discussion of Hussein Agrama's analysis of the Abu Zayd trial, in which the Egyptian state incorporated a notion of *hisba* from classical Sharia but in which the form it took apparently "differed dramatically" in that it came "to be articulated with the concept of public order and the state's duty to uphold the morals of the society in congruence with the Islamic tradition" (*RR*, 87). What's most significant to Mahmood is the "striking resemblance between the Egyptian legal argument and those of the ECtHR" in the case of the Otto-Preminger-Institut versus Austria (*RR*, 87), where the court upheld the Austrian decision to ban a film offensive to "Christian sensibilities" (*RR*, 84). In both cases, Mahmood sees the law as upholding majoritarian interests—as she does in the case of the ECtHR decision to uphold a Turkish ban on a book deemed offensive to the majority Muslim population (*RR*, 87). So Muslims, who resort to the law, simply "remain blind" to the normative disposition of secular-liberal law to majority culture (*RR*, 88). Since Mahmood does not say so, I do not know if she believes that there is a nonsecular, nonmodern, illiberal juridical tradition that does not privilege the majority or if this is a problem that is constitutive of the law itself. In other words, it's not clear if there is something in the very process of the codification necessary to law that then simply means that law favors order—emanates perhaps from the need for order—and that order itself can only be maintained by catering to a majority whose cooperation is its necessary adhesive force. On this reading, codification requires normalization and normalization requires social adhesion, which can only be achieved by catering to, perhaps even morally bribing, the majority. In the conceptual terrain in which Mahmood's argument is articulated an attendant and crucial question is: What precisely is an illiberal state in modernity?

As it stands, it seems as if the interchangeability of secular, modern, and liberal marks the redundancy of secularism as a descriptor. What is really being contested, then, is the structure of actually existing institutions, which by the fact of their currentness are secular. Moreover, all those interchangeable things are also Protestant-Christian "in contour." If the argument seems a little circular, it does because it is.[4]

The other side of Mahmood's argument is the explanation of moral injury, and how Muslims experience it. The argument is motivated as an address to liberal confusion. "Moral injury," as felt in the Danish cartoon controversy, is something liberals don't understand, and to them it must be made intelligible. Interestingly enough, the person who is presented as most baffled is Tariq Ali, liberal only in some rather philosophically elastic conceptual universe and increasingly a reluctant proponent of radical Muslim groups, like the Taliban, for their "anti-imperialist" tendencies; in this way the argument accrues and grows, gathering different groups and persons of various affiliations, so it includes progressives, liberals, or anyone who does not get it, yoked together by a puzzled secular orientation. Mahmood's project is to show a way out of such puzzlement.

The conceptual resources Mahmood draws upon to explain how Muslims experience the moral injury that leads to religious pain come with a peculiar inadvertency. There is a certain care with which Mahmood points out that there were "heterogenous impulses" at play in the controversy and that no "single causal narrative" can explain the events that ensued upon the publication of the cartoons; and yet, despite these cautions and caveats, a figure of a "devout" Muslim is produced in negative contrast to whatever is modern, liberal, secular, Protestant. This contrast, then, stabilizes a notion of a Muslim identity constituted by religious pain and a particular susceptibility to the kind of moral injury sustained in the Danish political cartoon affair. The stabilization occurs as a consequence of Mahmood's procedure in establishing why the moral injury is unintelligible to the puzzled, and of the way she produces a map of the impasse between liberal confusion and Muslim pain through an account of what she designates a "semiotic ideology." This semiotic ideology, then, is what separates the two sides in the controversy and makes moral injury unintelligible to those of a secular, liberal disposition.

In order to explain how this ideology functions, and to provide a way of transcending its limitations, Mahmood turns to Webb Keane's work on Protestant missionaries, W. J. T Mitchell's notion of images and icons, and Kenneth Parry's discussion of Aristotelian notions of schesis and their use in the second Byzantine iconoclastic controversy. It is an impressive, even dizzying, marshaling of secondary conceptual resources. Keane's work on Protestant missionaries enables the insight that there are limits to a Protestant "semiotic ideology," most clearly evinced by the "shock" experienced by "proselytizing missionaries" on first contact with natives for whom material objects were invested with "divine agency." These natives apparently considered the exchange of material objects an "ontological extension of themselves." In the process they managed to dissolve the "distinction between persons and things" (*RR*, 72). The missionaries' "dismay" at the "moral consequences" of "native epistemological assumptions" has "resonances with the bafflement many liberals and progressives express at the scope and depth of Muslim reaction over the cartoons today" (*RR*, 72–73).

A way out of this confusion is ostensibly offered by Mitchell's understanding of icons. Mitchell's insistence that vision is not reducible to "language, or sign, or discourse" and that the field of "visual reciprocity" is constitutive of social reality is of great use to Mahmood (*RR*, 71). Mahmood's gloss on this is to suggest that "not all semiotic forms follow the logics of meaning, communication, or representation" (*RR*, 71). This explains, then, the inability of liberals and missionaries to understand what precisely it is that images do. The point for Mahmood is that "a devout Muslim's relationship to Muhammad is predicated on an "assimilative" model rather than a "communicative or representative" one (*RR*, 76). This devout Muslim's relationship with the Prophet is based not just on following his utterances as collected in the form of the hadith but instead on emulation. In what is essentially an explanation of how Sunnah functions, she describes how "devout Muslims" "try to emulate how he dressed; what he ate; how he spoke to his friends and adversaries;

how he slept, and so on" (*RR, 75*). At this point, an astonishingly sacramental quality creeps into Mahmood's prose: "These mimetic ways of realizing the Prophet's behaviour are lived not as commandments but as virtues where one wants to *ingest*, as it were, the Prophet's persona into oneself" (*RR, 75*; italics mine). This is remarkably and significantly in line with discussions of affective piety and traditions of *imitatio Christi.* The metaphor of "ingestion" seems to derive from a notion of communion, shared by the Eastern and Catholic Churches, except that in this context the transformation it theorizes sets up a bodily merge between Muhammad and devout Muslims, instead of Christ and Christians.

Mahmood's metaphor also reminds us of the intellectual contexts of the 1980s and 1990s that saw a resurgence of interest in European Catholicism and premodern notions of Christianity. It is this milieu, which must also, I think, be taken into account when the framing of contemporary arguments about religion is being analyzed. Talal Asad's work is very much part of this intellectual moment. A fundamental conceptual strut of Mahmood's position is based on an argument Asad popularized in the late 1980s. He suggested it is a modern and thus, on Asad's terms, necessarily colonially inflected concept of religion that suggests that religion requires belief and assent to a set of propositions. Asad is perhaps one of the major disseminators of a critique of this concept of religion, particularly as it may pertain to misunderstandings of Islam and very much a part of the intellectual context of the fin de siècle of the twentieth century. For Mahmood, one of the reasons liberals and Protestants do not understand native/ Muslim (the conflation is slowly consolidated) attachment to images or religious figures is that they are too reliant on this Protestant-modern notion of religion.[5] Mahmood's metaphor of ingestion is the very antinomy of this ostensibly modern notion of religion. Ingestion gives you transmuted being, not discursive belief. But as Mahmood's metaphor makes clear such a critique of modern religion is itself part of a certain Christian nostalgia that undergirds the contemporary turn to religion, and links it also to another, Modernist, context. The idea of a different, unruptured mode of religious identification, one that overcomes relations between subject and object, thought and feeling is what T. S. Eliot argues for when he laments the "dissociation of sensibility" that ostensibly sets in at the end of the seventeenth century. Once we remember the Modernist context, even the turn to Byzantium seems overdetermined—one has only to think of Yeats.[6] As I suggested in the previous chapter, the intellectual formation of which Asad and Mahmood are leading proponents is as much driven by Modernist and Anglo-Catholic anti-Reformation thought as it is by Weberian conceptions of the relation between the rise of Protestantism and the consolidation of the modern capitalist order.

Mahmood supplements the notion of ingestion with Kenneth Parry's reading of the importance of Aristotelian notions of schesis in Byzantine iconophilia in the second iconoclastic controversy. What this reading of Byzantine Christianity is supposed to offer is a precedent for understanding modes of identification between subject and object of veneration that do not attribute arbitrariness to the attachment between image and deity or native and image/object. A different model of relation along with the metaphor of ingestion allows for completion of a different semiotic ideology—one that can provide a counter to the liberal-Protestant version.

It is particularly the iconophiles' defense of their doctrine of "consubstantiality" against charges of idolatry that interests Mahmood. The relation between image and deity is one, as she presents it, in her reading of Parry of "homonymy and hypostasis: the image and deity are two in nature and essence but identical in name" (*RR*, 77). In order to explain this further, Mahmood turns, very briefly, to a historian: "In the words of the historian Marie-José Mondzain, to be the 'image of' is to be in a living relation to" (*RR*, 77). Mahmood's expansion of this is that schesis "captures this living relation because of its heightened psychophysiological and emotional connotations and its emphasis on familiarity and intimacy as a necessary aspect of the relation" (*RR*, 77).

What one might expect after this is a discussion of images of Muhammad and their living relation to the Prophet and of the Danish political cartoons as some particularly offensive perversion of such iconographic impulses, since Mahmood has already told us it is not the representation per se in the cartoons that is objectionable—an argument, in any case, that would be hard to sustain given Mahmood's conceptual recourse to iconophilic rather than iconoclastic thought. But Mahmood has also already set up the meaning of icon as metaphorical and not literal: an icon is not just an image; it can also be "a cluster of meanings" that can suggest "a persona, an authoritative presence, or even a shared imagination" (*RR*, 74). The icon is thus "a form of relationality that binds the subject to an object or imaginary" (*RR*, 74).[7] In any case, once the icon is established as

any sanctified relation between entities, things, or persons, it is perhaps not a complete surprise when Mahmood takes the template of
Parry's discussion of Byzantine uses of schesis to apply to the relation
between Muhammad and the Muslim rather than Muhammad and
his image. Mahmood begins the paragraph that follows the one about
the relation between image and deity with the following sentence, and
it is the execution of the shift that intrigues me here: "What interests
me in the iconophile tradition is not so much the image as the concept
of relationality that binds the subject to the object of veneration" (*RR*,
77). At this point, it is not at all clear whether the relation in question is between the image and the deity, which is what the preceding
sentence is about, or between Muhammad and the believer. What, in
other words, is the object of veneration here? Is the relation of image
to deity a relation of veneration? Moreover, is image to the Muslim as
Muhammad is to the deity? How does one map one relation onto the
other without careful elucidation? Is the Muslim, on these terms, the
image of Muhammad?

The passage that follows is, in my view, one of the two cruces of
the essay, and in it Mahmood begins to attempt to clear the way for
what is nothing less than a new theory of Muslim worship. I will
quote it at length.

> This modality of relationship is operative in a number of traditions
> of worship and often coexists in some tension with other dominant
> ideologies of perception and religious practice. The three Abrahamic
> faiths adopted a range of key Aristotelian and Platonic concepts and
> practices that were often historically modified to fit the theological
> and doctrinal requirements of each tradition. In contemporary Islam,
> these ideas and practices, far from becoming extinct, have been
> reconfigured under conditions of new perceptual regimes and modes
> of governance—a reconfiguration that requires serious engagement
> with the historical relevance of these practices in the present.
>
> Schesis aptly captures not only how a devout Muslims relationship
> to Muhammad is described in Islamic devotional literature but also
> how it is lived and practiced in various parts of the Muslim world.
> (*RR*, 77)

It is still not clear which modality of relation is at play here, or even
before we get to its modality, which relation is at stake here. Is it the
relation between image and deity or prophet and follower? Or both,
or is it that one can substitute for the other?

The more intriguing line running through this passage is the
quiet creation of this mode of Muslim worship as nondominant, and

potentially a minority, within Muslim global practice—a minority also within a group of Muslims who start out in the article as *the* offended minority within Europe. At the same time, Mahmood's procedure allows for the creation of this mode of worship as potentially representative because it is intended to explain "religious" and "Muslim" pain, not the pain of some Muslims. As Mahmood will argue later in the article, it is in relation to this, not necessarily representative, form of Muslim self-constitution that the "Judeo-Christian sensibilities that undergird secular liberal law" might have to be changed in order to accommodate the Muslim minority in Europe. (I will return to this fascinating moment later.) In this passage, the modes of devotion Mahmood describes in the essay are "new" "reconfigurations" at odds with "dominant" largely unnamed ideologies, and these modes are not confined to European Muslims—the prime players in the controversy. In fact, some of the most important mobilizers in the Danish cartoon affair are not mentioned at all.[8] It turns out that these modes of worship are spread through a variety of largely unspecified Muslim contexts—although as a source of evidentiary material, Egypt runs large through the article and its footnotes.

Mahmood is creating a new-old Muslim mode, which names a global polity through a complexly analogical procedure. What Byzantium offers is a precedent for understanding antiliberal/ anti-Protestant modes of identification between subject and object of veneration. The use of Aristotelian notions of relation combined with the metaphor of ingestion allows for the completion of a different semiotic ideology. This counter-ideology could be said to comprise a Catholic-Byzantine mode of thinking as opposed to a Protestant one. An intriguing side effect is a remerging of the Eastern and Catholic Churches through the creation of a Byzanto-Catholic Islam offered in response to modern/liberal/Protestant/secularism, and created through this analogical assembling of a semiotic counter-ideology. There is a reciprocal creation, thus, of a counter-Enlightenment, even Counter-Reformation, mode of European affective, constitutively embodied, thought offered as a mode of antisecular, anti-Protestant, antiliberal religiosity and of a Muslim mode of affective embodied devotion and ethical thinking also offered as a mode of antisecular, antiliberal, anti-Protestant being. These modes of thought and being are both connected through Abrahamic variations on Platonic and Aristotelian thought and illuminated through an assemblage of Catholic-Byzantine concepts.

In addition, what this recourse to Byzantium and ingestion and icon also enables is for Mahmood to assert that to insult the Prophet is to actually hurt a Muslim. In other words, to inflict a pain a Muslim has no choice but to feel, or perhaps only the devout or the non-dominant Muslim has no choice but to feel. Those who adhere to the "normative conception of religion as belief" tend to assume that "the epistemological status of religious belief" is "speculative" and thus "less 'real'" than the materiality of race and biology" (*RR*, 81). Mahmood aims to reconceptualize the materiality of "religious belief" in order to explain the nature of the injury felt by Muslims. Religious offense is moral injury that causes a pain it would be wrong to see as merely psychic (hence the term *psychophysiological*) and is in fact akin to racial assault but not entirely reducible to it, yet the pain turns anything perceived as offensive into physiological as well as psychic attack—that the theological premise of such identification itself might be considered idolatrous, and thus hugely suspect, by radical, militant, yet minority (depending on regional and national context), or state-sanctioned or state-complicit branches of Sunni Islam is something that she registers only in her passing invocation of dominant ideologies.[9]

The form of the analogical procedure here works not only to produce an affinity between colonizing missionaries and present-day liberals and progressives but also to occlude the iconoclasm of many contemporary and historical forms of Islam, including those professed by many of the actors in the Danish cartoon controversy. Would the dismay of the Protestant missionaries have been distinct from that of Muslims encountering Hindu "idols" or Muhammad's relation with "false gods" in Mecca? What are we to make of the Taliban's hostility, bafflement, or, for that matter, affective response to the Bamiyan statues or the Saudi establishment's hostility to the pilgrims who look for graves of revered figures from the Muslim past in Mecca and Medina, an act that is considered idolatrous by the establishment. In other words, who is akin to the missionary here, and how many degrees of separation does that confer from the liberals? What of the desecration of Muhammad's gravestone by the Wahhabis as far back as 1804?[10] What also of those who today blow up Sufi shrines, or attack Shia Ta'aziyeh processions? Can liberal "bafflement" be shamed into understanding by an embarrassing, or worse, genealogical association? Can, in turn, such a procedure externalize a notion of an iconoclastic "semiotic ideology"—shared by segments of modern and early

Islam and, equally, resisted and transformed by other segments—as somehow only an arid symptom of a liberalism or modernity or secularism, or all of the above (at this point I am simply not sure what to call it), Protestant-Christian in its contours? In other words, can an Islam conceived in Byzantine-Catholic terms, stabilized by opposition to liberal, Protestant, secular modernity, do away with some of the most intense and consequent divisions, precisely over icons and iconic attitudes, in a range of diasporic and Muslim-majority contexts today?[11] As we shall see in the next chapter, the use of aesthetic iconic traditions from Catholicism and Byzantium is instead being used to *contest* neo-orthodox Islamism, which is frequently perceived to have radically iconoclastic impulses. A more interesting question might be: How does a presumptively Barelvi notion of Islam—referred to by Modood in the context of *The Satanic Verses*—merge with Wahhabist, Salafist, and perhaps even Deobandi strands in the metropolitan context, and how are the Wahhabi influence and colonial context of Deobandism forgotten? In other words, it might be worth pausing over how the historical affinities and differences are reswirled into just "Islam" in the metropole.

If the production of this countersemiotics is to enable better, and equal, coexistence across lines of "religious difference" it raises a host of difficulties. The "devout Muslim" produced through an analysis of his or her "religious pain" is one who feels an injury unintelligible to liberal, modern, Protestant seculars, shares a relation to icons and iconic objects and imaginaries that are akin to, and even share, Byzantine-Aristotelian notions of the icon, manifests a late-twentieth-century semiotic theory advanced by Mitchell and an epistemology (held by tribal natives) akin to that which confused early Protestant missionaries. But this Muslim then gets to stand in as representative for Muslims in general, and his or her pain is invited to begin to set guidelines for how Europe should learn to deal with its migrants.

In the second of, what I think of as, the two cruces of this essay, Mahmood brings together the antilegalism of her critique of secular modernity and the consequences of her explication of moral injury and Muslim pain. She argues, as against positions advocated by Modood, that Muslims who turn to the court or to the state simply do not understand that to turn this kind of injury into a legally prosecutable crime is to fundamentally transform or destroy that very "religiosity." Given its predication on entirely different conceptions of the "subject religiosity, harm and semiosis" to turn it over to the "logic of civil law is to promulgate its demise (rather than to protect it)" (*RR*, 88). This leads, then, to what is either the bold naming of an impasse or the equally bold, though implicit, suggesting of a solution:

> Ultimately, the future of the Muslim minority in Europe depends not so much on how secular-liberal protocols of free speech might be expanded to accommodate its concerns as on a larger transformation of the cultural and ethical sensibilities of the Judeo-Christian population that undergird the cultural practices of secular-liberal law. (*RR*, 89)

Since secular-liberal law, even when it upholds Muslim majoritarian interests (as in the ECtHR decision in the case of Turkey), is Judeo-Christian at the level of "cultural and ethical sensibility," it will, in fact, transform Muslim religiosity. I am not interested here in disagreeing with Mahmood on the efficacy, let alone ethics or politics, of turning to the law to impose various forms of censorship; I am interested in trying to understand what, if anything, is being advocated. Since Muslims apparently share some sensibilities with Jews and Christians, which sensibilities would require transformation on the terms of the essay? Should Jews and Christians become less Jewish and Christian? Should Christians become iconophilic affiliates of the Eastern Church or more Catholic? What are Jews to do? Is it instead that the underpinnings of the law need to become more Eastern Christian/Catholic and thus potentially more Muslim? Since it is the shared, if refracted, Aristotelian and Platonic strands of thought that run through the Abrahamic religions which are used to explain Muslim practice, it is not clear whether law has to become less Judeo-Christian or more in line with the kind of Islam in line with aspects of law assumed to be more consonant with anti-Protestant strains of Christianity.

The problem manifest here runs through the essay. When I try to describe Mahmood's analogical procedure, I am not at all suggesting that it is comparison per se that ought not be undertaken. Neither do I wish to deny similarities and continuities between the three religions. Of course, there are shared philosophical traditions and theological impulses in the three Abrahamic religions, and to the extent that both Asad and Mahmood are attentive to these, the turn to religion of which they are part is intellectually useful. But my intention is rather to question the way in which Mahmood's procedure covers divisions within societies and turns them into historical monoliths, which so conceptualized are then made to do analogical work that, in turn, occludes consequent divisions and the complexity of political formations in the present. A procedure that shows the contestations that attend repeated divisions over icons and iconoclastic thought in Byzantine and Western Christian societies—the iconoclastic controversies and post-Reformation struggles—that shows how similar divisions are lived in Muslim contexts, and how they might be reproduced through contact and emulation in different Islamicate societies and diasporic contexts, is very different from a procedure that uses anticolonial and anti-imperial sentiment in order to stabilize (and create) monolithic identities even while parenthetically disavowing such monolithicism.

Moreover, my point is not at all to question Mahmood's skepticism about enshrining anti-Protestant religious impulses into civil law (which she has also suggested is immanently Protestant), or to question her mention, in passing, of the problem of the nation-state as it cross-cuts the issue of minorities. Indeed, once one shifts locations, critiques of the entwinement between religious concepts and law, foregroundings of the problem of the nation-state's relationship with minorities—especially as it intersects with colonial history, postcolonial crisis, and a newly explicit imperialism—acquire crucial though very different, if connected, valences. It is to these that I would now like to turn.

REGIMES OF FEELING

In the context of Pakistan, the question of the relationship between minority, identity, and law gets at the very heart of the problematic of the postcolonial nation-state. The battle around what is called the "blasphemy law," although the word "blasphemy" does not occur in it, confronts us with the most challenging questions that comprise the predicament of the postcolonial state: how are institutions to be formed or re-formed in the context of decolonization? How are the configurations of law and sensibility within structures of colonialism to be rethought, or even undone? In the age of renewed religious nationalism, how are we to configure, or for that matter even recognize, what is indigenous? How is religious indigeneity to be secured? What is its relation with religious orthodoxy?

Postcolonial critics and theorists of South Asia have tended to focus on the Indian state's relation with religion and religious minorities. From this perspective it is the avowedly secular state's failure to incorporate religious minorities, while honoring their difference, that marks the limit or failure of secularization. According to Gauri Viswanathan's subtle and inflected account of belief and conversion in modernity, secularization in India has always been a "fraught process," in large part because parliamentary reform has not been able to absorb religious minorities as "citizens."[12] For Viswanathan this is because, in India, state formation is "basically incorporation of the subjects into a colonial state"; after independence this process transforms into absorption into a "hegemonic state in which the social relations sanctioned by colonialism continue virtually uninterrupted."[13] The continuities between the colonial and postcolonial state are important. Equally important, however, is that religious conflicts in South Asia seem also to have intensified in ways that reveal the reconfigurations of power in the post-Independence states. In the Indian context the destruction of the Babri mosque and the violence in Gujrat may be the most extreme signatures of this intensification. These postcolonial reconfigurations invite more sustained study of majoritarian action, agency, and responsibility within the not quite new nation-states.

The postcolonial state's combination of rupture and continuity with the colonial state requires more work on what the postcolonial state has added to these social relations, and the global, Cold War context of these additions. In Pakistan, the Sunni Muslim majority has come increasingly to define the denominational inflection of the state; and the marginalization of minorities as citizens does not emanate from the failure of state-sponsored secularization to ensure "absorption." It issues instead from attempts to secure the religious underpinning of the postcolonial state, under conditions of the large-scale, Cold War–enabled decimation and neutralization of progressives opposed to these attempts, combined with the addition of the sensibilities of a specific religion to penal laws designed to manage colonial populations by letting them have their religion. Increasingly, it is a state with a particular Islamic inflection that deprives minorities of their status as citizens, sometimes because it is attempting to secure a particular meaning of Islam and to create a proper Muslim persona—by way of the control of the image of the Prophet—in and through the structures of the state. The most powerful instrument of this consolidation has been a military government's addition of a series of amendments to British penal law. The centrality of the military's shaping of state structures itself invites a more sustained conceptualization of the praetorian element in structures of governmentality than is possible here. The peculiar combinatory of normalization through the juridical sphere of the law and the sovereign power of the military in the process of promulgating the law throws up a paradox, for it suggests the normalization of the exceptional. The military's relationship to the National Assembly during the Zia period, and more generally over the national history, suggests the ongoing necessity of conceptualizing the role of structures of state, including militaristic ones, in the formation of the juridical sphere.

Viswanathan has been critical of the reduction of religion to "wounded sentiments" in the Rushdie affair and has, in my view, rightly seen a recourse to the language of the wound as a "permissible secular gesture" that has the virtue of not "pandering to religious absolutism" on which these sentiments are based.[14] Such a privileging of "the subjectivity of sentiment over the objectivity of creed steers clear of antiheretical presumptions while still holding fast to the ideal of cultural relativism."[15] It is not incompatible with Viswanathan's argument to emphasize that, in the Anglophone context, the language of the wound, when invoked in relation to the religions of South Asian former subject populations, issues from colonial law, shaped in turn by the need to produce a governable population.

It is, of course, not surprising to say that the protection afforded the religious feelings of the colonial subject is entangled with the need to produce a more governable polity and that such governance was assumed to require managing relations between the different religious populations of the Indian subcontinent. As far back as 1785, in his oft-quoted preface to Charles Wilkin's translation of the Bhagavad Gita, drawing upon the idiom of English sentimentalism, Warren Hastings connected the "conciliation" of "distant affections" with the "exercise of dominion." The mode of this conciliation was the gathering and dissemination of local knowledge; it was indeed in the guise of what one might characterize as a certain "respect" for indigenous religious knowledge that the consolidation of colonialism was to occur:

> Every accumulation of knowledge and especially such as is obtained
> by social communication with people over whom we exercise a
> dominion founded on the right of conquest, is useful to the state: it
> is the gain of humanity: in the specific instance which I have stated,
> it attracts and conciliates distant affections; it lessens the weight of
> the chain by which the natives are held in subjection; and it imprints
> on the heart of our own countrymen the sense and obligation of
> benevolence.[16]

What is often emphasized in the discussion of colonial law is the production of knowledge and its relation with colonial conquest.[17] A more systematic understanding of the colonial production of religious affect and its imbrication with the institutions of religious knowledge, "custom," and code is also required. The relation between sentiment and subjection would underpin an emphasis on indigenous law and custom, and this foundational entanglement of affect and the consolidation of conquest was to prove extraordinarily consequential in the codification of Hinduism and Islam in India. The explicit entanglement of knowledge, the "right of conquest," and the need to find a way to win over the affections of the people in Hastings's introduction is remarkable. The production of such conciliating knowledge is also part of the project of a creation of a fiction of reciprocity in the figure of colonial "benevolence" to be imprinted on the "heart" of the English. This benevolence is to be fortified by the "virtue" rather than the "ability" of the employees of the East India Company, for it is on this virtue that the Company must rely for the "permanency of their [*sic*] dominion."[18] English virtue and the conciliation of native affection are to remain forever connected. Bernard Cohn has made the case that Hastings invented the emblematic figure of British imperialism, the colonial administrator who knows the natives.[19] One might add that the political use and efficacy of this figure lies in his anthropological knowledge of native difference, a knowledge undergirded by a blend of benevolence, virtue, conciliation, and domination. The anthropological administrator thus invented is a sentimental figure.

That this sentimental idiom would explode into Burke's sensational rhetoric, which was attended by visions of abject Indian suffering and famously of female bodies, wrenched from homes made sanctuaries by religion, so brilliantly discussed in Sara Suleri's seminal essay on the impeachment of Warren Hastings, is a symptom of the ubiquity of the idiom in the formation of "imperial sensibilities," even in their ostensibly critical guise.[20]

The law configures the subject population as a body to be engaged and humored ("conciliated" one might say) at the level of feeling; that is, it produces an understanding of the native's relation with religion as a series of affects, a mesh of feelings rather than principled commitments or propositions, even as the knowledge produced in colonial institutions fixes and codifies religious practice and belief. On the terms of the colonial state, it is these feelings that required protective governance; the penal code is to assist in the management of the realm of native emotion. Conquest and plunder were to be followed by conciliation.

It is perhaps unsurprising that the first draft of the code was authored by a law commission chaired by Thomas Macaulay in 1837.[21] Sentimentalism and liberalism converged in the juridical sphere of the colony, shaping the discourses of law and knowledge, creating religious affect as a mesh of relations of power—of the colonizer to dispense the salve and of the colonized to demand and exercise power by avowing religious feeling—and, in the postcolonial aftermath, enabling the discursive power of the praetorian state under Zia-ul-Haq, whose addition of five amendments to the British colonial code is central to the state's attempted capture of its citizens' Muslim persona—indeed, to its creation of an affective sphere in which every citizen is required to develop a relation of feeling to the icons of Islam chosen by the state.

Of the four articles in the chapter (XV) pertaining to "Offences Against Religion" in the Indian Penal Code of 1860, two explicitly invoke religious feelings. In article 297, the object is to protect "funeral ceremonies," places of burial, potential desecrations of the dead from people who have "the intention of wounding the religious feelings of any person, or of insulting the religion of any person, or with the knowledge that the feelings of any person are likely to be wounded, or that the religion of any person is likely to be insulted thereby, commits any trespass" in any place that might be associated with burial or funeral ceremonies.[22]

In article 298 the solicitude for the religious feelings of the colonized is more central to the juridical aim:

> Uttering words, &c., with deliberate intent to wound the religious feelings of any person.
>
> Whoever, with the deliberate intention of wounding the religious feelings of any person utters, any word or makes any sound in the hearing of that person, or makes any gesture in the sight of that person, or places any object in the sight of the person, shall be punished with imprisonment of either description for a term which may extend to one year, or with fine, or with both. (*IPC*, 139)

The only amendment added by the colonial government (295–A) in 1927 was in response to the conflict that ensued upon the publication of the pamphlet, *Rangīlā Rasūl* (The Libertine Prophet), when the article most explicitly committed to containing communal public disorder was deemed inadequate to convict the author of the text.[23]

The original article 295 reads as follows:

> Injuring or defiling a place of worship, with intent to insult the religion of any class:
>   Whoever destroys, damages or defiles any place of worship, or any object held sacred by any class of persons with the intention of thereby insulting the religion of any class of persons, or with the knowledge that any class of persons is likely to consider such destruction, damage or defilement as an insult to their religion shall be punished with imprisonment of either description for a term which may extend to two years, or with fine, or with both. (*IPC*, 138)

Amendment 295-A adds outraging "religious feelings" back into the article where in the original article the crime is "intent to insult." Perhaps most significantly, it links these feelings to religious "beliefs." In the Pakistan Penal Code, the substitution of "the citizens of Pakistan" for "His Majesty's subjects" for those whose religious feelings need to be protected establishes it as the most ecumenical of the amendments, for, unlike the post-Independence amendments, it configures those who can be injured as Pakistani and not only Muslim:

> Deliberate and malicious acts intended to outrage religious feelings of any class by insulting its religion or religious beliefs:
>   Whoever with deliberate and malicious intention of outraging the religious feelings of any class of the citizens of Pakistan, by words, either spoken or written or by visible representations insults the religion or the religious beliefs of that class, shall be punished with imprisonment of either description for a term which may extend to ten years, or with fine, or with both. (*PPC*).

Reading the language of the colonial code helps dispel a certain confusion that might have been felt around the Rushdie affair, the rhetorical field of which comes increasingly to seem like part of the long afterlife of colonial law. At the time, commentators, such as Roald Dahl, critical of Rushdie, were prone to say that Rushdie "knew" what he was doing. One might have wondered: What is it that he should have known? What was the stake of such knowledge? Why, in an age that was otherwise so comfortable with the unconscious prompts of speech, action, or writing, was knowing so important? Article 295 clarifies the genealogy of that use: in the article, the punishment is for anyone who acts "with the knowledge that any class of persons is likely to consider such destruction, damage or defilement as an insult to their religion." Article 295-A adds the written text to the list of injury-causing objects. It becomes clear that knowing as conscious knowledge, as that which should have activated a prohibition within himself that would have negated Rushdie's writing of the novel, is related to the legal requirement of "intention" that, in these articles, attends prosecution. "Knowing" in this context suggests a normalization of the law, the linguistic adaptation of the juridical aim of containing trangression and keeping social order while managing unruly subject populations. "Knowing" also relies on an assumption that as a former "native," Rushdie has particular access to the feelings of his people and is thus particularly culpable. This proximity then ensures his status as traitor.

Lingering access to the language of the law, shaped by complex processes of historical diffusion, feeds into contemporary British policies of official multiculturalism that seek to turn the management of Britain's racially different populations over to religious community leaders, and into also the recourse to the notion of religious pain by a proponent of state-sponsored multiculturalism such as Modood, which then is explained in its "Muslim" variation, almost two decades later, by a Foucault-inspired critic of legalism such as Mahmood.[24]

After Independence, the colonial laws come to play a complex role in securing the identity of the nation as Muslim. In their current form, the Pakistani laws regarding offenses against religion, consisting of five amendments added under the military dictator General Zia-ul Haq and the original articles and one amendment of chapter XV of the colonial code, represent an attempt to fill in a particular Islamic content to the religious feelings mentioned in the original code. They do not represent an erasure of colonial liberalism's protection of the natives from religious pain, simply its attachment to a particular group. The praetorian state attempts the creation of the proper Muslim persona and its relation to Muhammad through military-executive fiat, that is, through the militarized sovereignty of the state, through, in effect, the militarized control and production of iconography and of the citizen's relations with icons and iconic objects. Perhaps the amendments that do so most explicitly are the ones pertaining to the Prophet and his family:

> 295-C: Whoever by words, either spoken or written, or by visible representation or by any imputation, innuendo, or insinuation, directly or indirectly, defiles the sacred name of the Holy Prophet Muhammad (peace be upon him) shall be punished with death, or imprisonment for life, and shall also be liable to fine. (*PPC*)

The first amendment to 298—the article originally most directly concerned with protecting religious feelings from being wounded—specified that those who are not to be insulted include the family, the caliphs (in a clause that seems intended to target Shias who tend to be critical of the first three caliphs), and the friends of the Prophet, using the same language of implication and innuendo: "Whoever by words, either spoken or written, or by visible representation or by any imputation, innuendo, or insinuation, directly or indirectly, defiles the sacred names of any wife (Ummul Mumineen), or members of the family (Ahle-bait), of the Holy Prophet (peace be upon him), or any of the righteous Caliphs (Khulafa-e-Rashideen) or companions (Sahaaba) of the Holy Prophet (peace be upon him)" (*PPC*). The punishment is imprisonment of up to three years, a fine, or both.

It is 295-C that is usually referred to as the "blasphemy law," when the term is used in the singular, and one might argue that it represents an attempt to give full juridical force to attachments to Muhammad. The ones that also incurred life imprisonment (295-B and 295-C) and, in the case of insults to Muhammad (295-C), now the death penalty, are used disproportionately in accusation against Christians. The vagueness of its language makes it a particularly useful weapon in the hands of those seeking to settle petty disputes.[25] The mandatory death sentence, added under Nawaz Sharif's first government, suggests that it is this very vagueness of "Imputation, insinuation, and innuendo, directly or indirectly," that requires the punishment of death in the framing of the amendment, as if the ephemerality of the accusation demands the ultimate corporeal finality for its complete and proper embodiment, perhaps even its reality—as if only the death of the accused can secure the truth of the accusation.[26] The refraction of the spirit of the law in the social imaginary is represented by the fact that although none of the accused have been executed by the state, many have been murdered during trial or on release. The addition of the two amendments to the one added after the *Rangīlā Rasūl* controversy reveals a haunting of the Pakistani imaginary by a colonial history of religious strife, a trauma endlessly to be replayed on the bodies of the nation's minorities. The minority's identity as citizen is erased through the production of the citizen's proper relation with the icon.

A constitutional amendment, which is a crucial precursor to the additions to the penal code attacked the Ahmaddiyya minority through an act of theological targeting.[27] Thus when Zia embarked on his process of Islamization, and instituted the changes to the penal code, which was an attempt to reconstitute every aspect of Pakistani society, the space for those legally declared minorities, the Christians, Ahmadis, Parsis, Sikhs, and Hindus, had already shrunk significantly. The space for minorities began to be whittled away with the passing of the Objectives resolution of the Constituent Assembly of 1949, with its emphasis on Islam as the grounds of the state.[28] Subsequent negotiations over the question of the sovereignty of Islam in the state in the three constitutions of 1956, 1962, and 1973 further normalized the marginality of minoritarian citizenship.

In the amendment, Ahmadis are defined as non-Muslim through theological targeting. The amendment devolves on the proposition that Muhammad is the last prophet. The doctrinal name for this proposition is Khatm-e nubūwwat (the finality of prophethood), evident in the third part of the amendment:

> 3- Amendment of article 260 of the Constitution.
>
> In the constitution, in article 260, after clause (2) the following new clause shall be added, namely—A person who does not believe in the absolute and unqualified finality of The Prophethood of Muhammad (Peace be upon him), the last of the Prophets or claims to be a Prophet, in any sense of the word or of any description whatsoever, after Muhammad (Peace be upon him), or recognizes such a claimant as a Prophet or religious reformer, is not a Muslim for the purposes of the Constitution or law.[29]

The density of Ahmadi belief, practice, and theology has been reduced, by those opposed to the Ahmadis, to what is presented as one theological essential. The Ahmadi belief that their leader, though subordinate to Muhammad, received a revelation is placed against their self-understanding as Muslims, and the finality of Prophethood is invoked to declare them non-Muslims.[30] The offense and injury, caused by perceived or actual challenges to the finality of prophethood, are modes of expressing a passionate attachment to the Prophet. They now haunt the national imagination and are a cause of considerable anxiety and fear for Ahmadis and Christians.[31]

As if performing the centrality of the Ahmadi question to the project of the nation-state, two of the five penal amendments are constructed to target and exclude a particular religious group, the Ahmadis, from the Muslim religious fold and manifest a rather sustained attempt to manage attachments to the Prophet, disallowing those excluded from any attachment or affiliation to him and arrogating to the state the power to curtail its forms and representations. The detail is exhausting, but the amendments are worth reading in full. The sheer length of the articles and the compulsive list of prohibitions emphasize the centrality of the Ahmadi question to the enterprise of securing the content of the Islam forming the ground of the state. The detail suggests, moreover, a will to power that requires the complete eradication of the grounds of the perceived enemy's religious being. It is not the privatization of belief and practice but its complete *confiscation* that is at work:

> 298–B: Misuse of epithets, descriptions and titles, etc., reserved for certain holy personages or places: (1) Any person of the Quadiani group or the Lahori group (who call themselves 'Ahmadis' or by any other name) who by words, either spoken or written, or by visible representation- (a) refers to or addresses, any person, other than a Caliph or companion of the Holy Prophet Muhammad (peace be upon him), as "Ameer-ul-Mumineen", "Khalifatul-Mumineen", "Khalifa-tul-Muslimeen", "Sahaabi" or "Razi Allah Anho"; (b) refers to, or addresses, any person, other than a wife of the Holy Prophet Muhammad (peace be upon him), as "Ummul-Mumineen"; (c) refers to, or addresses, any person, other than a member of the family "Ahle-bait" of the Holy Prophet Muhammad (peace be upon him), as "Ahle-bait"; or (d) refers to, or names, or calls, his place of worship a "Masjid"; shall be punished with imprisonment of either description for a term which may extend to three years, and shall also be liable to fine. (2) Any person of the Qaudiani group or Lahori group (who call themselves "Ahmadis" or by any other name) who by words, either spoken or written, or by visible representation refers to the mode or form of call to prayers followed by his faith as "Azan", or recites Azan as used by the Muslims, shall be punished with imprisonment of either description for a term which may extend to three years, and shall also be liable to fine. (*PPC*)

> 298–C: Person of Quadiani group, etc., calling himself a Muslim or preaching or propagating his faith: Any person of the Quadiani group or the Lahori group (who call themselves 'Ahmadis' or by any other name), who directly or indirectly, poses himself as a Muslim, or calls, or refers to, his faith as Islam, or preaches or propagates his faith, or invites others to accept his faith, by words, either spoken or written, or by visible representations, or in any manner whatsoever outrages the religious feelings of Muslims shall be punished with imprisonment of either description for a term which may extend to three years and shall also be liable to fine. (*PPC*)

Promulgated in what was called Ordinance XX in 1984, the attachment of these amendments regarding Ahmadis to the article most concerned with protecting the religious feelings of various groups suggests that the very act of being an Ahmadi inflicts a wound on Muslims, that any claim to being Muslims by Ahmadis is a cause of Muslim religious pain. When I first drafted the preceding sentence, I was responding merely to what I saw as the rhetorical logic of the framing of the amendments, but since then I have discovered that this equation has a diffuse social circulation. In 2010, Nawaz Sharif, announcing his sympathy for Ahmadis following suicide bombings of two mosques, in which eighty were killed, called them "brothers and sisters." There was condemnation from many clerics for his declaration of such kinship. From across the border in India, the Ahrars, a militant group formed in 1929, ferociously opposed to the Ahmadis, apparently insufficiently occupied with the discrimination against Muslims there, found time to respond. Their leading cleric declared that Nawaz Sharif had "hurt the sentiments of Muslims" by calling the Ahmadis brothers. Showing a blissful lack of anxiety about mediatic representation, they provided this information through an article from the *Hindustan Times* prominently displayed on their website. The news functions as a mode of self-declaration, indeed, as a form of promulgation.[32]

At stake is a precise conception of Muslim interiority and an attendant assumption regarding its transparency to the state. The gauge of the authenticity of Muslim interiority is thus a commitment to a doctrinal proposition. On the one hand, the amendments seem to privilege an orthopractic understanding of religion, and Islam, whereby even engaging in a practice is a way of usurping its identity; on the other hand, by their very commitment to the doctrine of the finality of prophethood, they insist that such a practice is dependent on a content assigned to belief—that is, a theological claim with propositional content that requires assent.[33] The amendments encode the attempt to strip any possible expression—in practice or utterance—of being Muslims from Ahmadis and thus to take away their very identity. The requirement that Ahmadis have to be prevented from "posing" as Muslims is a complete denial of the ontological possibility of them being Muslim; that is, they can only impersonate Muslims.[34] While impersonation is the only action possible by Ahmadis it can turn Muslims away from being Muslim because it invites others, through proselytization and presumably the seduction of emulation, to engage in similar posing. It is this apparent impersonation that then has to be prevented by stripping language from them. Even as the very language of devotion is taken away, they are the ones construed as inflicting the injury.

The genealogy of the word *posing* in the anti-Ahmaddiyya amendments both demands an attention to the question of belief's content and illustrates with particular trenchancy the problem of the transformation of minority and nationalism over the course of decolonization. "Posing" comes directly from Abul Ala Mawdudi's English-language version of the 1953 polemic, "The Qadiani Problem."[35] The pamphlet was written to demand the removal of Muhammad Zafarullah Khan, the foreign minister at the time and the author of the Pakistan Resolution:

> But Qadianis penetrate into the Muslim Society posing as Muslims; they propagate their views in the name of Islam; start controversies everywhere, carry on proselytizing propaganda in an aggressive manner and continuously strive to swell their numbers at the expense of Muslim society. They have thus become a permanent disintegrating force amongst Muslims. How can it, therefore, be possible to show the same kind of toleration towards them as is shown towards other passive sects?[36]

Mawdudi appended two documents by Muhammad Iqbal to authorize this sense of a threat to Muslim society from the group: a letter to *The Statesman,* which had published Iqbal's original, 1934 pamphlet against the Ahmadiyya ("Qadianis and Orthodox Muslims") and a response to Nehru ("Islam and Ahmadism," also published as "Reply to Questions raised by Pundit Nehru") who had asked why Iqbal had felt the need to write the first piece, published in 1935. Although Iqbal's complete oeuvre is more aesthetically and philosophically complicated than these essays suggest, and can even be taken to authorize certain notions of Muslim selfhood and dignity, one might speculate that it is a complex double pressure that leads to this very dark contribution to the status of minorities.[37] The first lies in the necessity of an unruptured Muslim identity. The second is in the effect of English on the position he articulates. He produces these statements in Anglophone texts, Mawdudi circulates them in English as well as Urdu, and the law itself is in English. In this Anglophone context, Islam becomes subject to a defensive language of differentiation and becomes permeated by the exigencies of power in the colonial state. Paradoxically in the postcolonial context the Anglophone frame is crucial to the violence of the law, whose defenders repeatedly cast it in anti-Western and anticolonial terms—in terms, in other words, entirely determined by a "Western" audience. The genealogy of the law reminds us that the colonial administration was the first audience to whom Iqbal addressed his demands.

It must be said that, in these essays, Iqbal's fear is not of secularism or of religion's expulsion from the modern world but of more, other, religions. In "Qadianism and Orthodox Muslims," he presents both Bahaism and Ahmadism as instances of pre-Islamic Magianism, which, according to Iqbal, relies on a "constant expectation" of prophets because continuity of prophethood is necessary in the Magian context (*QM*, 92). The result of the "Magian attitude" is the "disintegration of old communities and the constant formation of new ones by all sorts of religious adventurers" (*QM*, 92). The return to the pre-Islamic past in such practices entails permanent communitarian revolution and ensures the possibility of new religions. For Iqbal, "since Islam . . . claims to weld all the various communities of the world into one single community" it cannot "reconcile itself with a movement which threatens its present solidarity and promises of further rifts in human society" (*QM*, 92). What makes Ahmadis so threatening to this solidarity is the challenge they pose to the Muslim community because "the integrity of Muslim society is secured by the Finality of Prophethood alone" (*QM*, 92). Because Ahmadis claim to be Muslim and engage in practices that are associated with Muslims they undermine the community from within; they are, in other words, internal threats that very locally undermine the vision of global homogeneity—the world as one single community—that constitutes Iqbal's utopia in these essays.

Ayesha Jalal has argued that within Iqbal's thought the insistent opposition to Ahmadis issues from the effects of the internal politics of the Punjab.[38] On my view, that regional issue intersects with a very precise conception of interiority and a theological intimacy, which shapes the intensity of the disavowal and makes it so necessary to ensure that the "externals" of practice be shown to be at odds with Ahmadi inwardness, that Ahmadis be shown only to be capable of posing as Muslims, since "Qadianism" "retains some of the more important externals of Islam with an inwardness wholly inimical of the spirit and aspirations of Islam" (*QM*, 93). This denial of the possibility of inwardness is predicated on the importance of the proposition of prophetic finality to Muslim interiority.[39] For Iqbal, Ahmadis can only appear to be Muslims because their belief puts them at odds with Islam, and thus their practice must be empty: they cannot possess, what is to Iqbal, a specifically Muslim interiority. Their very intimate challenge comes from their ability to seem Muslim in practice and even in utterance.

The problem of appearing Muslim then becomes a crucial challenge to what Iqbal calls "the parent community" (*QM*, 96). For this, he says bitterly, figuring colonial adjudication as "care," "the liberal state does not care a fig" (*QM*, 95). It is the religious proximity of Ahmadis that makes them so much of a threat despite their very small number. "Parent community" figures religious heresy and theological difference as a disruptive child, and as a child, moreover, with the potential to take over, devouring the parents as it grows up. This figuration is an effect of what Mufti has identified as the "mapping" of the Indian Muslim *ashraf* "ideology of familial descent" from non-Indic sources on to "the political community or *qaum*" as a whole during the process of the "nationalization of society."[40] An ideology of familial descent produces a notion of the community as family— a rather tight-knit one, if Iqbal's rage is to be comprehended. Within this configuration, Iqbal's constitution of the Ahmadi threat is a way of ensuring that the Muslim community, imagined in kinship terms, remains intact. Iqbal's dismissal of Mirza Gulam Ahmed as "an Indian prophet," as opposed to the true Arab one, is rhetorically and politically continuous with the claim to non-Indic roots.

As Jalal suggests, Iqbal's involvement with the militant group, the Ahrars, is significant, as is the fact that, as she sardonically suggests, "basing Islam's much-vaunted unity in difference on the logic of internal exclusion was a novel invention for which Punjab's urban middle-class leadership can rightfully claim credit."[41] But I would emphasize that this local entanglement and its relationship with anticolonial struggle, through the Ahrar's desire to be more central in the politics around Kashmiri liberation, to which they felt marginal, and to which marginality they reacted with an attack on the All-India Kashmir council when an Ahmadi was appointed president, is articulated through a theological position.[42] That the Ahrars went on to fight with Shias in Lucknow suggests that the question of policing the boundaries of theological orthodoxy powers the intensity of the opposition.[43] It is, moreover, this theological claim that allows for the subsequent globalization of Ahmadi persecution.

The regnant theories of religion have tended to play down the propositional content of belief.[44] Such underplaying issues in part from a contemporary interest in embodiment and practice, but, as

Viswanathan has suggested, engaging questions of heresy, blasphemy, and apostasy requires that belief's content also be recognized. For Iqbal, it was certainly important in these essays, and that importance has proved historically consequential. He is even more clear and insistent about the propositional importance of the finality of the prophethood in "Islam and Ahmadism," his response to the baffled questions Nehru posed in "The Solidarity of Islam."[45] "This simple faith" is, for Iqbal, based on two propositions (*RQ*, 115). One is, of course, the doctrine of finality; the other is that "God is One" (*RQ*, 115). "The solidarity of Islam . . . consists in a uniform belief in the two structural principles of Islam, supplemented by the five well-known 'practices of the faith'" (*RQ*, 137). It is a similar commitment to doctrine and to keeping practice free of "heretical" innovation that motivates Mawdudi and the framers of the amendment.

Any political engagement with the status of religion has to confront what is to be done (or not done) when a belief is assumed to have been compromised. Framing the question of secularism as a problem of religious sentiment versus free speech, where free speech is assumed to be free secular speech and thus an expression of a hegemonic liberalism opposed to the religious other, simply deflects attention from the conceptual stakes and underpinnings of the political status of belief. It is not surprising then that one of the primary modes of this deflection has been a displacement of the problem onto artistic expression, the valuation of which is, in turn, figured as a residue of the aggressive Enlightenment valuation of man. It is perhaps equally unsurprising that Rushdie has become central to this deflection.

Iqbal's defense of the practice of the clerical designation of *kufr* (which he translates, strangely, as "heresy")—in cases of "minor theological points of difference as well as extreme cases of heresy" against "present day educated Muslims" who deplore the practice—sits oddly with his charge that Ahmadis should only expect to be treated badly as they declare everyone kāfirs (nonbelievers). On his own view, that practice might be construed as an extension of an orthodox habit. Yet, arguing in some sense against himself, he is insistent that these present-day, educated Muslims are wrong to see the practice as a sign of the "social and political disintegration of the Muslim community" (*RQ*, 116). For the "history of Muslim theology shows that the mutual accusations of heresy for minor points of difference has so far from working as a disruptive force, actually given impetus to synthetic theological thought" (*RQ*, 116). Declaring each other "outside the fold" ensures intellectual movement and becomes an engine (providing "impetus") of a project conceived, inconsistently, in Hegelian terms of attaining theological "synthesis." What, one might wonder, would be the antithesis?

Iqbal, one need hardly point out, is not a traditionalist. He celebrates reformers from Wahhab to Al-Afghani and attacks, in bullet point form, and, in this order: "Mullahism," "mysticism," and "Muslim kings" (*RQ*, 128–29). But for him acceptable designations of other people's heresy are those that ensure that the Muslim community stays itself, especially since Western colonialism has so endangered it. The problem is one of limits to community, what must be excluded, and to imagination, to the structures of thought, language, filiation, and affiliation that enable the self-policing, or ongoing self-creation, of that limit. In the sustenance and clarification of that limit the Ahmadis seem to play a crucial role in this late stage in Iqbal's thought.

For Iqbal, political humiliation and the embattled condition of Muslims worldwide is combined with the problem of Muslim minority in India, and it is this connection that allows him recourse both to an analogy with the German state that arose after the defeat by Napoleon at Jena and to Jews in seventeenth-century Amsterdam.[46] The separation of Ahmadis from the Muslim majority that he wants the colonial government to institute is justified by an invocation of Spinoza: "Situated as the Jews were—a minority community in Amsterdam—they were justified in regarding Spinoza as a disintegrating factor threatening the dissolution of their community" (*RQ*, 112). Mawdudi's "disintegrating force" in *The Qadiani Problem* is, of course, a slight modification of Iqbal's "disintegrating factor." Iqbal is careful to distinguish the leader of the Ahmadis from Spinoza—there is apparently no comparison of intellect between Mirza Ghulam Ahmed and the philosopher (*RQ*, 111); and, moreover, the Ahmadis are a bigger threat (*RQ*, 112). The example clarifies what is acceptable in order to ensure the cohesiveness of the community. Expulsion from the group—disinheritance—is an acceptable price for solidarity: "Politically, then, the solidarity of Islam is shaken only when Muslim states war on one another; religiously, it is shaken only when Muslims rebel against any one of the basic beliefs and practices of the faith. It is in the interest of this *eternal solidarity* that Islam cannot tolerate any rebellious group within its fold. Outside the fold, such a group is entitled to as much toleration as followers of any other faith" (*RQ*, 137; italics mine).

For Iqbal eternal solidarity is fundamentally related to what looks like his equivocation on nationalism. In response to Nehru's question about whether Iqbal's objection to Indian nationalism extends to Ataturk, that is, to nationalism per se, Iqbal gives a remarkable answer. It is worth quoting at length:

> It is not difficult to see the attitude of Islam towards nationalist ideals. Nationalism in the sense of love of one's country and even readiness to die for its honour, is a part of the Muslim's faith; it comes into conflict with Islam only when it begins to play the role of a political concept and claims to be a principle of human solidarity demanding that Islam should recede to the background of a mere private opinion and cease to be a living factor in national life. In Turkey, Persia, Egypt and other Muslim countries it will never become a problem. In these countries Muslims constitute an overwhelming majority and their minorities, i.e. Jews, Christians, Zoroastrians, according to the law of Islam, are either "People of the Book" or "like the People of the Book" with whom the law of Islam allows free social relations, including matrimonial alliances. It becomes a problem for Muslims only in countries where they happen to be in a minority and nationalism demands their complete effacement. In majority countries Islam accommodates nationalism; for there Islam and nationalism are practically identical; in minority countries it is justified in seeking self-determination as a cultural unit. In either case, it is thoroughly consistent with itself." (*RQ*, 136–37)

It might be argued that no matter what the "eternal" and majoritarian claims here, Iqbal is writing very much from within his position as a religious minority in a colonially governed empire, in which the regnant nationalism, Indian nationalism, cast in terms of territory or defined in terms of regional belonging, nonetheless cannot accommodate Muslim difference. One might see Iqbal's recourse to an "eternal" Islam as an attempt to transcend the limits of the material conditions of Muslims in post-Rebellion India. On such a reading the transcendent escape is a response to a worldly dilemma. The guarantee of a permanent eternal union can only be a deferred promise but one that mirrors the pre-Independence condition of the Muslims.

One might argue, then, that the demand for solidarity comes from the phenomenological inconceivability of Muslim emancipation even as it is articulated as a fierce aspiration. But, in the context of the post-colonial nation-state carved out for many of the Muslims of India, this call for solidarity acquires a different cast. I do not wish to suggest an inevitability to the way Iqbal's views on Ahmadis are adopted. They could, and but for a series of decisions made by Bhutto and

Zia, they might well have been ignored. If "Muslim" participation in Indian modernity has always included the claim of being non-Indian, as Mufti has argued, progressive culture in Urdu (historically contiguous with Iqbal) has also included the attempt to reveal "the Indian environment of this claim."[47] Yet if the persecution of Ahmadis is an effect of empire, then theories of empire and of anti-imperialism need to find a vocabulary for the cannibalization of the perceived internal enemy in situations of disempowerment. Equally important is an account of what happens when memories of disempowerment do not catch up with reconfigurations of power and domination.

Mawdudi's use of Iqbal's attack on the Ahmadis and its complete codification by Zia's military regime suggest that it is the (militarized) sovereignty of the state as Islamic in a particular way that is to be ensured by the designation of the theological enemy. As this genealogy demonstrates, the relentless and systematic persecution of the Ahmadis issues from the need to ensure control over the parameters of the ground of the Islam that will form the basis of the Pakistani state's sovereignty.

The proposition that Muhammad is the last prophet has come to shape the boundaries of the nation and of the state.[48] That is, a variety of pan-Islamism, which is antinationalist (in that it is opposed to Indian nationalism) but which yet forms the grounds of the Pakistani nation-state, took a proposition regarding the finality of prophethood and made it central to securing the boundaries of Islam. After Independence, designating the Ahmadis outside the fold is to help resolve the tension between the "eternal solidarity" of Islam and the borders of the nation-state. The relation between the Ahmadis and Muhammad devotion suggests that the Muslim persona and the state's limit are both bounded by a legally sustained (one might even say juridically manufactured) relation to the icon.

WOUNDED ICONOCLASTS, SURREPTITIOUS ICONOGRAPHIES

In one of the most stunning passages in the chapter "Religious Criticism" in *Genealogies of Religion: Discipline and Reasons of Power in the Christianity and Islam*, correcting yet another Western misapprehension about the traditionalism of Muslims, Talal Asad writes:

> Actually, innumerable foreign techniques were absorbed into Saudi
> society before the oil boom in the seventies with little or no objection

from the 'ulama: new forms of transport including paved roads, new
modes of building and printing, electricity, new medicines and types
of medical treatment, and so forth. Clearly, something more complicated is involved here than a traditional opposition to moderniza-
tion by the ulama. As a start I would propose that what the ulama
are doing is to attempt a definition of orthodoxy—a (re)ordering of
knowledge that the "correct" form of Islamic practices. In effect,
what we have today is essentially part of the same process by which
long-established indigenous practices (such as the veneration of saints
tombs) were judged to be un-Islamic by the Wahhabi reformers of
Arabia (see Abdul Wahhab A.H. 1376, 124–35) and then forcibly
eliminated. That is, like all practical criticism, orthodox criticism
seeks to construct a relation of discursive dominance.

    I argue that the critical discourses of Saudi ulama (like those of
Muhammad Abdul Wahhab before them) presuppose the concept
of an orthodox Islam. Muslims in Saudi Arabia (as elsewhere) disagree profoundly over what orthodox Islam is, but as Muslims their
differences are fought out on the ground of that concept. It is too
often forgotten that the process of determining orthodoxy in conditions of change and contest includes attempts at achieving discursive
coherence.[49]

The passage starts out with a seemingly simple refutation of a fac-
tual error on the part of Western commentators, who appear not to
understand the modernity of the Saudi clerics. But it transforms into
a defense of orthodox erasures of Muslims perceived to be otherwise.
Asad is sanguine about the forcible elimination of indigenous religious practice, since like all "practical criticism" orthodox criticism
seeks to construct a relation of "discursive dominance." The destruction of lifeworlds is just an effect of "practical criticism," which itself
is emptied of content by being abstracted into *all* practical criticism.
One can only assume that the alternative to religious criticism is the
"secular criticism" advocated by Edward Said. Twenty years later
this implicit opposition, and the crucial role of Said's secular criticism as the negative delineation of Asad's conception of religious criticism, is laid bare in his contribution to *Is Critique Secular?* in which
the "worldly critic"—the critic, in other words, of Said's *The World,
the Text, the Critic*—stands as the figure against whose purported
excesses the argument is made.[50]

    There are two moves that are particularly significant here. The first
is the reduction of Islam to "orthodox" Islam. According to Asad,
Muslims disagree widely over "what orthodox Islam is." He does not
say that they disagree over what Islam is—which, obviously they do.

Not every practicing Muslim aspires to orthodoxy or even to anti-secular criticism. The slide from "religious" to orthodox Islamic to simply Islamic is, I'm going to have to say it, puzzling. More significant is the argument that, as Muslims, their claims are fought out on the ground of that concept. It is the very presupposition of the stability of that ground that is at issue even when orthodox clerics fight among themselves. Otherwise the practice of declaring each other kāfir would be unintelligible. It should be added that orthodox practices in Saudi Arabia are linked to the Pakistani ones that motivate attempts to secure the discursive dominance of the orthodox upon the legal code. The Jamaat-i-Islami, the party that was central to the bid to persecute and marginalize the Ahmadis, has always sought to emulate Saudi practice, as, of course, did Zia-ul-Haq. In fact, Asad's article is written at the end of an eleven-year period in which Zia secured these practices in Pakistan while strengthening the relationship with Saudi Arabia, at the same time, of course, as being strengthened by Saudi help—a period in which the assassination of Shias by militias had begun in the Punjab.

To understand Asad's disregard for the cost of such orthodox practice, one might turn to a passing reference to Shi'is in his polemic against Rushdie: "No Sunni collection contains a hadith prohibiting the consumption of prawns, a prohibition followed only by Shi'is. . . . The question that an informed reader may want to ask is why the rules of the hadith are presented as having been revealed by Gabriel, and further why sectarian rules are presented as though they were accepted by all Muslims."[51] Setting aside for a moment the question of referential literalism, one might yet wonder why it is that a Shia prohibition is presented as sectarian. If Islam is not a monolith, as Asad frequently reminds us, then why does a practice associated with a particular group have to be produced as sectarian? Why is it not just one more Muslim practice? But, as I have suggested throughout this book, the ostensibly antiessentialist project of questioning the monolithicization of Islam has simply come to attach itself to securing the equation of orthodox or radically conservative Islam, in some cases just even Sunni Islam, with Islam as a whole. Challenges to that equation are either to be discredited by some association with the Enlightenment, or the West, or colonial modernity or, as witnessed here, to be renamed as "sectarian." It is not that the term *sectarian* does not apply in some cases; it is rather that in this particular case the word is used to dismiss a practice's association with Islam. In light of Saudi Arabia's complicated relationship with its Shia population and Asad's reproduction of Sunni orthodoxy as Islamic orthodoxy such a detail is consequential. There is nonetheless something contradictory here. In 2011, defending the Muslim Brotherhood in the face of skepticism about their role in the Egyptian revolution, Asad mentions his support for Hamas and Hezbollah, the Shia militant group in Lebanon.[52]

On terms that concede the importance of religious pain as a socioethical and political category, the erasure to which Ahmadis are being subjected in the amendments to the penal code is an effect of the priority given to the religious pain of the majority. This "pain" is caused by their ostensible disregard for, or alleged defilement of, a theological proposition presented as fundamental to orthodoxy, and is itself predicated on the complete denial of the possibility of Ahmadi religious pain. The persecution of Ahmadis is further normalized in passport and identity card applications. Citizens applying for either are asked to sign a statement declaring Ahmadis non-Muslim. The signature is a remarkably explicit example of "hailing," indicating the systematic interpellation of Pakistan's citizenry, through the targeting of one group. The national community is to be secured through this collective attestation.

More than twenty-five years later and in a context made ever more violent by the U.S. presence in Afghanistan, such interpellation works in tandem with the extrajudicial but fully juridical power evident in a pamphlet demanding the conversion of Ahmadis to Islam from a group giving its location in Faisalabad.[53] The document's chilling openness about its religious vigilantism deserves a close reading. The group, which calls itself the World Congress for the Protection of the Finality of the Prophethood, is happy to give its address and phone number, revealing the impunity with which it functions even as it issues a notification of imminent murder (Fig. 1). Combined with the unselfconscious declaration of coordinates, it is the inadvertently parodic tone—produced through a combination of menace and the creepily caressing generosity of Bollywood gangsterism—that allows it to represent the normalization of the persecution it unleashes and of which it is a part.[54]

The pamphlet is framed as an invitation from "good" (*acche*) Muslims to Ahmadis to become "true" (*haqīqī*) Muslims. The unselfconscious sense of moral superiority and of entitlement is perhaps most evident in the recurrence of the word *da'vat* (in this context literally "invitation"). It occurs eight times in the page-long pamphlet. *Da'vat* can mean an invitation to Islam, a call, a more general invitation, and a feast. It is no surprise that it is derived from the Arabic *dawa* (to call). In everyday use it frequently suggests an invitation to a party or a feast. The generosity and hospitality such linguistic associations suggest are dear to the writer of the pamphlet:[55]

> Tārī<u>kh</u> gavāh hai ke Musalmāno<u>n</u> ne <u>gh</u>air Musalmāno<u>n</u> ke sāth acchā bartā'o karte hū'e unko Musalmān hone kī da'vat dī aur voh Musalmān ho ga'e aur jin logo<u>n</u> ne Musalmāno<u>n</u> ke acche bartā'o ke bāvujūd Islam kī da'vat qabūl nahī<u>n</u> kī unkā hashar bhī tārī<u>kh</u> men maujūd hai. Is līye ham āp ko acche Musalmān hone ke nāte ḥaqīqī Musalmān hone kī da'vat de rahe hai<u>n</u>. Agar āp ne is ā<u>kh</u>rī aur qīmtī mauqe ko hāt se ganvā diyā to tum logo<u>n</u> kā bhī vahī anjām ho gā jo Murad Cloth House aur dūsre murtid aur kāfir Mirzā'iyo<u>n</u> vālo<u>n</u> kā hū'ā thā

> History is witness that, treating them well, Muslims invited non-Muslims to become Muslims and they converted. And the fate of those who did not accept the call, despite their being treated well by Muslims, is also available in history. This is why, as good Muslims, we are inviting you to become true Muslims. If you squander this valuable, last chance you will face the same fate as the owners of Murad cloth and other apostate and infidel Ahmadis.

The author's sense of being a "good" Muslim is fundamentally linked to his or her perception of the historical generosity of Islam, and the group is presented as a historical conduit that will further the teleological ends of missionary largesse. The "invitation" to convert is a form of rescue from the punishing judgment of history: "jin logo<u>n</u> ne . . . Islam kī da'vat qabūl nahī<u>n</u> kī in ka hashar bhī tārī<u>kh</u> me<u>n</u> maujūd hai" (the fate of those who did not accept the call to Islam . . . is also available in history).

The word *da'vat* allows a certain historical inversion to become visible. The pamphleteer threatens a few lines down to report the targets to the Lashkar-i-Jhangvi, the Taliban, the Jaish-i-Muhammad, and all the "religious organizations" (*maz̤habī tanz̤īme<u>n</u>*). The fear intentionally solicited by the reference to the murdered Ahmadi owners of Murad Cloth House in Faisalabad is then fortified with the threat to give the names of the targets to the militant groups. The jihadi groups the pamphlet names are profoundly anticustomary. They object to all the forms of lived and customary Islam in South Asia. The Bakhtinian concept of carnival is useful here. The very aspects of festive sociality that allow for the occasional suspension of social rigidities in South Asian shrine culture and Sufi Islam are anathema to them. They are ferociously iconoclastic and opposed to the carnivalesque sociality the word summons. *Da'vat* restores the sense of a fundamental fissure in Pakistani society, a fissure created by the denial of customary, religious urban and rural social practices. The illusion sometimes created is that these groups are accessing some historically authentic Islam and thus accessing a premodern cultural formation, but their claim to revival is fundamentally modern, anticommunity, anticustomary, and indeed anticultural.[56]

A SHIFT IN SENSIBILITY

Such a genealogy as I have undertaken in the previous pages yet provides insufficient resources for minorities working from within the context of the nation-state and its multiple institutional and ideological apparatuses. Following the murder of Shahbaz Bhatti, the Christian Member of the National Assembly, Asiya Nasir, gave an extraordinary speech in the National Assembly. Complexly steeped in a history of progressive Urdu literature and Jinnah's claims about secular citizenship, crossbred with the blood-soaked language of national sacrifice, it offers a tragic compendium of a vernacular history of the aspiration for emancipation and citizenship from the position of those who are not numerically strong enough nor sufficiently politically powerful to demand a nation of their own. Nasir's speech embodies the paradox that it is from the ground of the nation that the minority framed by law must speak and the simultaneous fact that that act can call that very ground into question.

Both Bhatti's and Taseer's murders were seen as responses to the most recent attempts to repeal the laws initiated by a democratically elected representative in the assembly. For those who supported the murders, they were caused by the attempt to repeal Pakistan's blasphemy laws. If Taseer's murderer was celebrated by some, in terms borrowed from Iqbal's commemoration of the murderer of the man who had authored *Rangīlā Rasūl*, as a Ghazi (surely an invitation to the grimmer yields of genealogy), Taseer himself could be assimilated into a narrative of a secular-liberal, flamboyantly Anglophone elite. Underlying such an assimilation is the specter of "decadence" as a cultural symbolic substitute for a more socially analytic conception of the dynamics, economic and cultural, of class and power.

Availing himself in particularly heightened rhetoric of the ventriloquial discourse of a variety of media analysis—in which the attribution of a view to the media is enough to put it outside the pale of subscription by the right sort of radical—"liberal" "elite," and "pro-Western" are indeed the terms in which one commentator in *Counterpunch* excoriates Pakistan's Anglophone media after Taseer's murder: "Pakistan's English print media faux liberal and elitist have been in furor over the recent political murder of Salman Taseer, governor of Punjab, by his own bodyguard."[57] Moreover, the author implicitly defends the laws by suggesting that the problem is with their "abuse," not with the particular law (295–C) under which Aasia Noreen, the woman whose case Taseer had chosen to take up, was convicted and sentenced to death. In the process, he represents attempts to repeal it, and outrage at the murders, as emblems of imperial complicity: "Pakistan's wealthy and faux liberal elites, by carrying their treachery to extremes, by agreeing to rain death on Pakistanis from the skies, are losing the argument in Pakistan. Going off on a limb, the governor began attacking Pakistan's blasphemy law, which has been abused by some Pakistanis to settle personal scores. Is it a fault in the law or its execution?"[58] One need hardly defend the impressively rapacious and frequently culturally deracinated wealthy upper class of Pakistan in order to defend the cause of the minorities, but the invitation to equate the two is overdetermined by the invocation of Rushdie: "Pakistanis worried that this was only the start of a campaign to repeal the law and open the floodgates for Salman Rushdi-style [*sic*] smearing of the Prophet."[59] The author's linking of concerns about the Rushdiesque "blasphemies" that might be unleashed with related speculation that the initiative to "repeal the laws" might have been inspired by "foreign embassies" is part of a political shorthand in which Rushdie's name can work to summon a vast network of subliminal associations of treachery. Within this paragraph, this system of association is locked down by suggesting that the "law maker" who introduced the bill was a part of the "pro-Western Pakistan People's Party," which party, the author does not point out, was also democratically elected; neither does he tell the reader that the party abandoned Taseer on this issue.[60]

The form of circulation of Rushdie's name in a context such as this and in the banner in which the pope and Rushdie are associated (see Figs. 2 and 3), as those who have insulted Muhammad, is difficult to name, especially when one recalls the case, one of those over which the

Pakistani bishop John Joseph committed suicide in a bid to get the blasphemy law overturned in 1996, in which a Christian man had been accused of praising *The Satanic Verses*.[61] In the banner both the pope and Rushdie are called "disrespectful dogs," and viewers are asked to throw shoes at them and earn divine reward. Most striking is the effect that putting Rushdie next to the pope is meant to induce. The children looking at the images are being invited into an oppositional collectivity, a dark sociality, through their indignation at the insult to the Prophet: the confirmation of the insult lies in the presence of Rushdie's image. The photographs were taken on the Prophet's birthday, and the banners turn that occasion of customarily festive and generous piety into a punitive one.

As I suggested in the first chapter, at play is a new, inverted form of what Foucault identified as the author-function. In this new function, the name of the author does not certify or elevate his own work but serves in an equally transformative and occlusive way to simultaneously certify and obscure acts of violence—in this case, ones (at least initially) underwritten by the state.[62] The intellectual history informed by Foucauldian skepticism about the ostensibly emancipated autonomy of the author, which was very much part of the autocritique of literature in the 1980s and 1990s, has seeped into political commentary in ways that allow this inverted author-function to produce its alchemical effects.

Shahbaz Bhatti's murder is, however, less easy to assimilate into the elites against internal subaltern narratives that have come to underpin critiques of secularism. Bhatti's own position as a Punjabi Christian does not carry the same Anglophone aura, and given the language of caste that is used in anti-Christian discrimination cannot be subsumed easily to the same elite cultural position—neither, of course, can Nasir's speech. Elected to a seat reserved for minorities, affiliated with the conservative Islamist party, the JUI, clad in a black chador, she addressed, eerily, the portrait of Mohammad Ali Jinnah and spoke to it, and him, as might an accusatory petitioner. For thirteen devastating minutes she embodied and revealed, without necessarily intending to do so, the contradictions of the status of religious minorities in the nation-state. Nasir's speech, which deserves the close and careful attention she demands of her fellow assembly members and, implicitly, in her shifting address, of the entire nation, is in some ways an elegy produced from within the space of complaint. Of Jinnah, she asks, why did you ask us to join you on the endeavor to build Pakistan? Of the constituents of the assembly, she asks why there had been no prayer for Bhatti and, instead, only a two-minute silence. The complaint is also part lament for the impossibility of elegy in the absence of recognition of the dead, an attempt, in other words, to notice the national conditions within which, to use Judith Butler's very suggestive idea, a life is ungrievable.[63] Within the parallel economies of metropolitan anti-imperialism and "local" religious nationalism, it is the murder that cannot be called itself. Nasir's speech is thus Antigone's demand for a proper burial for the man she names her brother ("merā bhā'ī qatal hū'ā hai," "my brother has been murdered").[64]

Nasir flanks her speech with extended quotations from Faiz Ahmed Faiz, and then, as if in an allegory for the relation between political rhetoric, narration, and politics, which must culminate in the necessary banality of political action, she starts again to declare an ending with a symbolic "token" "walkout." After reading a long section from the Faiz poem, "ham jo tārīk rāhon men māre ga'e" (We Who Were Killed in the Dark Lanes), Nasir goes on to say that she will not address the speaker or the house or the PM and turns to the portrait of Jinnah, points to it, and says:[65]

> Mohammad Ali Jinnah āj main tum se mukhātib hūn kyūnke mera bhai qatal hū'ā hai. Āp ne ham se kahā tha ke āo ek ghar banāte hain. Us pāk sar zamīn ka nām Pakistan rakhen ge aur us pāk sar zamīn par na ko'ī Hindu hoga na ko'ī Christian hoga na ko'ī Musalmān hoga balke ek parcham ke sā'e tale ham sab ek honge. Qā'id-i Ā'zam āj main āp se sawāl kartī hūn ke jab Pakistan kī takhlīq ho ga'ī aur jab ham āp ke kehne par is ghar men āga'e tho hamāre sāth kyā salūk ravān rakha gaya? Janāb-e 'speaker' main is aivān se pūchna chahūngī ke kyā qusūr tha mere bhai ka? Sirf yehī ke voh is mulk-e Pakistan ko Qā'id-i Ā'zam ka Pakistan dekhna chāhtā tha?

> Mohammad Ali Jinnah: today I address you because my brother has been murdered. You said to us: "come with us together we will make a home. We will name that pure land Pakistan. And on that pure land, there will be no Hindu nor Christian nor Muslim instead we will all be one in the shade of one flag." Quaid-e-Azam, today I want to ask you: once Pakistan's creation was complete and once we had arrived here, on your suggestion, what kind of treatment were we given? [then she shifts her address to the Speaker] Mr. Speaker I would like to ask this assembly: what was my brother's fault? Only this: that he wanted to see this country- Pakistan as Quaid-e-Azam's country" [as the country envisaged by Jinnah].[66]

The epigraphic invocation of Faiz, figuring the subject as the one killed in the dark lane, is poised against the shade of the flag and an intimacy in the imagined invitation from Jinnah. If the darkness disappears the subject, dispersed and wandering in the lane, by disappearing the very fact of murder, the shade of the flag, under which rest is to enable the making of a house, figures a national space offering the comfort of a community configured in familial terms—the connotation of "ghar"" is both home and house. "Sā'e tale"" (under the shade) is moreover a tender image, one that registers the intensity of a yearning to be allowed to belong in one's own home—a belonging suggested by the possibility of rest, and of the creation of conditions for that rest: a building of a home together in the shade. The invitation of the shade is a contrast to the wandering travel in dark roads, a wandering that acquires an additional valence through the explicit fear of exile and religious cleansing that Nasir raises, later in the speech, when she asks if Pakistan is only a nation for Muslims, as, she says some "extremist" (*intihā-pasand*) journalists are arguing in the media, and whether the Christians should leave and take up residence elsewhere. Significantly, the word Nasir uses to indicate residence elsewhere, "thikānā," has little connotation of comfort.[67]

Nasir's use of an imagery of shade and rest is an attempt to take back the language of community configured in familial terms in Muslim *ashrāf* ideology, and to expand the ambit of the family, to stretch what was already a metaphorical inscription to provide a more secular understanding of nation imagined as family. What makes the unity of this community possible ("ham sab ek ho<u>n</u>ge," "we will all be one") is the dissolution of religious identity into political identity, promised by Jinnah in his speech on August 11, 1947, a part of which she quotes in translation: "na ko'ī Hindu hogā, na ko'ī Christian hogā na ko'ī Musalmān hogā" (no one will be Hindu, or Christian or Muslim).[68]

The lines from Jinnah that are so often quoted might be said to go against the very grain of metropolitan multiculturalism, which cannot imagine political action as distinct from the articulation of difference and identity, in fact, from assertion of difference as a political claim. The presence of Jinnah's lines in Nasir's speech, so fully absorbed into a vernacular history, reveals a paradox: such a call for the recognition of difference may, in fact, not be intelligible without the possibility of a secular separation of state and religious identity. The reference to Jinnah functions as an assertion of the necessity of preserving, or perhaps even creating, the conditions in which religious difference is publicly and safely possible.

The contrast between Jinnah's speech and Nasir's claim that minorities are more than able to protect the last prophet makes it strikingly evident that the difference Jinnah sought to protect in his speech is publicly inaccessible to her even as she invokes these words. Her implicit allegiance to the finality of prophethood in her designation of Muhammad as the last prophet, "ambiyā'-e i<u>kh</u>titām," is a measure of this unavailability of religious difference, against which her invocation of Jinnah remains grimly poised:

> "ham ambiyā'-e i<u>kh</u>titām aur namūs kī hifāzat karnā baṛi acchī tara se jānte hai<u>n</u> ko'ı masıhı ya aqlıyat ye tassavur bhī nahı<u>n</u> kar saktā ke ham kisī nabi kī shān me<u>n</u> gustā<u>kh</u>ī kare<u>n</u>."

> We know very well how to protect the honour of the last prophet. No Christian or minority could even imagine that we [*sic*] would insult the glory of any prophet.[69]

The equation of the acceptance of the doctrine of finality with respect for the Prophet is quite remarkable when expected of minorities who recognize other prophets. What is sometimes argued is that Islam recognizes other prophets and monotheists as people of the book. The Muslim notion of respect for the people of the book relies on the fact that Muhammad completes history and supersedes the prophets who have preceded him—that they are part of a history conceived as Muslim through a conception of Islam as the teleological end. It needs to be asked: What does it mean for the state, or its inhabitants, to require Christians to accept the teleology on which this idea relies?

In addition to the two Faiz poems, Nasir quotes a few lines from a poem ("<u>Kh</u>ūn phir <u>kh</u>ūn hai") by Sahir Ludhianvi, written upon the assassination of Patrice Lumumba.[70] It might take a while to realize upon hearing the speech that the quotations are all transcribed and sometimes mistranscribed from a short and harrowing documentary, *Burning Alive*, about the attack on Christians in an incident in Korian, a village near the town of Gojra, in which more than forty houses and two churches were torched and seven Christians burned to death.[71] Incited by clerics who also called the Christians "American agents," the mob attacked while the police failed to intervene. In the film, the poems from Faiz are rendered in his own voice, but significantly the documentary concludes with Ludhianvi's poem and a final declaration of the inauguration of a new struggle. The documentary begins with a rolling text image of a verse from the Bible superimposed upon a scene of houses burning, which is followed by some of the details of what transpired. Then as a prelude to the narration we hear Faiz, to whom the narrator later refers as "umīd o zindagi ke numā'indah shair" (the exemplary poet of hope and life), reciting a section of "ham jo tārīk rāho<u>n</u> me<u>n</u> māre ga'e" (We Who Were Lost in the Dark Lanes). The film concludes with another segment of Faiz reading from "Lahū ka surāgh" (Trace of Blood), another one of his poems; and then the narrator mentions Ludhianvi whom he calls a fellow traveler of Faiz, more precisely a "ham qāfilah shair" (a poet and fellow traveler) and concludes with a quotation from Ludhianvi.

Even as footage rolls of looted homes, houses burning, the burned bodies of those killed being carted away, and of the police milling about as the violence unfolds, the narrator poses some telling questions:

> "Ijtimā'i qatal magar qātil kaun?" (Collective murder, but who is the murderer?)[72]

Before that, picking up on the Faiz poem with which the short began, he asks:

> "Tārīk rāho<u>n</u> ka safar kab tamām ho gā?" (When will the travel on the dark roads end?)[73]

The first question demands an answer from all of society, for if a murder is collective, the question of collusion, of participation, indeed of what allowed the collectivity to come about, requires direct moral confrontation. The second draws upon Faiz and Ludhianvi to articulate its protest. The documentary thus stages a confrontation between two collectivities, *both* constituting aspects of the Pakistani public:

1. The group opposed to the existence of Christians, fully socially constructed on the documentary's terms, by the law—as the narrator says "'dictator' to khair 'dictator' hote hai<u>n</u> lekin siyāsati hakūmato<u>n</u> ne bhī mujrimānah ghaflat ka muzāhirah kiya unhone<u>n</u> na sirf takfīrī qavanīn ko khatm karne me<u>n</u> sanjīdagī ka muzāhirah nahi<u>n</u> kiya balke in qavānīn se paidah hone vāli sūrat-e hāl ko bhī samajhne kī kabhī koshish nahī<u>n</u> kī" (After all dictators are dictators, but even elected governments have displayed criminal negligence. Not only have they shown no seriousness in removing these laws, but they have also not tried to understand the situation arising from them).[74] One might call this group a fully

juridical collectivity authorized by penal laws that have a
colonial genealogy.

2. A second group constituted by a critical claim to citizenship
    articulated by turning to poetic expressions of critiques of the
    state, of the failures of nationalism, indeed of tyranny, injus-
    tice, and cruelty, attempting instead to use Faiz and Ludhi-
    anvi to argue for repairing a torn collective self. The poetic
    imagination serves thus to create a collectivity that attempts
    to imagine a more inclusive notion of citizenship. Figures such
    as Faiz both comprise such collectivity and enable its ongoing
    constitution.

Nasir's transcription of the poems from the documentary contributes
to an archive whose foundations are stabilized through citation and
repetition.[75] Nasir appears not to have read the poems in a text but
in fact heard them in the documentary and used them accordingly;
her transcription reveals, moreover, how the poetic imagination can
circulate to create a collectivity—however momentary and fluid the
existence of such a formation.

Nasir's first quotation—from a poem that Faiz wrote in prison,
after being arrested for the Rawalpindi conspiracy case, inspired by
the letters of Ethel and Julius Rosenberg—restores the Cold War history, shared by Pakistan and the United States, through a collusion
between the military and the United States, that has so shaped the
present within which Nasir speaks. A history that has now turned
in fully upon itself, of which the dramatically visible early moment
is the attack on the Twin Towers in 2001. In the documentary, the
exacerbation of the persecution of Christians is linked to that event,
although the narrative makes clear that the persecution far precedes
2001.

Faiz's extraordinary ability to write about the Rosenbergs while
in prison himself, to identify their loss of each other as an exemplary
loss, is figured in a classically Urdu idiom. The identification is presented through a kind of affiliation, evident in the use of "ham" (we)
of "ham jo tarīk rāhon men māre ga'e" (we who were killed in the dark
lanes/highways).[76] That larger sense of a polity, which crosses boundaries, brought together by injustice makes it into Nasir's speech, via
the documentary, surfacing as a demand for recognition and justice
within the national space. A demand reinforced through the (slightly
misremembered) quotation from Ludhianvi, where she substitutes the

word used for blood, "khūn," in the poem with "lahū," in one of the
moments in the speech where, overcome, she speeds up, stumbles, or
misspeaks:

> zulm tho [*sic*] zulm hai baṛhtā hai tho mit jātā hai
> lahū tho lahū hai tapke gā tho jam jā'e gā.
>
> Cruelty is cruelty if it increases it gets erased
> Blood is blood if it drips it will congeal.[77]

She goes on to pick up the concluding line of the film that this congealed blood will prove a point of departure for a new struggle, but
what she chooses to conclude with is the penultimate quotation from
Faiz, from a poem that mourns the erasure of the unimportant dead—
as if Bhatti's murder and Aasia Noreen's plight reinforces for her the
despairing sense of ongoing erasure to which the documentary seeks
to bear witness:

> kahīn nahīn hai kahīn bhī nahīn lahū kā surāgh
> na dast-o nākhun-e qātil, na āstīn pe nishān
> na surkhī-e lab-e khanjar, na rang-e nok-e sīnān
> na khāk par ko'ī dhabbā, na bām par ko'ī dāgh
> kahīn nahīn hai kahīn bhī nahīn lahū kā surāgh
>
> pukārtā rahā be-āsra yatīm lahū
> kisī ko bahr-e sama'at na vaqt tha na dimāgh
> na mudda'i na shahādat hisāb pāk hū'ā
> ye khūn-e khāk-nashīnān tha rizq-e khāk hua
>
> Nowhere, nowhere at all is there any trace of the blood
> Not on the murderer's hands, nails, or sleeve
> No redness on the lip of the dagger or on the tip of the spear
> No stain on the soil and no blot on the rooftop
> Nowhere, nowhere at all is there any trace of the blood
>
> The helpless, orphaned blood kept calling out,
> Noone had the capacity to listen, nor the time or mind for it
> No plaintiff no witness so the account was purified (closed)
> This was the blood of those who dwelt in the dust and was
> consumed by the dust.[78]

These lines from Faiz are from a poem he wrote in 1965, after the
elections, which Fatima Jinnah ostensibly lost, followed by riots in
Karachi in which many were killed by the government. The poem
mourns murder and injustice through a deployment of metaphors
of blood that has not stained the murderers, their weapons, or their
clothes. The blood, which keeps calling out ("pukārta raha be asra

yatīm lahū"/"the orphaned hopeless blood kept calling out"), disappears back into the earth, to which it is closer for it is the blood of the lowly. The poem courts the implication that all the dead must revert to the earth. Yet because it is the blood of those who are considered beneath notice, the murders disappear as murders because those killed are not worthy of justice. The poem provides the witness unavailable in the realm of injustice it indicts.

Through these quotations, Nasir invokes what one might call a literature of disappearance—a literature that attempts to figure the particular kind of loss that comes with the politics of disappearance, which might be the exemplary form of Cold War state power, with its peculiar combination of surveillance—which seeks to peer at that which is least visible—and invisibility. Disappearance paradoxically demands continuous grief—as within the matrix of that kind of power, the dead cannot be laid to rest—and simultaneously installs, even institutionalizes, the ungrievability of the dead because disappearance cannot be accompanied by burial. It institutionalizes thus an absence of rest. Within this larger matrix of ungrievability, grief is inescapably repetitive, not, it must be said, because of a remembered trauma, but because of an ongoing one.[79]

But if the absence of blood from the weapons of the murderers represents the impossibility of justice—for not only is there no sign of guilt, there is no sign, no evidence, of the murder—Nasir's demand for the recognition of the contribution of Christians to the nation, which is also, and fully, a plea, is itself presented through a metaphor of blood: "ham ne iss dhartī ko apne lahū se sīnchā hai" (we have irrigated this land with our blood).[80] This incarnadine irrigation then establishes a relation that is fundamentally corporeal between the human body and the world's body, through the transformation of blood into water that keeps the land alive. This connection is meant to overcome the ideality of the theologically bounded conception of nation, which excludes minorities. Nasir assimilates Bhatti's murder to this larger contribution "kal hī mere bhai ne apna tāzah lahū diyā hai iss dhartī ke liye," (only yesterday has my brother has given his fresh blood for this land).[81] The irrigation becomes a transfusion for the land, made sacrifice because the amount of blood given results in the death of the donor.

Nasir's (and the documentary makers') density of citation is an attempt to restore a history erased by the project of turning the history of the region into one conceived only in religious nationalist terms, a religious nationalism whose security is achieved through the delineation and ongoing iteration of a theological principle. If the citation of Jinnah's speech attempts to seize the charismatic if—given his oscillations on the question—ultimately unstable authority of Jinnah in order to authorize a secular conception of the state, to retain hold of a different concept of the nation in order to authorize dissent from prevalent forms of power, the allusions, woven together into a political poetics of blood, work to restore the bodily presence of the minority in the area, the land, over which different conceptions of the nation, and different nationalisms, seek to settle. Blood that does not stain reveals the moral stain of unprosecuted murder, blood that clots and strengthens ("jam jāta hai," "becomes congealed") has the power to cause some transformative upheaval for justice, and blood shed by minorities in the service of the national project (Christian nurses who died at Partition) and the state (a murdered minister) reveals a history in a condition of perpetual erasure because the contribution, the national labor (the work of irrigation) cannot be recognized. Put together, these metaphorical meanings, all suggested within the speech, reveal complex varieties of suffering, within the nationalist state, of which the disappearance of history is the absent and yet, as Nasir configures it, overwhelming sign.

In the context of a political environment pervaded with metaphors of martyrdom and sacrifice, Nasir's declaration that Bhatti is a *shahīd* (martyr) is another demand for recognition within the very terms of the languages of the state and, more subtly, for some equivalence to be granted to the religions that feed those languages. Her mention of those who die in the service of Christ is also an insistence for the state's recognition of martyrdom as a condition that can be achieved by its "non-Muslim" subjects. The poetry of blood she invokes is an oppositional poetry by poets for whom blood is a sign of injustice and a signal for dissent, both against the state and against varieties of Muslim identitarian nationalism, and, in the case of Faiz, also against Ayub Khan's secular militarism. At the same time, the importance of Christ's blood in Christian theology and piety gives these metaphors of blood an additional and religiously particular emotional resonance.

A note is in order about the confusion that speaking of nationalism induces in this context. This nationalism is complex because it issues from a demand for a state, but in its inceptionary moment its opposition to Indian nationalism, in the form we see it in Iqbal, is based on a transnational conception of the demands of faith, practice, and sociality upon Muslims. For Iqbal, these obligations of faith and practice are to be seen as constitutive of Muslim identity, and that identity is then presented as the principle underpinning the demand for the state. The available language of the nation-state is not fully adequate to this phenomenon, which acquires its nationalist purchase in the form of the achieved state but whose conceptual mutability issues from an Iqbalian pan-Islamist conception of Muslim identity and collectivity as *transnational*, a conception that requires the local policing of the boundaries of religion in the service of its "eternal solidarity" and geographically diffuse instantiations.

As is so often the case, the history of discrimination within the postcolonial state has an intricate relation with a pre-Independence context, upon which the discrimination draws in a completely counterintuitive manner. For the language of anti Christian discrimination issues from the idiom of caste bigotry—Christians are attacked as *churas* and *achūt*, as sweepers and of low caste. Immediately after she speaks of the invitation from Jinnah, Nasir refers to the Christian participation in the Boundary Commission discussion about the partition of Punjab. A small number of Punjabi Christians had sought to remain in eastern Punjab. A larger group sought to join the western part that would become part of Pakistan. The language used at the time to defend the choice is revealing, and, with the hindsight of the half century that has followed, heartbreakingly ironic:

> Our people have been living with the Muslims for a long time and they have become Muslimised more or less in culture and outlook. They trust the Muslims more. They dress like them. No doubt there have been stabbings of Christians but this was probably due to a mistake as they were taken as Muslims. They are economically as poor as the Muslims. With Muslims they have a religious affinity. After all the Prophets of Islam and Christians are the same. If somebody talks discourteously about Christ, a Muslim will take up the cudgels and even take to violence more than a Christian himself. They believe in the sacred things we believe in. There is a great affinity between the two communities, especially in the villages.[82]

Underlying this sense of affinity is an idea that many Punjabi Christians are lower-caste converts and would still be subject to caste discrimination in a predominantly Hindu context. The presumption of affinity on historical (shared prophets) and theological (shared monotheistic and "people of the book") grounds combined with an awareness of the absence of caste as an Islamic theological category apparently makes a Muslim-majority nation a more attractive option than a Hindu-majority one:

> The question of Chhoot, Chhat, i.e. untouchability is a great sore in their hearts and these people have suffered a lot from the social prejudices of non-Muslims. I have been in the villages and I know. I am their representative and have to express their feelings. In non-Muslim villages we have no graveyards and are not allowed to draw water from wells.[83]

Nasir's assertion that Christians came into Pakistan of their own choice is an insistence on a recognition of this history and, at the same time, calls the originary moment of Partition into question, acting as it does as a reminder of the inaugural problem of minority that underpins the Pakistani state. The current crisis is represented as a betrayal of the trust evinced by Christians in the moments preceding Partition, a trust relying both on this Punjabi Christian commitment to Pakistan and on the idea that the nation built for a particular minority might be more sensitive to the needs of the minorities it gathers into its borders, such as Christians, Parsis, and Sikhs, and the new minorities its borders create—the Hindus within. The crisis Nasir struggles to name issues from the paradoxical sense that the nation built for a segment of the Muslim minority in India might have been expected to be more responsive to the problem of other minorities but seems unable to escape a consciousness of that very formation in a condition of Muslim minority. A sympathetic awareness of Muslim minority lies in the conclusion of the Christian arguments at the boundary commission: "The bulk of our population should be allowed to go to the West Punjab where most of us live and want to live. The weight of our number and our percentage of population should go to the Muslims, to make their majority bigger or to make them from minority to majority in all their claims."[84] The solution at the time is a pooling of minority in order to achieve a majority—a nonsecular Christian dissolution into Muslimness to achieve a shared majority enabled through overlapping prophets and a shared monotheism. Most important, of course, is the material condition of living and having lived on the land that is about to be sliced in the service of nationalisms articulated in terms that render them invisible.[85] Nasir's speech, and the conditions that occasion it, shows that what remains inaccessible more than sixty years after Partition is the knowledge that Muslims are now the powerful majority.

Nasir's reminder of the betrayal of Christian fealty at Partition comes as an accusatory cry:

> Kaise log hain āp log? Kaise insān hain āp log? Jab hamāre 'vote' kī
> zarūrat thī, Pakistan banāne kī zarūrat thī tho hamen sāth le līya
> aur jab Pakistan ban gaya tho aqlīyat keh kar dīvar ke sāth lagā diyā.
> Phir hamen 'discriminations' ka sāmna karna parha, kabhī hamen
> 'untouchable' kabhī hamen achūt keh kar hamāre bartan alag kar
> diye ga'e kabhī hamāre. . . . kabhī hamāre masīḥā ko chīn līya gaya.

> What kind of people are you? What kind of humans are you people?
> When you needed our vote, when you needed to make Pakistan then
> you gathered us with you and after Pakistan was created we were
> declared minorities and put against the wall. We had to face discrimi-
> nations then. Sometimes we were called untouchable and sometimes
> *achūt* [also untouchable] and our plates were separated. . . . Some-
> times our messiah was taken from us. [86]

For Nasir, the abjection that attends the status of legal minority is fully entangled with the discrimination encoded in the language of untouchability (of the *achūt*). For both the status of minority and the figure of untouchability are markers of separation, indeed of segrega-tion. The separation of the cutlery, the insistence on separation dur-ing the particular sociality of a meal, signals a fundamental rupture in the social and a complete failure of the originary promise in the intimacy she imagines in the invitation from Jinnah. The separation Nasir indicts is very visible in Noreen's case. The incident is a varia-tion on the archetypal fear of a member of a lower caste drinking at the well and thus contaminating the water. The dispute, which cul-minated in the accusation of blasphemy, is said to have begun with some Muslim women with her refusing to drink water that Noreen had brought them and in response to which refusal she is said to have become abusive. The history that haunts the inability of the Muslim women to take water from the hands of a Christian in a village in a nation created to protect Muslim difference poses yet another chal-lenge to the narrative of that creation.

Nasir declares her awareness of the threat to her own life by equat-ing herself with Noreen. The shared first name heightens the sense of the plight shared by the Christian population: "Iske bād Aasia Bibi ko takht-e dar (takht-e bakht?) par lita den ya Asiya Nasir ko golīyon se chalnī kar den āp aqlīyaton kī āvāz ko nahīn dabā saken ge" (After this [Shahbaz Bhatti's murder] whether you lay Aasia Bibi down on [she seems to mean a bier] or riddle Asiya Nasir with bullets, you

will not be able to suppress the voice of minorities).[87] It is a plight
that is exacerbated by an imperial encounter in which Christians are
then inscribed as traitors by the religious actors, newly antagonistic
to Empire, who are affiliated with organizations that have a history
(that significantly *predates* the current conflict) of persecuting minorities. She feels yet the necessity of declaring that the loyalties of the
Christians are not to America or the West but to Pakistan, for they
have "sworn," she says, "to protect this garden" (ham ne is gulshan
ke taḥaffuẓ kī qasam khā'ī hai).[88]

The need to declare one's loyalty and to use that loyalty as a
demand for protection might well be the problem of the minority in
the nation. It is a dilemma heightened in conditions of war and imperial adventurism. In these conditions, the double bind of minoritarian identity is subject to a double erasure. For to speak of injustice is
to court the possibility of being called a traitor or of being accused
of producing "recruitable" narratives. Yet one might wonder what
might be the condition of those who have fled in the face of threats.
When confronted with racism as "Pakis" in Britain or subject to an
Islamophobia that cannot tell brown people apart, what should the
refugee or asylum seeker say? How, moreover, should postcolonial
intellectuals respond to these dilemmas?

The globalization of "local" conditions and histories requires
tensile responses. The convergence of concerns about the status of
minorities in Europe and America with wars that have been waged
since 1989 can obscure these histories in intellectual discourse. Yet
thinking about minorities elsewhere cannot be disconnected from
metropolitan contexts. For in these contexts immigrant populations
are increasingly encouraged to articulate political claims in terms of
identitarian alterity—in terms, that is, that call upon histories from
elsewhere. These political claims have the potential to affect religious
and "cultural" identities on a planetary scale, for as we know, and I
have sought to demonstrate further, narratives travel across time and
space, sometimes with devastating consequences. Modood's claims
about religious pain with which I began this chapter are built on arguments about the particularities of South Asian forms of devotion,
which are said to be invisible to metropolitan "host" populations. To
make his case he draws upon the persecution of Muslims in the West
and in India but also obscures the costs of that pain for others in the
very spaces whose historical and "cultural" authority he summons in
support of his argument, all the while erasing the colonial genealogy

of the juridical construction of that pain. The absence of Pakistan from his narrative is perhaps most significant. If a history and present of injustice toward people with whom one shares beliefs or practices or histories is one's own, in what sense is injustice by people with whom one shares beliefs, practices, and histories not so? What, in other words, are the ethics of transnational belonging?

The conceptual problems that confront us have everything to do with the disparate but yet fully discursively entangled locations from which postcolonial intellectuals write. As I struggle with the question of what it is about the current configuration that makes Muslims as a majority inconceivable, it seems appropriate to pay renewed attention to what Mufti has termed the "crisis of minority in its global diffusion."[89]

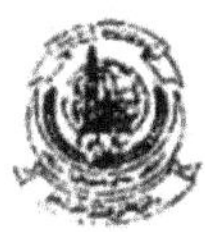

عالمی مجلس تحفظ ختم نبوت

Alami Majlise Tahaffuze Khatme Nubuwwat

22-CO-OPERATIVE BANK BUILDING INSIDE CIRCULAR ROAD FAISALABAD: P HONE 2633522

حوالہ نمبر ____ AMTKN ____ تاریخ ____ 11 . 3 . ____

اسلام علیکم ورحمۃ اللہ

ہم آپ کو عالمی تحریک تحفظ ختم نبوت ﷺ کی طرف سے اسلام قبول کرنے کی دعوت دیتے ہیں اور احمدیت و مرزائیت سے توبہ کرنے اور مرزا غلام احمد کو مجھوٹا اور رسول پاک ﷺ کو آخری نبی ﷺ ماننے اور مذہب اسلام میں آنے کی دعوت دیتے ہیں اور امید کرتے ہیں کہ تم سید منظر احمد ولد سید حسن محمد مرحوم بمع اہل وعیال احمدیت کی تبلیغ اور کافرانہ حرکات سے توبہ کر کے مسلمان ہو جاؤ گے اور یہ بھی امید کرتے ہیں کہ تم اسلام اور رسول پاک ﷺ کی تعلیم کی طرف آ جاؤ گے اور ہماری اس دعوت کو باخوشی قبول کرتے ہوئے مسلمان ہو جاؤ گے۔ تاریخ گواہ ہے کہ مسلمانوں نے غیر مسلموں کے ساتھ اچھا برتاؤ کرتے ہوئے ان کو مسلمان ہونے کی دعوت دی اور وہ مسلمان ہو گئے اور جن لوگوں نے مسلمانوں کے اچھے برتاؤ کے باوجود اسلام کی دعوت قبول نہیں کی ان کا حشر بھی تاریخ میں موجود ہے اس لیے ہم آپ کو اچھے مسلمان ہونے کے ناطے حقیقی مسلمان ہونے کی دعوت دے رہے ہیں اگر آپ نے اس آخری اور قیمتی موقع کو ہاتھ سے گنواہ دیا تو تم لوگوں کا بھی وہی انجام ہوگا جو مرزا و کلاتھ ہاؤس اور دوسرے مرتد کافر سر زائیوں والوں کا ہوا تھا ہم تمہاری جماعت کے بڑے کافروں جو کہ مرتد اور کافر ہیں اور جن کی سزا صرف اور صرف موت ہے ان کو بھی اسلام کی دعوت دے رہے ہیں لیکن اکرم نے بمع اہل وعیال اسلام کی دعوت قبول نہ کی اور مرزا غلام احمد کو نبی ماننے سے انکار نہ کیا تو انجام کے تم خود ذمہ دار ہوں گے۔ یاد رہے کہ تمہارا گھر، بچے ہماری ہٹ لسٹ پر ہیں اور تمہاری تمام منفی حرکات کا ہمیں باخوبی علم ہے۔ یہ خط تمہیں بھیجے کے ساتھ ہی اطلاع کیلئے تم لوگوں کے نام بھیجتے ہیں اور تمام ضروری معلومات لشکر جھنگوی، طالبان، جیش محمد اور تمام دیگر مذہبی تنظیموں کو بھی بھیجی جا رہی ہیں تا کہ اگر تم لوگوں نے اسلام قبول نہ کیا تو تم لوگ نچ کر نہ جا سکو۔ تم لوگوں کو کھلم کھلا اجازت ہے کہ تم یہ خط جس مرضی ایجنسی یا تھانہ میں دکھا سکتے ہو اور اپنی حفاظت کیلئے جو کچھ کر سکتے ہو کر لو تم لوگوں کے بچے کی سوائے اسلام قبول کرنے کے اور کوئی جگہ نہیں بچتی۔ آخر میں اس لئے ہم امید کرتے ہیں کہ تم لوگ مرزائیت سے توبہ کر کے اسلام کی پناہ میں آ جاؤ گے تو دنیا اور آخرت کے تمام خطرات سے محفوظ ہو گے۔

امیر
عالمی مجلس تحفظ ختم نبوت
22 کوآپریٹو بینک بلڈنگ اندرون سرکلر روڈ فیصل آباد

※ ※ ※ 22 کوآپریٹو بینک بلڈنگ اندرون سرکلر روڈ فیصل آباد: فون 2633522 ※ ※ ※

Figure 1. Pamphlet "World Congress for the Protection of the Finality of Prophethood"

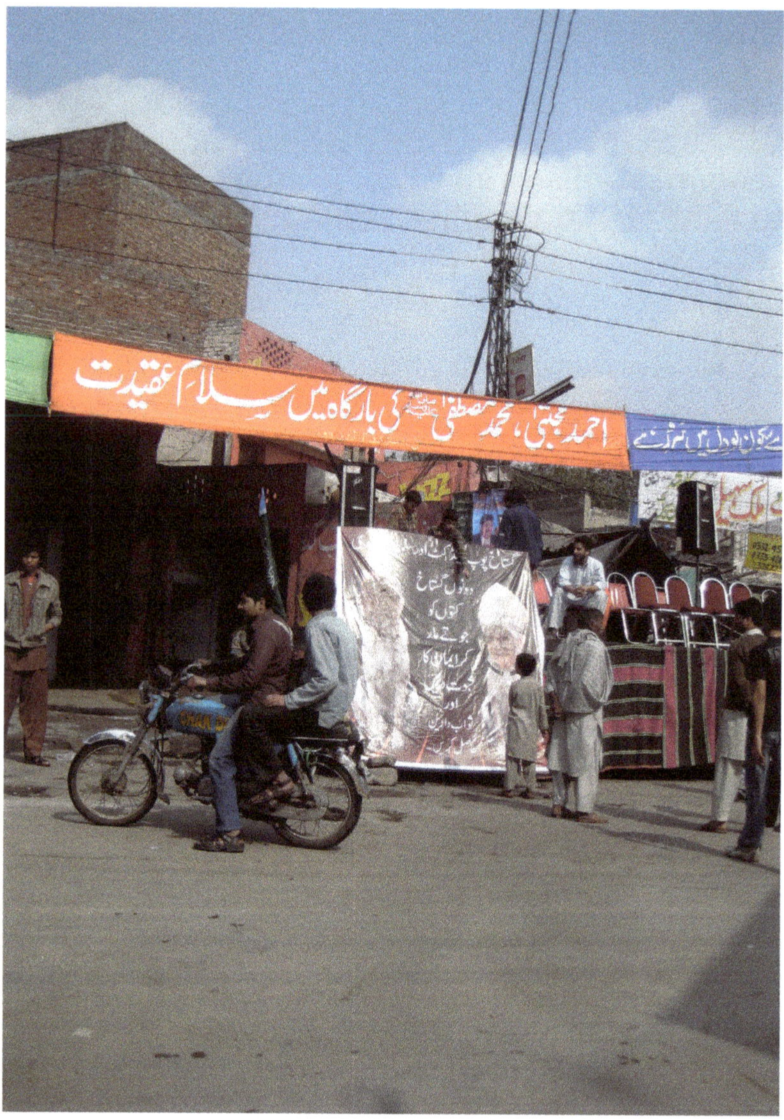

Figure 2. Eid Milad-ul-Nabi Day, 2011, outside Delhi gate of the walled city of Lahore. The banner reads: "Disrespectful Pope Benedict and Salman Rushdie. Give proof of faith and earn God's favor by throwing shoes at both disrespectful dogs."

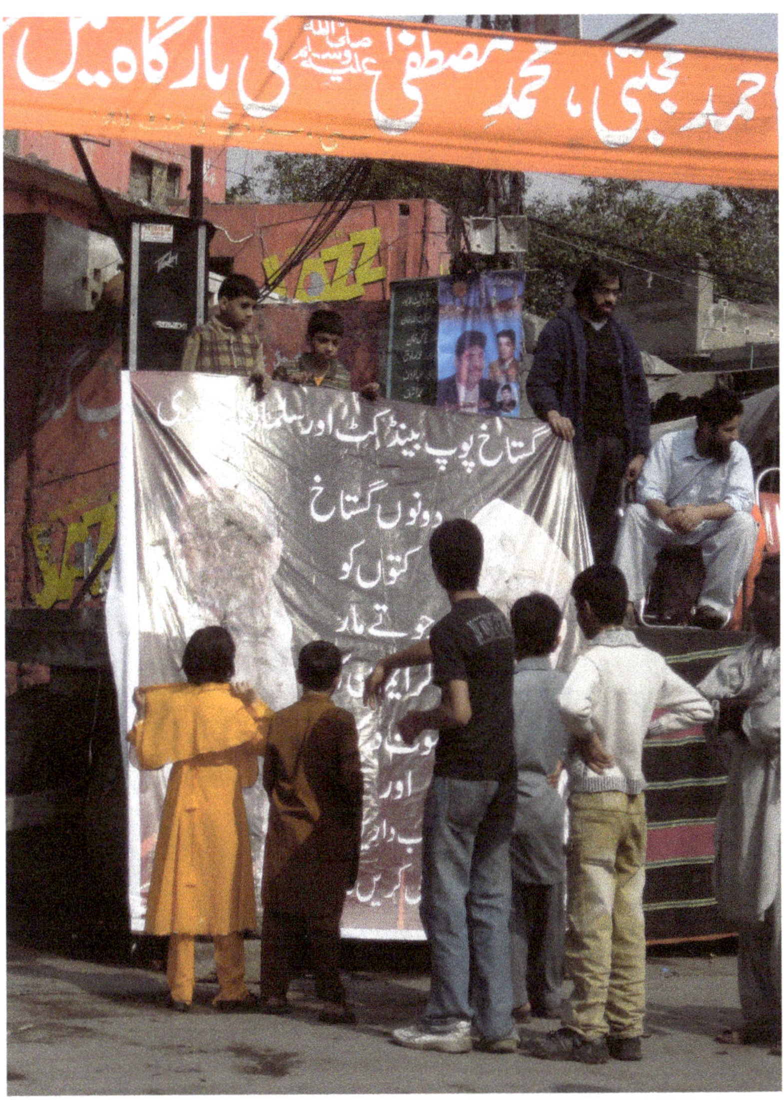

Figure 3. Eid Milad-ul-Nabi Day, 2011, outside Delhi gate of the walled city of Lahore.

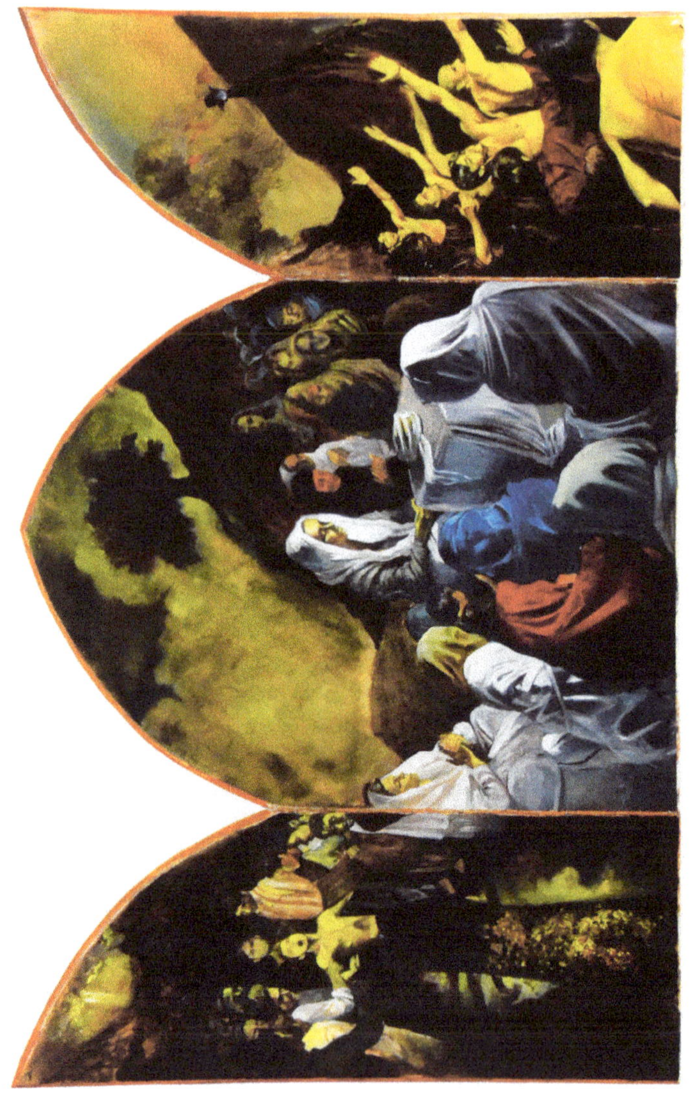

Figure 4. Komail Aijazuddin *First Majlis*

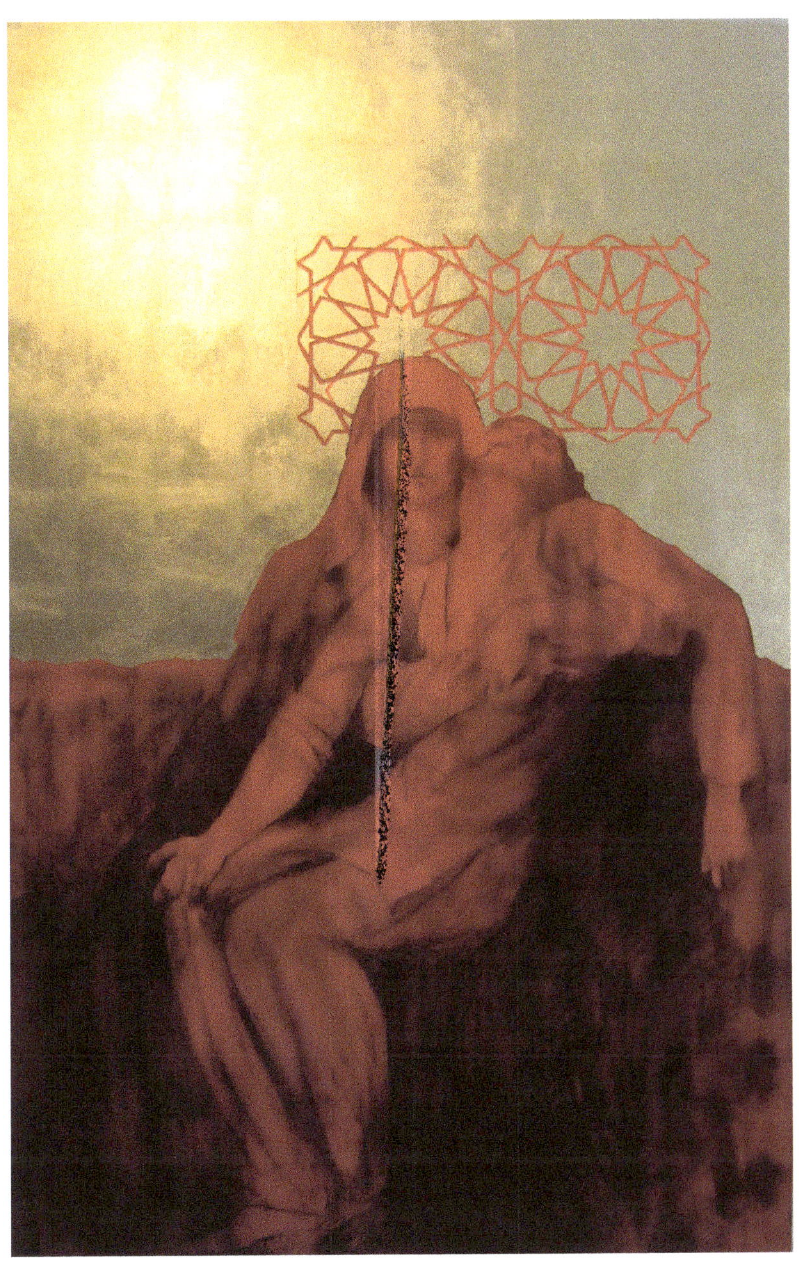

Figure 5. Komail Aijazuddin, *Pieta*

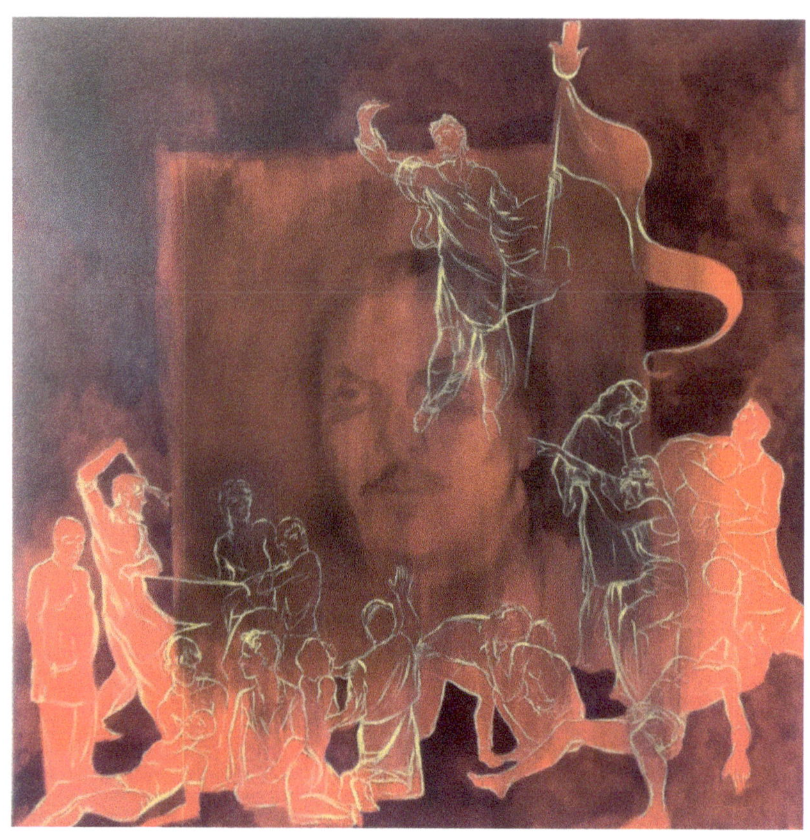

Figure 6. Komail Aijazuddin, *The Accusation*

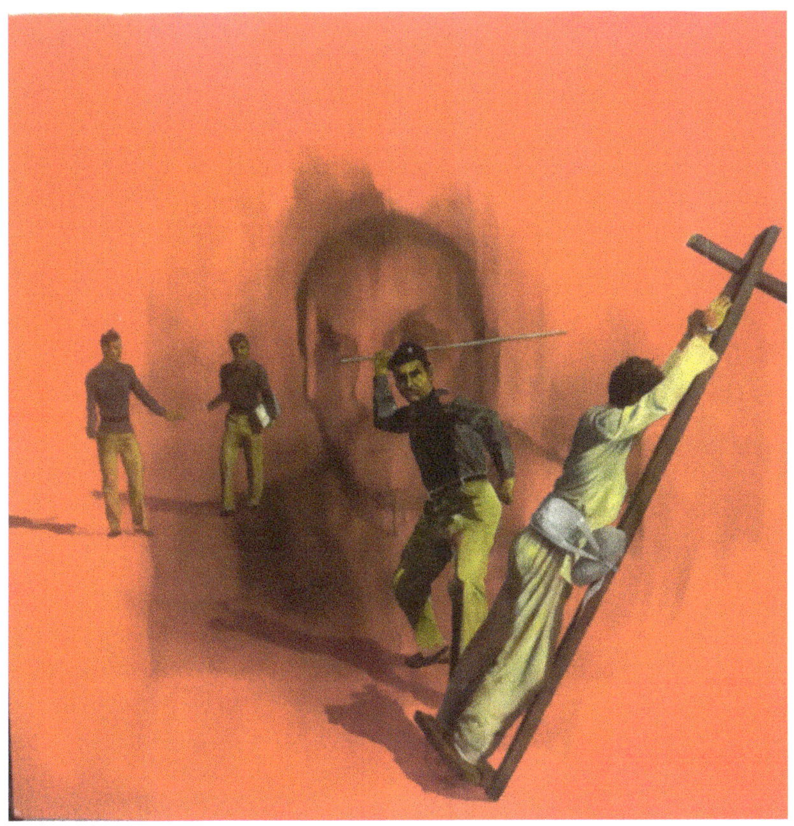

Figure 7. Komail Aijazuddin, *The Flagellation*

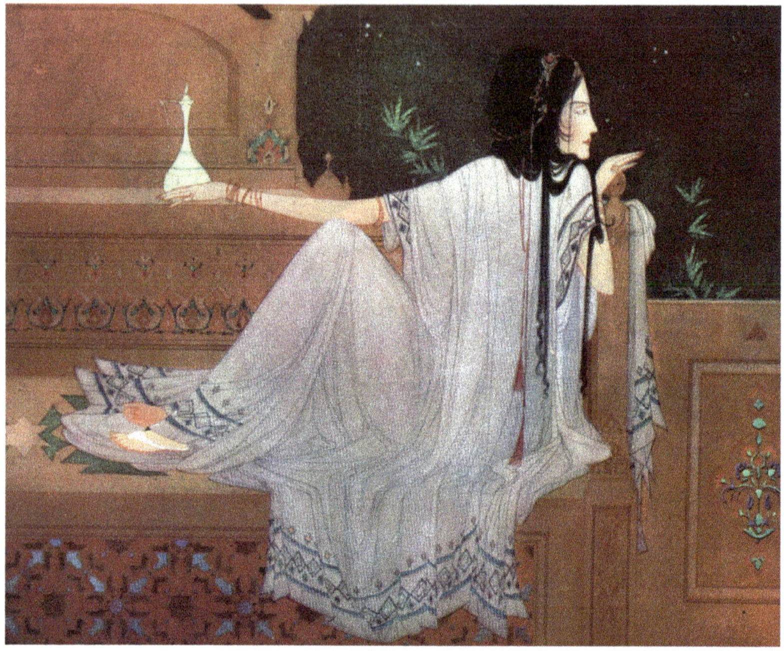

Figure 8. Abdur Rahman Chughtai, *The Wasted Vigil*. All rights reserved by Arif Rahman Chughtai, representing Chughtai Art Home Lahore, courtesy of Arif Rahman Chughtai.

Cold War Baroque

Saints and Icons

IMPERIAL THEOLOGY

The proposition that most political concepts are really secularized theological concepts has come close to attaining the status of intellectual doxa.[1] I am not interested in ascertaining, or disproving, the truth of this formula. Although one might suggest, by way of simple counterweight, that an equally accurate way of characterizing the same history of political thought is that all theological concepts are simply political concepts with metaphysical flourishes adapted to the historical necessities of their moments of production. Most concepts, conceived as political by such an intellectual history, are ideas of how to establish sovereignty—man's or God's—over the web of earthly social relations; that is, they are philosophical responses to the dilemma of establishing the grounds of human authority over other humans, the earth, the universe itself.

Syed Qutb, perhaps the most complexly important thinker for the contemporary moment, recognizes this. In *Milestones* he is insistent that submission to God's sovereignty is a means to freedom of man from man-made laws.[2] In that text, the moment when this notion turns on itself is when it becomes clear that the sovereignty said to be God's is to be claimed by the purified subject, who has submitted properly to God. Only upon the achievement of such purification can God's laws be implemented. In such a case, even when sovereignty is claimed not to be man's, it reveals itself to be in search of a purified vessel for its eventual proper expression. Qutb's repudiation of man's sovereignty seems to be a claim for man's sovereignty after all, but it is attained through an ostensible self-emptying made available through a moral program. For Qutb, the theological is indeed fully political, and the political produced through a combination of a critique of Marxism, nationalism, and all human impurity and ignorance. The latter comes in *Milestones*, with a complete rejection of fourteen hundred years of Muslim history as all of Muslim culture and society are deemed Jahilya. Purification entails not only the repudiation but also the destruction, indeed the extinction, of Muslim history, Islamicate literature, art, and devotional practice, in other words, of all of Islamicate and Muslim lifeworlds. Qutb's rejection of history is a form of claiming sovereignty through a return to an originary moment of embattlement, one that paradoxically erases more than a thousand intervening years of power, and extraordinary cultural production, a range of societies, and, it must be emphasized, social collectivities.[3]

Nonetheless, whichever way one tilts in the priority one gives to the theological or the political, that is, whether one decides that most political concepts are secularized theological concepts or most theological concepts are political concepts with metaphysics added, it is clear that contemporary discussions of politcs and secularism have been particularly interested in the surreptitious operations of theology in the most secular-seeming spaces.[4] The interest of these various interpretations of political theology lies chiefly in their exposure of the ostensible delusions of secularism, that is, in their outing of its false and fallen consciousness.

The emphasis on exposing secularism in the cause of making its mystificatory theologies visible has had the effect of obscuring a convergence that I call imperial theology: the nexus of American, varieties of third world nationalist or postcolonial praetorian, and Saudi Arabian anticommunism, and the cultivation by these convergent groups and agents of iconoclastic and antiaesthetic brands of Islam.[5] In the post–September 11, 2001, wars, it is this convergence that has turned in upon itself, producing religio-political effects that can only be understood locally when the global investments in the production of local religion are reconfigured and mapped. In the Afghan-Pakistani contexts, this promotion of an imperial theology and the subsequent implosion of the alliances that produced it have resulted, in turn, in what I am calling a baroque moment—a moment of involution, of a history that is collapsing in on itself, where the realignments of power and religion are producing aesthetic responses that share features of the historical Baroque: ornateness (even ornate floridity), a profound preoccupation with endlessly layered religious ideas and devotional and theological aesthetics, a preoccupation with the torn and suffering body, an attempt to expose the layers of the intricate historical webs of the present through a play on and multiple uses, sometimes ironic or comic, of theological ideas and varieties of iconicism. Moreover, in literary narratives this encounter between theology and Cold War politics has generated a fascination with the figure of the spy, the double agent, the soldier and brutalizing policeman, of the (often defeated) communist and, of course, the conservative Islamist, but also of the poet, the painter, and the aesthete. The works that comprise this formation seem profoundly antitheodicean even if there is a certain grimly amused use of a narrative structure that may almost seem (parodically) providential in a work such as Mohammed Hanif's *A Case of Exploding Mangoes*, which I discuss at some length below.[6] The most striking element of this formation is its explicit use of icons and theological and devotional aesthetics in the service of complexly secular visions.

The literature on the Baroque is vast, much of it sparked, as is well known, by Heinrich Wölfflin's *Renaissance and Baroque* (1888).[7] The traits I associate with the baroque can be found listed in Rene Wellek's compendium of scholarship on the term in "The Concept of the Baroque."[8] My conception could be said to be present in a series attributions of the Baroque but reflects my own perception of characteristics important to the moment and formation I am describing. Cold War Baroque is not seventeenth-century Baroque. It does, however, share certain formal tendencies and, perhaps more significant, signals a longer political *durée* marked by the ongoing problematic of the restructuring of religion—and the relationship of that reconfiguration with the problem of the nation-state and the status of citizenship and minority—in modernity.[9]

There is a certain historical irony in the association of the Baroque with the Counter-Reformation. For in the contemporary moment the rise of Protestant power and, in the case of the United States, a Protestant empire's cultivation of scripturalist and iconoclastic varieties of Islam has produced a secular aesthetic formation, which heavily utilizes icons, and resonates with the "Counter-Reformation" because it opposes the machinations of a Protestant empire whose very existence and consolidation is a post-Reformation effect. Insofar as the collection of aesthetic practices I describe oppose the effects of a successful Protestant empire, they are, of course, "countering" an aspect of the Reformation, or more precisely of its afterlife, and yet, because of shifts in power over time, these aesthetic practices are far removed from the sphere of the political power available to the historical Counter-Reformation. This is not to downplay the effect of the Counter-Reformation but rather to note the importance of the shifts of the balance of power within Christendom. What I am describing is not a derivative formation but instead a grounded, dialogical one that responds to immanent features of the new theology and a historical geopolitics by putting the iconographic registers of the Baroque to highly inverted secular use. Although the formation I am describing is fully engaged with politics and both new and old histories, the set of practices of representation of which it is comprised are not in any narrow way simply "reflective" of politics or history. Instead, following T. J. Clark, I would argue that these practices have a certain "cognitive power," that they have something to tell us which exceeds mere illustration.[10] In fact, these are a set of emergent practices that recognize and organize a history and a series of political, institutional, theological, and fundamentally social transformations that are yet to be named and theorized. At the same time, these practices participate in those very transformations not only *revealing* their complexity, but actively complicating them. This formation demands, moreover, a renewed attention to the capacities for critique and contest within aesthetic practice.

The revival of academic interest in the Baroque under the rubric of the neobaroque is a welcome reminder of the continuities between the historical Baroque and visual and literary forms in the Americas, where the aesthetic forms of the Empire have been further subjected to indigenization and themselves been transformed in the process.[11] The form of the Baroque I am interested in here provides a further fold in the question of the Baroque in the present. Unlike the Latin American situation, its point of departure is a Protestant empire. Moreover, what interests me in this context is its explicit engagement with theological confrontations in Muslim-majority societies and disaporic contexts. Yet the space of direct contact with the Latin American neobaroque is the global Anglophone novel and the influence of the Latin American practitioners of the Marvelous Real upon it. The most visible name in this carrying over is, of course, Salman Rushdie, on whom the influence of Latin American fiction is well known and whose own influence on the career of the global Anglophone novel is hard to overstate.

In *A Case of Exploding Mangoes*, his satirical conspiracy novel about Zia-ul-Haq's death and his collusion with the United States during the 1980s, the period widely thought to have decisively secured the transformation of the political and cultural landscape of Pakistan, Mohammed Hanif, perhaps the most unsentimental Anglophone Pakistani novelist and a fierce moral intelligence, writes: "In the name of God, God was exiled from the land and replaced by the one and only Allah" (*CM*, 42).This follows a long list of God's names and the places from which they were removed, as if the full extent of the erasure of culture under Zia can only be registered by a relentless recuperating list of the expunged alternatives:

> All God's names were slowly deleted from the national memory, as if a wind had swept the land and blown them away. Innocuous, intimate names: Persian Khuda, which had been handy for ghazal poets, as it rhymed with most of the operative verbs; Rab, which poor people invoked in their hour of distress; Maula, which the Sufis shouted in their hashish sessions. Allah had given himself ninety-nine names. His people had improvised many more. But all these names slowly started to disappear—from official stationery, from Friday sermons, from newspaper editorials, from mother's prayers, from greeting cards, from official memos, from the lips of television quiz-show hosts. From children's storybooks, from lovers' songs, from court orders, from telephone operators' greetings, from habeas corpus applications, from interschool debating competitions, from road inauguration speeches, from memorial services, from cricket players' curses, and even from beggars' begging pleas. (*CM*, 42)

"Deleted" insists on the agency behind the erasure. As Hanif presents it, there is something systematic here: an editorial project of culture, executed through the control of language and, more significantly, through an attempted transformation of forms of devotion—forms fully entangled with the most ordinary actions and objects of life. Hanif is aware that the historical turn to what is perceived as a purified and authentic Islam is connected to what is presented and perceived as a turn to a "pure" Arabic mode, which, in turn, ahistorically figures Arab as Saudi and theologically aligned with Wahhabism. In the novel the deletion of the local lifeworlds—first presented as the erasure of names and thus the gouging out of inscriptions of a local language—is fundamentally linked to Zia's consolidation of his power after the coup in which Bhutto was deposed and the Cold War machinations that were the cause for the American presence in the region.[12]

Hanif figures the destruction of these alternatives as part of a complex interaction between regional and local understandings of religion. Many of the erased alternatives are local names of God, pervasive in utterance, poetry, music, Sufi practice, and shrine culture, permeating the most mundane practices of daily life. The paradox is that the disenchantment of daily life is an effect of a particular brand of a militaristically mandated, regionally (by Saudi Arabia) and globally (farther afield—by the United States) supported version of religion.

"Cold War Baroque" is then an apt rubric for the responses that try to map, organize, reveal, and critique the history of these deletions and that, in their narrative version, write a cast of spies, soldiers, torturers and the tortured, military leaders, religious fighters, communists, and right-wing Islamist militants, responses that at the same time try to undo these expurgations, foregrounding and using that which has been targeted for "deletion." The political history that enabled these deletions has itself been redacted, and many of these responses attempt to recuperate that history as well, employing ingenious variations on historical fiction with a variety of aesthetic and narrative devices associated with magical realism and devotional poetry while calling upon genres such as spy novels, thrillers, canonization narratives, even rape revenge stories.

The point has been made regarding Rushdie that in South Asia his books were read as history. It bears repeating. That postcolonial studies achieved ascendancy in a moment when high antihumanism and antifoundationalism were—and continue to be—institutionally powerful, forming the "spontaneous philosophy" of the humanities and social sciences, has meant that the very active political engagements of a great deal of postcolonial literature have been defanged and domesticated to conceptually curtailed effect.[13] The aesthetic practices I describe here cannot be recognized in their complex articulations if their capacity for critique and their social and political interventions are underplayed in the ostensible service of epistemological sophistication. What the literature I am describing has in common is an attempt to produce histories of the destructive effects of Cold War theologies through fictional phenomenologies. The point is not at all that what is produced is conventional history—although, of course, that, too, is a contestable category—neither does it invite an interpretive literalism seeking meticulous correspondences between verifiable events and those presented in the texts but rather that the achievement of critique ought to be recognized. It is, indeed, in the critique and through the formal devices used to enable that critique that history is produced.

In Hanif's novel, the protagonist—a soldier who is tortured and is enlisted into being a coconspirator in the murder of the military leader—and the ISI colonel, named after the current head of the military, Kayani, who turns him, are strange emblems of the hidden history of the enterprise of imperial theology and the Cold War clientelism that was one of its sustaining mechanisms. A theology that was, moreover, supported and promulgated by an imperial network, which also operated through what has is some circles come to be known, with the awe that a blurring between the world of pulp thrillers and political reality needs must induce, one of the largest covert operations in history.[14]

In literary narratives, Aslam and Hanif clarify the shape of this formation, which is evident in Aslam's novels (which I will discuss in the next chapter) in a poetics of hyper-aestheticism and sentimental excess, a complex substructure of Sufi thought and aesthetic practice, and a relentless proximity between exaggerated, grotesque, and almost unbearably violent imagery and images of powerful, wrenching beauty. Hanif's voice is more unsentimental, less ornate, but equally relentless in its recuperation of these hidden histories and in its complex engagement with theological aesthetics (especially, as we shall see, in *Our Lady of Alice Bhatti*), and even through a fairly straightforward use of magical realism in *A Case of Exploding Mangoes*.[15]

As my invocation of the Baroque suggests, the formation crosses aesthetic media. Perhaps the most visually striking examples can be found in the work of a young painter, Komail Aijazuddin, who in early 2012 exhibited a series of "altarpieces."[16] Aijazuddin's very deliberate use of iconography associated with Christianity, and especially Catholicism, to present themes from Shia narratives, and the martyrdom of Husain at Karbala is of deep theo-political significance. For it is an assemblage that brings together the fragments of religious practices and minoritarian faiths that have been systematically marginalized over the course of the national history he engages but which were particularly shattered under the reign of Zia-ul-Haq.

The altarpieces both attempt to recuperate increasingly marginalized, though continuously lived, Shia practices and stories and explicitly link them to Christian practice, by way of the conceit of the altarpiece. The conceit is historically multiple: even as it draws on an aesthetic history from a tradition from within Western Christianity, it links the Christians with Shias through an implied context of minority. The altarpieces tend to be around two and a half by three feet and are meant to be like those used in private chapels. The private devotion implied by the scale resonates with an ongoing practice in South Asian Shia homes, particularly in Karachi, of having small *imambargahs* (spaces for Shia commemoration, especially during Muharram) in the house, which are often only used during the first ten days of Muharram. That an altarpiece can be shut, and the iconography thus hidden, is significant. For instead of signaling, as it might in a different context, a special sanctity reserved for particular occasions, in this case it suggests that the images can be quickly hidden should the need arise. The hands painted on many of the altarpieces are, of course, the standard icons of Shia practice, the *alams*—the hand of Fatima—which can be found in *imambargahs* with heavily worked pennants hanging from them, suggesting the standards carried into battle by Husain and his followers. That they are on the outside of the altarpieces reveals the defiant use of an icon of Shia protest. Turned horizontally, as Aijazuddin occasionally presents them, they become icons of the Sephardic Jews. This blurring of the lines between the Abrahamic religions is part of Aijazuddin's ongoing practice—a blurring that is both dissident and historically restorative insofar as it seeks to make visible and thus produce a perception of shared parts of the Abrahamic theological traditions and cultural practices and icons, a perception that in its engagement with the historical materiality of present-day Pakistan acts as a form of historical reorientation.

For Aijazuddin, the story of Karbala, and the embattled group of seventy-two, facing a much more powerful army, is also increasingly the story of secular embattlement in Pakistan.[17] Aijazuddin, who studied in the United States, has said that his position has changed since he moved back to Pakistan. At first, he had intended merely to find ways to figure the Shia narratives within a frame of marginalized religious practice; he shifted to seeing the Karbala narrative as also analogous with the plight of a secular, aesthetically inclined position, one that can draw on these stories and their devotional and theological import to insist on the history, often aesthetic, with which they have been so profoundly interwoven—a history that includes Urdu literary genres, like the *marsiya*, written by poets as canonical as Mir Anis.[18] It is perhaps unsurprising that it is Aijazuddin's move back to Pakistan that makes him more insistent about the threat to forms of secularism. At the same time it must be emphasized that his version of secularism is not anathema to religious practice or religious lifeworlds. After the assassination of a Shia doctor and his young son, it is with great attachment to Shia religious narratives and practice that, in his persona as the gossipy newspaper columnist Fayes T. Kantawala, he wrote: "The protest had the air of a majlis about it, of the Shia dirge and elegy. It occurred to me that a full-on procession of people doing maatam [flagellation] in front of governor's House was as good an expression as any of collective outrage and grief." Even more powerfully in another column he had a few months earlier identified the current plight of Shias in Pakistan with the tragedy at Karbala:

> A war has been declared on Shias. They-we-are being picked out and killed all over the country. Muharram isn't over yet—not at the time of submission of this piece, God help us all—and already we've suffered three terrifying attacks on gatherings.
>
> That we, the Shias of Pakistan, have now entered our own Karbala here is more than a little ironic.
>
> When you see us march and hear us wail this week, know that we do it not only to protest the assault on our icons, but also the one on ourselves.[19]

It is not surprising, then, that the tenderness regarding some of these religious narratives and practices is evident in the altarpieces. One of Aijazuddin's most powerful altarpieces, *The First Majlis* (Fig. 4), tries to imagine and figure the first commemoration of Husain's death. Each panel of the triptych figures a different type of remembrance of Husain's martyrdom. In one side panel a young man walks on burning embers, watched and helped along by his fellow mourners, in a practice known as *āg kā mātam*, or flagellation on fire.

In the other side panel, young men flagellate themselves in unison in a representation of the practice of *mātam* while the standard reaches into a dark and angry sky. The central panel presents a vision of women keeping each other company while listening to the tale of martyrdom, within an encroaching darkness, which seems ready to engulf. The sky in the background is mottled and brown, suggesting a tumultuous mourning. The landscape, itself tormented and in upheaval, seems to threaten the assembled women, while the tree looks ready to slide down the side of the mountain, away from the women but yet as if it cannot bear to stay rooted.

The vision is of a sociality structured by mourning, and, in the side panels, by a deep, angrily inconsolable grief and by commemoration.

The painting frames people tending to each other in mourning, as suggested by the man helping the younger man walk on fire in the left panel, young men self-flagellating in passionate unison in the right panel, and women sitting together sharing the story of the martyrdom in the central panel. It is a grief in which the earth itself, darkened, twisted, and in turmoil, participates. Such a vision needs must resonate with contemporary South Asian Shia devotional practice in the months of Muharram, when men and women attend several of these gatherings daily, especially women who can attend as many as four or more in a day, thus forming the community through participation in practices of remembrance. The darkness of the painting and the utterly bleak mood it evokes could well suggest a contemporary *majlis* on 'Āshūrah, except that the women, and the men in the side panels, are exposed to the threatening elements in a way that they would not be in present-day Pakistan. But, by dressing the men in Pakistani clothing, Aijazuddin makes the very earliest commemoration a South Asian act. Significantly, instead of Arabizing South Asian Shia culture he makes an Arab scene South Asian, thus laying a local claim to this inceptionary moment in Muslim history.

In another painting, *Pieta* (Fig. 5), which figures a dead son in a mother's arms but which is meant to imagine Husain's death within this frame, Aijazuddin again explicitly brings together Shia and Christian stories but this time in an interpretation of a Byzantine icon replete with a gold background. The figures in red acrylic and graphite and the scale add the modern element in the painting. The colors and the angle of the male body along with the mother's set expression, as in numerous variations on the Pietà, present a vision of the commingling of patience and suffering in mourning. The suffering mother represents the historical wrong represented by the death of a child, which is often explicitly figured in the presentations of the idea of Fatima's suffering, had she witnessed the events at Karbala, in many a *nauḥa* and *marṣiya*.

Set alongside *The First Majlis* and *Pieta* the other forms of remembrance of the multiple genealogies of South Asian culture in Aijazuddin's work acquire the weight of commemorative mourning, a mourning that, in this case, keeps the memory of injustice alive through the reworking of practices of commemoration from Shia martyrology, evoking the importance of the element of protest in Shia thought and practice that Hamid Dabashi has discussed in *Shi'ism: A Religion of Protest*.[20]

CONTRAPASSO FICTIONS

In a series of paintings of Zia, Aijazuddin's complex use of icons and iconography continues in less historically familiar and transparent forms. The paintings are imbued with an aesthetics of accusation and judgment. They challenge the viewer to remember, and to judge in the remembrance. If the altarpieces tend to make use of compositions from late Renaissance triptychs, if they use, consciously citing, the dark colors and exaggerated movement of line in body, fabric, and gesture of Baroque and Mannerist painting, the Zia paintings seem more contemporary in conception and composition. In each one of the four-by-four-foot paintings the much larger than life head of Zia in the background gives the impression of a paradoxically presiding spectral presence; that is, what strikes is that despite the disembodied, shadelike execution of the portrait in graphite, the figure seems powerful and strangely, emphatically present. The red acrylic wash recalls Shakir Ali's work by which Aijazuddin was surrounded growing up, since his family owns a number of his paintings, and, at the same time, makes the paintings seem bathed in blood. In each painting, the figures that are arranged on and around Zia's face complete what I can only call, blurring visual and written text, the compositional narrative. These paintings contribute to a national archive by adding their own (fragmented) narrative, even as they rely on historical stories that may not always be intelligible to their (nationally and confessionally multiple) audiences.

The Accusation (Fig. 6) pictures an astonishing fantasy of revenge imagined from the perspective of those marginalized by Zia's religious politics. The striking figure of a man in a *shalwar kameez*, holding up a Shia standard, with his feet on Zia's face, is meant to be Husain; and the painting is Husain's judgment, rendered in response to the accusation of the people affected by Zia's injustice. Husain's clothing makes him a local figure, quietly reversing the antilocalism of Zia's Saudi-facing and U.S.-backed politics. Zia's rather spectral portrait seems drawn within the painting on a monumental slab of unidentifiable stone, looking onto a scene of claustrophobic tumult. The figures arrayed below form a group in turmoil and disarray, full of pain, two dead bodies scattered across, fleeing and also seeking. In their midst is the figure of the woman who points accusingly at the face. The man who seems to be reaching to touch the face turns the face itself into an iconic object of veneration. The figures in the foreground on the right seem a little adrift. In the group on the left some are in conflict and one is collapsed, two are turned away from the face as if they cannot bear the sight. All are close to the face, as if encircling it in hell.

The painting puts different kinds of icons and valences of iconicity at play, contrasting Zia's status with Husain's, thus revealing Zia's lesser claim. This is rather unequivocally evident in the representation of the figure of Husain carrying the icon, calling upon the associations of protest, martyrdom, and commitment to justice the standard-bearing figure encodes. The painting, along with the series in which it occurs, could well be called "Nation and Icon" for it figures Zia as iconic, to at least some in the nation, even as to others he is a reviled figure only to be accused. In accord with these postures of accusation, the painting turns the heroic figure of Husain—carrying the most powerful icon, the *alam*, of a religious minority, rising out of this scene of misery and rage—against him in retribution as he stands with his feet and *alam* firmly planted in Zia's face. The figure of Husain is to rescue the nation afflicted by Zia. If one of Zia's projects was to permeate the nation with a Wahhabi-inspired Islam hostile to Shi'ism, Aijazuddin turns the emblematic figure of Shia heroism into the agent of Zia's punishment.

The Flagellation (Fig. 7) reaches into a photographic archive to render its judgment. There are fewer figures and less movement in it, yet the painting is even more disturbing. Positioned at an angle in the front right foreground is a man tied to wooden beams, which form a cross, being flogged by a policeman. The two policemen behind are closer to Zia's face. One seems almost to be carrying a book of laws or rules. It appears official, and he officious. The three policemen and the man being flogged seem more embodied as, unlike the silhouettes in *The Accusation*, they are painted in oils—almost as if in this blood-bathed environment only the torturer and the tortured can be given their fully embodied form. The representation of the flogging is based on a photograph taken after the Hudood ordinances were put into effect by Zia-ul-Haq.[21] By rendering a scene from a newspaper photograph the painting declares a certain documentary, even newslike impulse. And yet the painting's relation with its own mimetic impulses is more complex. It chooses to frame the rendering of that photograph within a larger set of relations. To translate Lukacs's thought about realism in the novel, one might say that its complicated realism lies in that it represents the relations between the event, those who make it possible by being the petty bureaucrats (the police) who serve the apparatus implementing the law, and the authorizing figure of Zia, who imposes, one might even say "authors," the law.[22]

Aijazuddin produces a representation of a structure of relations by combining portraiture and a mimetic rendering of a scene first framed in a photograph, and through an alignment of painting with photography, in what is a distinctly modern composition in which these genres are mixed, and yet at the same time subverting any easy association with a simple secularism by inviting a reflection on the genealogies of flagellation and flogging within Christian art and traditions and their intersection with Muslim theology and practice. The realism itself symbolizes and embraces a project of witness that demands the consolidation and memorialization of an archive of atrocity. The crosslike disposition of the beams links the Hudood Ordinances to the blasphemy laws, in which Christians have been disproportionately targeted. Together the Hudood Ordinances and the blasphemy laws—attempts to implement "Sharia" in Pakistan and put in place by an unelected military dictator—might be said to have provided the seal on the project of the religious right.

The title of the painting invites us to think of the minions of the militaristic state, the police in this case, as the praetorian guard flogging an innocent blasphemer, a Christic figure in working-class—as the nonstarched, unpristine *shalwar kameez* he is wearing indicates—Pakistani guise.[23] The title opens a formal history that enables a host of meanings and creates multiple associations whose semiotic work comes through an interaction between the image confronting us and a series of other images the name of the painting calls up. One need not assert the priority of language as a semiotic form to understand these associations; the cross within the painting refers back to so many other crosses and floggings. Yet the semiotic importance of language in these paintings is evident in Ajazuddin's decision to name this one *Flagellation* within a scene from a Pakistani context. Calling on the feature of icons that relies on the interplay between word and image, the name encourages an openness to linguistic association as well. The opening up of a connection between the Roman Imperial Guard and the militaristic apparatus—of which Zia was a product and which he did much to strengthen, through a linguistic transfer in "praetorian"—is precisely such an association. Though the word *praetorian* is not used, it is implied by the iconographic tradition made available by the titular reference to "flagellation." At the same time, this flagellation is at some distance from the Shia practices of self-flagellation Aijazuddin represents in his altarpiece. Those commemorate the unjust infliction of pain by the powerful, and pressure the national narrative from another perspective. A certain claim to national exception and historical distinction—predicated on the erasure of a variety of confessional histories—is undermined by the historical associations of praetorianism. The history of such iconography challenges the coherence of the nation's separateness, even indeed of the national religion's distinction.

Aijazuddin's is a vision that seeks both to accuse and to solidify an archive of an erased regional history and a shattered polity, haunted by Zia's specter. His commitment to figural representation, his tendency to opt for a certain bodily realism, is of a piece with the impulse to both render and consolidate this historical archive. At the same time, his use of a variety of iconic objects provides elements of judgment and allows for a certain fantasy of justice, even supernaturally rendered, to be a part of the fiction of the paintings. Yet this vision of retribution is antiprovidential. It cannot provide a narrative of redemption; it can only remember and imagine justice in the form of commemoration and, in the figure of Husain and his pennant, a mythic moment of vanquishment, for, from Aijazuddin's point of view, Husain's story is yet no evidence of divinity.

This encoding of a fictional wreaking of justice is also part of the generic frame and governing conceit of *A Case of Exploding Mangoes*, which can be characterized as both a satirical whodunit about Zia's death and as a variation on a rape revenge narrative. For although the novel's brutal yet hilarious fiction is that many of the characters desired, plotted, and had the opportunity to kill Zia, it is in the end the curse of blind Zainab, the woman accused under the ghastly Hudood Ordinances—more particularly the Zina laws— that propels the crow that destroys the plane carrying Zia. Although Zia is not the rapist, his laws are the reason that Zainab is imprisoned for being raped, since according to them she requires four Muslim male witnesses to prove that a rape has occurred. Because she is pregnant, in the absence of such witness, she is judged guilty of fornication. Gang-raped but in prison for fornication because her pregnancy is evidence of intercourse, Zainab is one Zia's most injured victims, multiply raped and then further brutalized by profoundly unjust and arbitrary laws. So important is her story that it seems that Noor's mother in *Our Lady of Alice Bhatti* might indeed be the same character.

Hanif figures Zainab's curse as the curse of the nation. For, on the novel's terms, Zia is the absent Muslim male witness who should be providing justice. That he ought to be a witness to the suffering of the people without whose consent he has chosen to govern is also how he understands his own duties, which is why, in one of the many hilarious episodes in the book, he wishes to go out like Haroun Al-Rashid, disguised as an ordinary man, seeking to see how content people are with his rule. That he is unaware of the hostility and contempt in which much of the citizenry holds him is simply an extension of the nonconsensual violence of his rule; it is also what exposes the delusions that he is loved by "his" people, that he has fulfilled his duty to the citizenry he has transformed willy-nilly into his subjects, and that his rule is an expression of God's sovereignty on earth.

The magical realist device of Zainab's curse is used to present a fiction of retributive, divinely facilitated, justice. The curse works alongside an inexorable sense dogging Zia that something terrible is likely to happen to him. Zia lives in a world of omens and portents, which he derives from his readings of the Qur'an. Although, as the novel tells us, he is aware, with the kind of consciousness an acolyte might have, that this practice would not meet with Maududi's approval:

> He had read enough Muaudi [*sic*] to know that the Quran wasn't a
> book of omens, to be used in worldly affairs, but like a child taking
> a peek at his surprise birthday presents, Genera Zia couldn't resist
> the temptation.
>   What is a lone man standing at the crossroads of history to do?
> (*CM*, 34)

Presenting Zia as so deluded as to appear a buffoon is part of the novel's structure of revenge. He imagines himself as an embattled savior—banalized in modern terms almost into a hero from a cowboy movie—although he is in fact an affliction to the nation and its citizens, and a disposable and disappointing prophet to the God he thinks he serves. Zia's sense that he might be destined for a fate like Jonah's, swallowed by the whale, turns out to be true within the fiction. But, unlike Jonah, he is not expelled. He simply dies with the exploding aircraft. The fear of Jonah's fate comes to him in one of his morning readings of the Qur'an when "his finger hesitated on verse 21:87 of the Quran" (*CM*, 30). Although he would spend the next two months and two days "dreaming about the innards of a whale," the rejoicing nation, the narrator tells us, was never to know that "General Zia's journey towards death had started over the slight confusion he experienced over the translation of a verse on a fateful day" (*CM*, 30).

As in Aijazuddin's *Accusation*, it is as fitting as any Dantean contrapasso that the punishment Zia experiences is borne across by a curse, and that he dies in the exploding belly of a military aircraft. His fear of the portent turns out to be justified, but that justification figures him, within his own metaphysical world, as a false and inadequate prophet. For, on the terms of Jonah's parable, he should have been spat out alive. It is yet another one of the novel's jokes that the portent turns out to be accurately ominous, and that the decisions Zia makes as a result of an anxiety about a confusion over Qur'anic interpretation turn out to ensure the very outcome he fears. His terror of divine abandonment and his fear of being left alone in the belly of the whale are met with the punishment reserved for the sinner who cannot be forgiven for having failed his people, for his prayers will not work. It is even more significant that the crime that involves assaulting the nation in the service of establishing a particular version of Islam should have its punishment begun in a confusion over scriptural interpretation, and even more specifically, Arabic translation. Zia's project was to produce a population infused with a particular kind of piety through the implementation of punitive laws; his death is effected in the supernatural operations of the curse of one of his most innocent victims, a curse that confirms his—on his own hero, Mawdudi's, terms—theologically inappropriate reading of the Qur'anic verse as a portent. Iftikhar Dadi has written of contemporary artistic practice in Pakistan that it is "beginning to look at discursive and scripturalist Islam . . . as a subject for complex artistic interrogation."[24] One can see such an interrogation of scripturalism in Hanif's work as well.

Spanning the two months leading up to Zia's death, the novel is temporally compact, but Hanif manages, through some very concentrated references, to critically usher in a longer national history. An exemplary moment occurs in the scene where Zia launches the attack on names other than Allah for God. Hanif presents Zia as both cleverly opportunistic in his manipulative use of religion and a zealot. In his first meeting with the top brass of the military he uses religion to wrongfoot the mostly secular, whiskey-swilling generals. Once he is done with what is a brilliant establishment of his authority after the coup in which Z. A. Bhutto was deposed, the novel reports the thoughts of his generals. They run the gamut from *"He really makes sense. How come I didn't think of it before?"* and *"I am going to prohibit the word* God *at home"* to *"A country that thinks it was created by God has finally found what it deserves: a blabbering idiot who thinks he has been chosen by Allah to clear his name"* (CM, 39–41; Hanif's italics). Even as Hanif incorporates a range of responses, in keeping with the novel's sustained attempt to crumble the Islamically monolithic Pakistan Zia sought to create, he manages to refer back to a strand of Muslim nationalism that imagines the nation as representing God's sovereignty, and thus as the achievement of divine intervention. In the scene, the venality, ingratiation, and hypocrisy of these wielders of national power work against the fantasy of being a conduit of divine sovereignty Hanif's allusion summons.

The very multiplicity of Hanif's farce, its determined attention to the comic banalities of everyday life in Pakistan in the 1980s—references to soldiers performing karaoke to George Michael's "Careless Whisper," people watching *Dallas*, wearing Levis manufactured for export, using "fake" Poison—reveals a commitment to producing a nonorientalized vision in his novels, one in which the representation of the sheer banality of contemporary life, of the cultural litter of modernity shatters a fantasy of being frozen in an aesthetic past while producing a critical fiction about an assault on aspects of that past. It is a demand, in other words, to attend to the present in its diurnal fullness without hagiographic sentimentalism.

At stake, of course, is also what has been done to that past, and some of the ways it is being used in the present. Under-officer Shigri is taken to the Lahore fort, built long ago by Mughals, to be tortured. The history of the fort, and its present, militates against any sentimental recuperation; as he crawls around in the dark, he is sardonically appreciative of the Mughal ability to build dungeons: "It's the kind of darkness that is ancient, manufactured by the sadistic imagination of the Mughals. Those buggers might have lost their empire, but they knew how to build dungeons" (*CM*, 136). Shigri has no idea of the more modern history of the fort, which was notorious for a long time as a place of torture. Although the novel doesn't tell us of that history except in the very elliptical reference in the thought Shigri has while in another cell in another location, "Who the fuck quotes poetry in prison unless they're a communist or a poet?" The fort is the place where Hasan Nasir the communist is said to have been tortured to death. Nasir's murder was the occasion on which Faiz, himself both imprisoned communist and poet, wrote "Khatm hū'ī bārish-e sang" (The Rain of Stones Has Ended).[25] The reference evokes the history of the struggles of the communists who resisted the various regimes, which were not always religious. The Ayub Khan regime invoked here was secular and was seen as creating a model developed modern nation. The role of writers and poets in progressive struggles in South Asia and more particularly in Pakistan is well known, yet attempts at suppressing them and the knowledge they produced are ongoing.[26] The suppression is continuous with the hiding of the role of both secular and religious militarism in the destruction of political processes and, perhaps even more damaging, of forms of sociality in Pakistan.

Hanif repeatedly constructs a critique of political institutions through the production of a fictional history of the institutions of state the novel satirizes. It is a complex form of fiction, which seeks to produce a historical narrative by imagining a hidden history. The subplot of Under-officer Shigri's confinement and torture in the fort imagines the military devouring itself, visiting upon one of its own a practice of counterinsurgency it has usually appeared to reserve for the civilian population. Indeed, historically the military's attitude toward this population could be described as one of permanent counterinsurgency, a form of governance, which has involved the manipulation and exacerbation of sectarian and ethnic tensions that have fragmented myriad historical forms of social life. The military's nationalism has continued and sustained colonial and imperial policies rather than reversing them. Writers and intellectuals such as Hanif, Nadeem Aslam, Ayesha Siddiqa, Zia Mian, and Pervez Hoodhbhoy are producing a growing body of work chronicling and critiquing its role, including quite specifically of secret service machinations.[27]

To use Fredric Jameson's very useful term here, Hanif has produced a cognitive map of a hidden history usually only understood or even referred to in conspiracy theories, political rumor, or, occasionally, the personal testimony of those who dare survive.[28] Shigri's entry into and subsequent imprisonment in the fort is also an encounter with this history (and present), an encounter that results in a cognitive remapping of his understanding of the nation he has chosen to "serve," of the military in which he has chosen to do so, and of the nation's vision of that military. In keeping with the references to Levis and *Dallas,* and "Careless Whisper," that is, with the attention to the banalities of everyday life, Hanif presents Shigri's approach to the fort in Kayani's custody, juxtaposing historical grandeur with mass production and modern consumption, in the anarchically humorous voice of a barely postadolescent male:

> In the historic city of Lahore, the fort is a very historic place. It was built by the same guy, who built the Taj Mahal, the Mughal emperor Shah Jahan. He was thrown into prison by his own son, a kind of forced premature retirement. I have never been to the fort but I have seen it in a shampoo ad.
>
> Do I look like the kind of person who needs a lesson in history at midnight? (*CM,* 86)

Two paragraphs down the same splendor is juxtaposed with the sinister apparatus of modern militarism: "The only signs of life in this deserted sprawl of useless splendour are two army trucks with their headlights on and engines idling" (*CM,* 86). At stake in the narrator's reflections on his approach to the fort is nothing less than the status of postcolonial nationalism. It is hard to overcome the sense that the question, "Do I really need a lesson in history at midnight?," is an allusion to *Midnight's Children,* for if that novel's governing metaphor imagines an involuted past that leads to the excesses and disappointments of decolonization which culminate in the twin atrocities of the 1971 war, leading to the formation of Bangladesh, and Indira Gandhi's emergency, Hanif's novel is no less about the betrayal of the people nationalism's promise was to liberate, by a governing, in this case, praetorian elite. To turn the fort into a center for the torture of the people within the nation is, of course, to turn the military's warlike capacities inward; it is also to turn the Muslim past that provides some of the narrative that authorizes, or just authors, the nation against its inhabitants. The splendor of the Mughal past, of the Muslim past, and, by extension, the historical narratives of nationalist glory have been transformed into a backdrop for shampoo ads and army jeeps. A far more sinister conscription is evident in the way that the fort has been turned into a warren of torture cells, which in the novel were built by Colonel Shigri, Under-officer

Shigri's father. Although he has known of his father's role in the war in Afghanistan (that he "was liasing between the Americans, who were funding the war, and the ISI, which was responsible for distributing these funds to the Mujahideen" [*CM*, 125]), it is in the fort that Shigri learns of his father's role in strengthening the apparatuses of torture in the nation and of his participation in the torture of its citizens: "To think that the hands that cradled you also put electrical wires to someone's testicles is not a very appetizing thought. A shudder of loathing runs through my body" (*CM*, 160). Mimicking as it does a bodily response that might follow electrocution, the shudder figures what it is to be tormented by the knowledge of what one's parents have done, more metaphorically, by the knowledge of the genealogy of one's own social production. Knowledge of truth in such circumstances as those Shigri encounters is a form of torture.

The absurdism, farce, and humor in the novel are part of Hanif's mechanisms for describing the phenomenological encounter with horrors too difficult to assimilate. The learning of difficult truths, including the contempt in which the civilian population hold the military, continues in the fort even as Shigri's painful bewilderment is expressed through his recurrent wonder at how the torturers managed to achieve "blood-spattered ceilings." These features work with the anger, restrained and tightened in Hanif's work through the very tonalities of farce and comedy, manifest in the fiction of revenge and metaphor of the curse. The cognitive mapping of the secret past of the nation is achieved through a fictional and formal combination that refuses sentimentality and nostalgia in the effort of a historical recovery that cannot, the novel seems to suggest, be effected without judgment. At the same time, the protagonist's familial and professional complicity in the militaristic apparatus and the imperial—American and Saudi—machinery that has guaranteed, underwritten, and grown it suggests that there is no escape from the genealogical burden of such knowledge. Comedy is a means of exposing such complicity. Combined with narrative structures that foreground and seem even to take a certain glee in revenge, it enables an understanding of the writing of history as a form of judgment, using, as Srinivas Aruvamudan has claimed of G. V. Desani and James Joyce, laughter as an ethical and destabilizing tool.[29] Comedy in Hanif's work enables an alienation effect that allows a critical distance from the characters and events. This particular combination of comedy and revenge suggests that literary narrative can have a special aptitude for such an exercise in history without too sentimental and morally paralyzing an empathy.

MURDER, MARTYRDOM, AND CANONICAL FICTIONS

In *Our Lady of Alice Bhatti*, Hanif's vision of the Pakistani body politic is presented through a novelistic frame that plays with canonization narratives, an intense engagement with Saadat Hasan Manto's famous short story "Toba Tek Singh," and the use of the hospital as a central location for much of the novel's action. These narrative strategies and tropes are united by the emphasis Hanif places on the body, which, vulnerable to being tortured, diseased, displaced, confined, and loved, quite literally, to death, is both the fundamental site of the nation (what is a nation without the citizen's body to populate it?) and, in its many orientations, a challenge (can every body be recognized as a citizen?) to that same nation. The body emerges as a locus of social forces and by being so resists any simple vision of the nation and society that claim to represent it. Everywhere in the novel is an attempt to disarticulate the national body politic, necessarily inflected with ideologies of state, from a multiple and varied society—that is, from a social body that demands attention to its many differentiations, indeed from a cluster of bodies that need to be rethought as "social" because of their many differentiations, thus prompting a meditation on the possibility of society in the presence of differentials of power and pervasive injustice. The social body is both body as formed by society and a cluster of bodies that, in their relation to each other, to institutions, discourses, and even to violence, forms a web of relations that, in turn, forms each body.

Hanif's representation of what I am calling the social body is not merely confined to the framing of a challenge to the nation-state's construction of its citizenry as an entity that reflects the hegemonic narrative of the nation and its identity. Hanif's meditation on love in the novel is both entangled with the problem of the nation (what sort of love does it allow between unequal citizens?) and exceeds it as an anti-Platonic philosophical reflection on the way love and the feminine object of love are formed by a society that idealizes women out of their bodies. So that when Teddy Butt encounters the sheer materiality of Alice's body, of her pubic hair, and of her walking around without her *shalwar*, he is unable to respond in any way that would signal care or appreciation. The Platonic mystery of love is hard to sustain in the presence of bodies that sweat, bleed, and grow pubic hair, and Hanif is particularly attuned to the violence of the demand that women's bodies be airbrushed out of existence.

At the same time, Hanif's representation of the body in society becomes a reflection on the inadequacy of a metaphysics of suffering, more broadly of transcendental narratives, to provide redress or explanation in the world. The body's encounter with power produces society as permeated with metaphysically authored forms of injustice, which when they do not reinforce injustice and the operations of power, provide nothing by way of relief and are called into question by the worldliness of the social body.

The almost anarchic irony that courses through *A Case of Exploding of Mangoes* is equally in evidence throughout *Our Lady of Alice Bhatti*. As deadly in its judgments as Hanif's first novel, the vision of an economically and socially varied Pakistan, often invisible in narratives that privilege—even if through a negative focus—elites is more central to the structure of this novel than *A Case of Exploding Mangoes*. Even in that novel the intimation of the desire to engage the social body, so often rendered invisible, is evident in the use of lists, which Hanif uses to stretch the boundaries of the generic frame of the novel, rupturing its refraction through the consciousness of the bourgeois subject and the narrow stylistic focalization such a consciousness invites. As I suggested earlier, the list is also an archival rejoinder to the official production of an Islamized state. Even a truncated version of the page-long list of those held up so that a VIP motorcade can pass in *A Case of Exploding Mangoes* conveys a sense of Hanif's effort to incorporate, indeed his demand to look at, the lives that constitute Pakistan—lives, in this scene quite literally, sidelined and stalled by the powerful he satirizes relentlessly in that novel. The motorcade is the modern spectacle of indifferent and occulted—one might think of the dark windows—power; and the clearing of the roads, the holding back of people going about their lives, is Hanif's metaphor for the cordoning off of the life of the society. The VIP motorcade is increasingly a symbol in Pakistani cultural production of the violence of the political elite and the marginalization of a disparate population, as, for instance, in the music video of "Umeed-e-Sahar" by the pop group, *Laal* (Red), in which a motorcade holds up a range of vehicles, including an ambulance.[30] It is a society that Hanif suggests is rife with ironies brutal (a blind woman escaped from prison who cannot be recognized as anything but a beggar), bleak (a seven-year-old condemned to hawk "dust-covered" chickpeas), and playfully comic (a drunk husband mock-fearfully chewing betel nuts to remove the smell of alcohol):

> A teenager anxious to continue his first ride on a Honda 70, a drunk husband ferociously chewing betel nuts to get rid of the smell before he got home, a horse buckling under the weight of too many passengers on the cart, . . . a seven-year-old selling dust-covered chickpeas, an old water carrier hawking water out of a goat-skin, . . . a husband and wife returning from a fertility clinic on a motorbike, an illegal Bengali immigrant waiting to sell his kidney so that he could send money back home, a blind woman who had escaped prison in the morning and had spent all day trying to convince people that she was not a beggar[,] . . . a black turbaned truck driver singing a love song about his lover at the top of his voice, a busful of trainee Lady Health visitors headed for their night shift at a government hospital. (*CM*, 82–83)

The ironic details work against the banalization of social life into the undifferentiated mass of society produced by national narratives that rely on homogenization and on a paradoxically brutal and violent sentimentality for their occlusive political power.

In *Our Lady of Alice Bhatti*, one of the ways in which Hanif demands attention to this social body is through his rewriting of "Toba Tek Singh," which occurs perhaps most fundamentally through his use of the hospital as a central location for the novel.[31] The mental hospital of "Toba Tek Singh" is replaced by the public hospital of *Our Lady of Alice Bhatti*, which also houses what the hospital staff and some of the patients call the Charya (crazy's) ward. The hospital allows Hanif to frame and foreground the violence that has gripped Karachi since the 1980s as it appears to those who have, quite literally, to pick up the pieces and who are yet glad to have that thankless and brutal job: "'A shift here and a shift there,' Noor whispered excitedly in Alice Bhatti's ear. 'And before they know it, you'll have a full-time job here.' They were surrounded by eight gunnysacks full of body parts that couldn't be identified and placed with any of the deceased" (*AB* 26). As Hanif frequently reminds his readers in his newspaper articles and interviews, the result of the violence has been ethnic battles between the MQM (Muttahida Qaumi Movement, the party that began by claiming to represent people displaced during Partition from India) and Pushtoon groups, internecine battles within the MQM, confrontations (and occasional collusions) between the MQM and the army, sectarian violence, jihadi action, and, as the novel makes very clear with the character of Inspector Malangi, a state that frames and tortures its citizens with impunity and chilling bonhomie.[32] Hanif calls upon a range of genres to frame the violence raging through Karachi since Zia's time to show the many fissures in the postcolonial nation and the attitude of counterinsurgency to its own population by the praetorian elements of the state that has resulted in the cultivation of armed groups with a variety of ideological inflections, suggesting Hanif's ongoing commitment to chronicling the social aftermath of Zia's reign.

The public hospital receives the bodies of the protagonists and many—perhaps the majority—of those caught in the crossfire of many of these battles. The centrality of the hospital within the novel makes visible the torn bodies that are too quickly forgotten in the many failures and incoherencies of postcolonial nationalism. If Manto's story foregrounds the psychic pressure resulting from the inconceivability of Partition, of the effect of the shifting of ground from beneath one's feet, and suggests that the patients in a mental hospital are best able to articulate that inconceivability, Hanif's use of the hospital returns us to a wrenchingly matter-of-fact awareness of the torn bodies littering the streets of the city and the country. The hospital is a starkly material reminder of the rent in the partitioned nation's fabric.

That the Christian nurse Alice's romance with the Punjabi Muslim wrestler begins in the Charya Ward locates the plot directly in an engagement with Manto's story. As if Hanif is addressing a question from "Toba Tek Singh" ("yeh Pakistan kyā hotā hai?"), "What is this Pakistan?," by first reconfiguring it as "What is love in this Pakistan?"[33] Teddy rescues Alice from the ward where she is assailed by its inmates and walks out from it carrying her, singing "*We are one under this flag. We are one. We are one . . .*" (*AB*, 36; Hanif's italics), turning that very rescue into a fantasy of union overseen by the emblem of the nation. The homage to Manto is clearly marked: the episode covers a chapter, early in which another Christian nurse, Hina Alvi, says, "But as far as I'm concerned, the whole country is a nuthouse. Have you read "Toba Tek Singh"? Nobody reads around here anymore. Manto wrote about the nutters in a charya ward and then ended up in one himself" (*AB*, 28–29). On Hina Alvi's terms, Manto's own breakdown in the new nation is merely a prefiguration of the insanity of the entire country; the Charya Ward is then a symbol of the mental state of the entire nation qua nation, that is, as the outcome of a nationalist enterprise that involved the carving out of a space within the Indian subcontinent. The segment of the Christian population in Pakistan that is usually thought of as lower caste is from the Punjab, and as I suggested in the previous chapter, the partition of the Punjab has had a tragically ironic effect on Punjabi Christians, the majority of whose leaders aligned themselves with the Pakistani cause at the boundary commission proceedings regarding Partition.[34] Their decision to align with Pakistan, a nation made for the Muslim minority, in which they might have expected to be treated better than Hindu-majority India, did not in fact protect Christians from the discrimination they so feared. The Charya Ward, by way of the allusions to Manto's story, becomes representative of the nation and of its birth in the founding act of violent partition. It might begin to seem overdetermined, then, that a love, born in such a space, between a Christian "untouchable" woman and a minor thug in the service of the state would end in the terrible atrocity of Teddy Butt throwing acid on Alice's face—that the acid is given to him by Inspector Malangi makes it a case of state-assisted homicide. The inspector's name "Malangi" (a somewhat Sufi, fakirlike, and mystically carefree figure) becomes a dark joke about the "encouragement" of Sufism by the state under Musharraf and of the implication of the variety of the range of orientations participating in the violence of the state. There is no aspect of society that is free of the taint of the violence unleashed by the securitized state.

Hanif's most structurally profound invitation to a meditation on the meaning of martyrdom, and consequently his meditation on the development of the post-Independence nation in which martyrdom and the language of the *"shahīd"* (martyr) has become central to the rhetoric of nationalism, occurs in the epilogue. Written as a letter by Joseph Bhatti addressed to the Vatican, the epilogue invites the reader to imagine the entire novel as a saint's life, a canonization narrative of sorts. Concluding the letter by asking the Vatican to reconsider its decision and canonize Alice after all, Joseph Bhatti writes, "And since Alice Bhatti's story can't be told without telling the story of her time at the Sacred, why not start the story when Alice Bhatti came to the Sacred, looking for a job?" This, the last line from the novel, is a challenge inviting us to begin again and reread the novel as a saint's life. Bhatti's attempt to get his daughter canonized represents a desire to find a redemptive account of her suffering, in which the tools of her destruction, the violence directed at her throughout her life, as a poor Christian woman in an environment where the poor, Christians, especially "lower-caste" ones, and women are humiliated and harassed, are turned into instruments of future and heavenly glory.

The reflection invited by Bhatti's letter is already present in the description of Alice's mother's funeral. What no one comes out and says aloud at that funeral is that the woman was raped and murdered by an employer while cleaning the stairs in the house where she worked. The priest's refrain about God—"He took her"—becomes a sinister pun about the circumstances of her death. A benevolent God's "taking" into heaven of one of his creatures raises the other question: why would he let one of his creatures be treated so? "He took her" says what remains unsayable in the scene—that she was raped—equates divine taking with the sexual kind, and suggests that divine benevolence was culpably absent from the scene of murder and rape. But for a moment Hanif allows for the entertainment of the possibility that divine intention might not have been: "When he wants to take you, He can make the marble staircase slippery" (*AB*, 119). A few lines down this divine agency is questioned again: "but it's not very likely that when you slip on that staircase you'll also accidentally scratch yourself on your left breast . . . [or] . . . that during that fall you'll somehow manage to spill someone's sperm on your thighs" (*AB*, 119). Then, yet again, the refrain: "He took her" (*AB*, 119).

Hanif's representation of the torment of the Muslim gardener who attends the funeral further troubles the temptation to transform horror into redemptive benevolence:

> The person sitting on the gardener's left . . . insisted that he had heard him saying "murder, murder, murder" during the prayer. The person sitting on the right of the gardener accused the person sitting on the left of spreading vicious rumours and violating the sanctity of a post-funeral meal. He even offered to swear on the Holy Bible to prove that the stranger was actually saying "martyr, martyr, martyr." (*AB*, 120)

This scene is a precursor to the more systematic reflection on trial narratives the epilogue invites. Divine agency and the insistence on divine benevolence suggest a providentialism compatible with a redemptive account of human suffering—so, too, does the possibility of martyrdom. But in this scene the potential interchangeability of "murder" and "martyr" suggests that the very idea of martyrdom is a redemptive misunderstanding, indeed, that the willful human mishearing of murder as martyr is a result of the temptation to find redemption in suffering. Martyrdom involves an erasure of the body and transforms suffering into a form of sacred virtue; it absorbs the disappearance of the body into a teleology that further rationalizes and thus abstracts suffering into virtue and reward.

The epilogue turns this slippage between "murder" and "martyr" into an ongoing critical reflection on the premises of the trial narrative in which suffering is a sign of redemption, or at the very least of some divine presence. Alice's own consciousness is crucially critical: "What kind of universe does He run? An exchange mart? Where was Himself when she was on the run from Senior's men, hiding in Charya Ward? Probably on His own lunch break. Or probably busy with this charya world that he has created?" (*AB*, 170). Alice's clarity extends to the plight of Muslims as well, as we hear when she reflects on those Christians who want to pass as Muslims: "They remind her of those people in French Colony who give their children these names in the hope that they'll pass as Muslas. As if there weren't already enough Muslas who were called Saleem or Salamat and who were as poor as the poorest Choohra" (*AB*, 181).

The novel's earlier claim that both "sacred texts and profane novels don't record everything" (*AB*, 20) has already set up an equivalence between the profane and the sacred that deprives the sacred of its priority even as it emphasizes the provisionality of the novel. But the epistemological and ethical authority of the canonization narrative is also called into question by the Vatican's racism, the class structure within the Christian community, by Alice's own lack of a devout religious sensibility, and the quotidian tribulations of poverty that affect the poor regardless of the religions they profess, and of which Alice and the Christian characters are more than aware.

The saint's tortured body may well be one of the more important features of classical saints' lives. Alice's death from an acid attack is the atrocity that could meet one of the requirements of canonization. But within the novel the tortured, acid-attacked, body that might qualify Alice as a saint is a culmination of the quotidian violence she experiences because she is poor, powerless, a woman, and a Christian. The flirtation with, and simultaneous aversion to, the grotesque, that is, with the excess and brutality of violence, is

important in the novel, whose representations of the varieties of violence matches and is interwoven with its many ways of thinking
the body for which Baroque excess and bodiliness provide powerful
genealogies and tropes. Hanif does not focus on her mutilated body,
and the reader learns of the actual attack only through an indirect
report, as if Hanif has deliberately denied the reader the prurient
spectacle of her destruction. The refusal to abject and simultaneously turn Alice's murder into a spectacle is of a piece with Hanif's
emphasis on Alice's shrewdness, sense of irony, and determination
to fight back. Perhaps the most significant instance of this occurs in
the way Hanif represents Alice's handling of the man who forces a
blow job on her in the Emergency Room. The deftness with which
she cuts the penis and escapes is central to Hanif's representation of
Alice's fierceness and dignity, whom he describes as "an all-weather,
all-terrain fighter" (*AB*, 175):

> Her twenty-seven-year-old body is a compact little war zone where
> competing warriors have trampled and left their marks. She has
> fought back often enough, with less calibrated viciousness maybe,
> definitely never with a firearm, but she has never accepted a wound
> without trying to give one back. And like all battle-hardened war-
> riors she has managed to preserve her gift for the fight but forgotten
> why she became a fighter in the first place. (*AB*, 174–75)

Despite the great tragedy of her murder and the many quotidian
injustices and trials she suffers, her ironic and assessing sense of the
absurdities that abound in the world she has to navigate militates
against any patheticization of her life. Indeed in *Our Lady of Alice
Bhatti*, Hanif's absurdism is a means of allowing Alice the dignity
of a certain emotional distance, which denies the reader the moral
comfort or the prurience of empathy. At the same time, it contributes to Hanif's refusal of what Paul Amar has recently called "the
politics of respectability."[35]

The fundamental challenge to the redemptive reading of tribulation and, through it, to the saint's life comes from the priority
given to the fact of Alice's poverty and her femaleness. In an episode describing Alice being measured for a shirt, Hanif weaves an
extraordinary meditation—presented as Mr. Dulhousie's, the tailor's, awareness of Alice's social circumstances and Alice's own
cognitive mapping of the way she inhabits her body in the world—
on the convergence of poverty and femaleness, and the consequent

formation of the body as a locus of unjust social forces. All this becomes clear because despite being malnourished to the point of emaciation she has opulent breasts and a figure that young girls dieting to the point of starvation would do anything to attain. Mr. Dulhousie knows that in the kind of house in which Alice grew up "starvation is passed off as fasting," the last week of the month dinner is bread soaked in water, "dhal and rice is a Sunday special and every fourth Sunday of the month is compulsory Lent" (*AB*, 93). As a result, Alice's ribs can be counted through her shirt, her collarbones stick out, and her ankles are "like a display from an anatomy lab" (*AB*, 93). Yet she has breasts that seem to have thrived, "despite the lack of a balanced diet" (*AB*, 93). Her very body—described by a nun, in a telling joke, as being "like a cross with tits" is a product of her poverty, and a source—crosslike—of tribulation.

This is also an engagement with Mulk Raj Anand's *The Untouchable* (1935). It is the father who wants to abstract her suffering into a redemptive metaphysical superstructure. Joseph Bhatti is a more satirical and destabilizing figure than the nervily masculine Bakha, whose masculinity is held up against the injustice of caste. Bakha is enraged by the way his sister is treated and his reflection on what has been done to her turns into an uncomfortably possessive eroticization of her body:

> Her slim, pale-brown figure, soft and warm and glowing . . . was so silent and subtly modest and full of a strange tenderness and light. He could not think of her being brutalized by anyone, even by a husband married to her according to rites of religion. . . . He loathed the ghost of her would-be husband that he conjured up. He could see the stranger holding her full breasts and she responding with a modest acquiescence.[36]

Hanif's presentation of Alice's reflection on her own breasts rewrites Bakha's eroticized horror at his sister's "violation," which leads him to think of her death as a blessing as it might free him from shame, and Anand's attempt to use Sohini to motivate the story by using the insult to her to retrieve Bakha's masculinity and then disappear her from the narrative.[37] Hanif privileges Alice's own consciousness of her body and the sociophysical navigations in which she has to engage in order to protect herself. Joseph Bhatti's attempt to get his daughter canonized is at some distance from Alice's own

consciousness, which is presented as profoundly antiredemptive—
repudiating both the abstraction into identitarian communal honor
represented by Bakha's anger and into an idealized religious redress
indicated by Joseph Bhatti's letter.

The irony that underpins Hanif's absurdism is aligned with
Alice's perception of her situation. In learning to navigate the attention her body attracts, Alice has acquired a darkly sardonic sense
of the world around her. It is a body Alice has learned to fear for
the uninvited attention it gets, and in attempting to not be noticed,
she covers herself as much as she can, pulls her hem down compulsively in order to draw attention away from her chest. At the end of
the chapter she even asks the tailor if he can make her chest seem
more flat. She has learned that being untouchable does not preclude
being touched, that those who would not touch a glass she has used
or take a banana from a bunch from which she has taken a fruit
have no qualms about groping her. As a nurse men have asked for
her attention and attempted to masturbate while she checks pulses
or looks down throats. On being rejected, one has threatened to cut
her up and throw her into a well. This leads into her reflection in
the chapter on the kinds of violence women suffer, a violence she is
determined—in a bleak moment of dramatic irony—to avoid:

> Alice Bhatti is not interested in understanding the rules but she also
> doesn't want to be the kind of girl who attracts the wrong kind of
> attention and ends up in the wrong place. . . . She doesn't want to be
> someone who walks around demanding to be hacked to bits.
>
> During her house jobs she worked in Accidents and Emergen-
> cies for six months and there was not a single day—not a single day
> when she didn't see a woman shot or hacked, strangled or burnt,
> hanged or buried alive. Suspicious husband brother, protecting his
> honour, father protecting his honour, feuding farmers settling their
> water disputes, moneylenders collecting their interest: most of life's
> arguments, it seemed, got settled by doing various things to a wom-
> an's body. (*AB*, 96)

The litany of violence, occasionally interrupted by recognition of
certain extraordinary women who have resisted and ended up in
prison, continues for two pages. Alice's remarkably lucid sense
of the violence that surrounds her and her—failed—refusal to be
destroyed by it are effects of a consciousness that her body and the
fact of bodiliness have given her. Clarity about the social world may
well be a result of her body's location in it and her own refusal to
delude herself, as a part of her desire for survival, about how that

world operates. Yet the novel carefully navigates the irrelevance of that agency in encounters with the arbitrary causal externality of violence. The plot refutes the fantasy that one can avert such violence by taking upon oneself the burden of erasing one's own body. Alice is not able to forestall Teddy's violence, which is propelled by a randomized violence that works paradoxically in concert with intricate social webs of injustice—hence, for instance, the significance of Inspector Malangi handing Teddy the acid, which reveals the randomness of the attack on women to be part of a more general structure of violence and inequity. Malangi's name implicates even a traditional Sufi structure in the violence of the state and in the more socially diffuse conditions of violence against women.

Hanif's representation of Alice's body, of the bodies in the hospital, of Noor's mother's cancer, of Noor's own habits of self-protection against molestation acquired in the Borstal come together as a profound reconsideration of the idea of the body politic. If one of the drives in modernity has been the increasing alignment of popular sovereignty with the modern nation-state and with national sovereignty, even a democratic majoritarianism does not allow for those who are at odds with the identities privileged by the nation's self-understanding to be recognized, nor is there any political or discursive space for the sovereignty of such identities to be expressed. Hanif's many bodies allow him to reveal the thought of the alignment between popular and national sovereignty to be a fiction—one that enables complex varieties of violence visited upon the bodies of those who are only nominally citizens. The notion of the body politic is deployed only to be pulled apart by the invitation to read the novel as a canonization narrative. Hanif's deployment of the possibility of reading the novel as a saint's life pushes powerfully against the anarchic vision of Manto's story. The mutual pressure enables a critical reflection on the varieties of sovereignty in collision in a nation-state that quite literally claims its sovereignty from God and Islam.

As I mentioned earlier, in *A Case of Exploding Mangoes*, Hanif made a joke through a general's thoughts about the nation that thinks it was made by God. The problem of the sovereignty of God is very much a part of the constitutional history of Pakistan, and the Islamic scholar Fazlur Rahman's reflections on the 1956 constitution's claims to be representing God's will are acerbic.[38] Qutb's reflections on the importance of subjecting oneself to God's sovereignty in order to create the possibilities for social transformation are not removed from the South Asian context even before the 1980s, for Qutb references Mawdudi's reflections in *Milestones,* suggesting a cross-fertilization of political theology that cannot be accounted for through an Arab-centric lens.[39] Qutb's form of subjection to the sovereignty of God reveals a reversal where such subjection leads to God's sovereignty being expressed in the religious state and the right sort of religious citizen. God's sovereignty turns out to be itself an authorizing relation for state power.

The questions surrounding the status of religious minorities foreground the problem of divine sovereignty in the modern nation-state; for it is not clear how the nation with its disparate population and its claim to representing a variety of bodies can then manifest divine Muslim sovereignty in or through (say) the Christian body. The nondemocratic theory of the monarch's divine right circumvents the multiplicity of the bodies that form the state and is better able to align the monarch's body with the body politic. Hanif's representation of the body politic, or, more accurately, of the polity's many bodies, reveals the incommensurability of divine sovereignty, national sovereignty, and the minority citizen's sovereignty; it becomes indeed an interrogation of what the possibilities of sovereignty, of subjectivity, and of citizenship are for the minority. Yet Hanif is careful not to idealize or romanticize the minority into an undifferentiated heroic mass, or group, with "recognition" as its political quest. For Alice's death is as much a product of her poverty and her femaleness as it is of her Christianity—it is, in fact, a result of the way those different social materialities converge on her body. Her own skepticism about religion, and thus the novel's positioning of her at some distance from a redemptive vision of her Christianity as a heroic minoritarianism, is in line with Hanif's representation of the Shia communist doctor who refuses to marry her after she becomes pregnant because of pressure from his mother: "For generations there has never been a single marriage outside our Shia clan, let alone a marriage into another religion. . . . He seemed to have discovered that the only chains he couldn't lose were those forged centuries ago in some Arab tribal feud" (*AB,* 180).

In the same vein, Hanif's skepticism about the absence of human rights lawyers who can descend on the courts to defend people from the blasphemy laws but are unable to respond to the ubiquitous, arbitrary injustice of the criminalization of the poor and thus to Alice's imprisonment for attacking a doctor who should not have left a student nurse alone with a patient, and who evades prosecution by offering her up in his stead, is part of his demand to look at the intricate structures of social inequity. Thus his reference to Pakistan's laws regarding religion is itself a brilliant instance of stylistic indirection: as Noor reflects on the unintelligibility of love he thinks, "Surely if there are laws against non-believers pretending to be Muslims, there should be a law against people with perfect eyes pretending to be blind" (*AB*, 78). Earlier on a lawyer has wondered whether it is even legal for Joseph Bhatti to recite the Qur'an (*AB* 45). The reference to the Ahmaddiya declared non-Muslim, who are according to the law not allowed to "pose" as Muslims, is worked into a more complex web of social, national, and even metaphysical—Platonic and religious—injustice. Even love is not possible in such circumstances.

Hanif's refusal to romanticize the question of minority while foregrounding the question of justice has everything to do with the way he represents the body without idealization. His vision of the body, his complex meditation on the question of sainthood, produces a dramatically critical Baroque. The social body is unwieldy and fully enmeshed in the mess and struggle of the world. One might offer as a precursor Caravaggio's Baroque as one finds it in *St. Peter's Crucifixion*, with its emphasis on the dirt and struggle in the infliction, and the endurance, of pain. The terrible worldliness of the dirt on the feet of the crucifier and Saint Peter's twisting body's refusal to fit the cross is fundamentally anti-Platonic, refusing any idealization of suffering. Hanif's representation of the body and Alice's tribulations, too, is anti-Platonic and reveals the power of the Baroque to produce a critique of the idealization of suffering through a confrontation with the social and worldly embeddedness of the body. This critical Baroque works against bodily abstraction. The point is not merely analogical or even straightforwardly genealogical, for Hanif's practice is no less illuminating of Caravaggio's work than Caravaggio's painting is of Hanif's vision. Hanif's refusal of a redemptive reading of trial is a refusal of resignation, indeed of Job as a model for human endurance.

Hanif's version of Cold War Baroque invites the reflection that saints are merely the ghosts of those the world murders. The geopolitics of the Cold War—the ideologies cultivated, the theologies nurtured, and the political structures dispersed throughout society in the context of that geopolitics—forms the very worldly historical machinery of that murder.

Theologies of Love

PLANETARY ICONOGRAPHIES

The year was 1985. Zia-ul Haq was in power. On a stage facing an audience of an estimated fifty thousand in a packed arena in Lahore, the very fine Pakistani singer Iqbal Bano sang an extraordinary rendition of Faiz Ahmad Faiz's "Wa-yabqā wajhu rabbik" (The Face of Thy Lord Will Abide Forever) which is also, probably because of the performance, more familiarly known as "Ham dekhen ge" (We Will See). Bano's performance that evening has become the stuff of political legend—so much so that people dispute the year and the place of the performance but not the effect of the event. For the poem about the upending of tyranny with its grand assertion of human selfhood, articulated through a quotation from the tenth-century mystic Al-Hallaj, "anā l-haqq" (I am the truth), written under a title that is a verse from the Qur'an, was received as a powerful repudiation of the sitting tyrant. The performance was to become such a political flashpoint that even in a recording from 1988, called "A Tribute to Faiz," one can hear the crowd erupt as Bano sings the lines "sab tāj uchāle jā'enge/ sab takht girā'e jā'enge" (all crowns will be tossed in the air/ all thrones will be toppled").[1]

The song turns the first line "Ham dekhenge" into a refrain, which sounds like a promise of a future, a longing for the possibility of one, and, subtly, a threat of justice rendered against the tyrant. The framing of "anā l-haqq" as the emancipatory cry—"uṭhegā anā l-haqq kā na'rah" (and the cry/slogan will rise: I am the truth)—places one of the greatest lines from Sufism at the center of the claim to social and political justice, and at the heart of the struggle for freedom from tyranny. In Faiz's full version, the line combines with the title of the poem, which states the abiding quality of divine being, to suggest the immanence of the divine in the human, linking that divinity to human freedom and the necessity of justice. Al-Hallaj's reputation as the great Sufi at odds even with other Sufis, the antinomian, in other words, of antinomians, provides a complicated corrective to the historical inversions of the present, indeed to its temporal parochialism. In the mid-1980s, Bano's performance was exultantly received as a rejection of the dictator whose tyrannical power was underwritten and made possible in its fullest extent by the United States. In the post–September 11, 2001, environment, U.S. think tanks, in a bid to encourage "moderate" Islam as an antidote to the forms of Islam that were until quite recently part of the U.S. imperium, have become advocates of Sufism, as did the military dictator Parvez Musharraf in 2008.[2] Sufi devotional forms are under a new and increasing threat because they can now be cast as collaborator devotionals. The effect is one that places a contemporary historical turn at odds with a longer internal history with complex philosophical, theological, and aesthetic stakes and valences.[3] The schematism of policy documents, which try to map and even axiomatize divisions within Islam with a view to increasing the power of the security state and its ideological apparatus, erases and imprisons these longer histories, reducing them merely to pawns in the great, doomed game and impoverished intellectual grid of global securitization. As one can see by reading the Rand Corporation report of 2003, *Civil-Democratic Islam: Partners, Resources, and Strategies*, they manifest a remarkable amnesia about the role of the United States in the cultivation of the most iconoclastic varieties of Islam.[4] Such schematism is, of course, itself an effect of the genre of the document, which encourages, even requires, the instrumentalization of knowledge in a manner that further necessitates historical reductionism, usually through the selective embrace of different moments in the history of the object of knowledge (in this case "Islam," all of it, all the time, for all time) of the documents.

The geopolitical historical entanglements at play in these ideological oscillations are everywhere evident in the work of Nadeem Aslam.[5] In a strikingly different tonal register than Mohammed Hanif, Aslam almost compulsively engages the divisions within Cold War Islam and is everywhere attentive to their swirled and ruptured (post)colonial histories. The crisis engendered by imperial-theological geopolitics is present in every one of his novels, *Season of the Rainbirds* (1993),

Maps for Lost Lovers (2004), and *The Wasted Vigil* (2008). Repeatedly in his fiction, Aslam stages an intricately aesthetic meditation on these histories, by putting them in play against, and with, one another through a series of formal confrontations and fusions: between poetry and the novel and, through ecphrasis, between painting and statuary and the novel. Almost as if he had set out to address the question: What forms would the novel have to take to embody earlier aesthetic histories? Or, to reformulate the question in Bakhtinian terms: how might a novel accomplish the work of "assimilating historical reality into the poetic image"?[6] The novels' aesthetic density comes, moreover, from their absorption, rather in the manner of epic, of other forms—elegy, pastoral, love lyric—and novelistic subgenres such as the spy thriller (*The Wasted Vigil*) and the murder mystery (*Maps for Lost Lovers*), the use of stylistic figures such as ecphrasis, and, in *The Wasted Vigil*, structurally central allusions to Greek tragedy and epic.

Aslam's work is a profoundly layered response to imperial theology. So aesthetically laden, even overwrought is the prose in the two novels on which I focus in this chapter that they invite the charge of *préciosité* leveled against the historical Baroque. In Aslam's novels baroque is a form of exacerbation and of hyper-aestheticism. It is moreover a principle of lateness, of repetition, and of rereading. Cold War histories, devotional aesthetics, literary forms are infolded, inverted, revealed to be caught in a cycle of seemingly inescapable yet endlessly torqued iteration. In a different stylistic vein than Hanif, Aslam shows us that *Baroque* in Cold War Baroque is the name of a polemicization of customary and regional devotional practices and aesthetics under the pressure of the theological divisions of modernity and the particularities of their politicization. At the same time, in its polemically responsive guise, Aslam's work makes available the insight that the historical Baroque was always a responsive formation, attempting to defend, elaborate, and reinscribe habits of theologically driven representation in the face of the Protestant iconoclastic attack.

Aslam's version of Cold War Baroque yields the baroque novel, which is, of course, a heuristic rubric that, in turn, gives us another heuristic rubric, that of a planetary baroque that extends beyond Europe and the Americas, in which Muslim aesthetic forms are enfolded in a manner that is not merely accidental or simply dependent on casual morphologies. This planetary baroque need not refer explicitly to Christianity and yet is entangled with its modern history, insofar as the conceptual world of the Reformation and Counter-Reformation exercised a pressure on the Empires that would come to shape colonial modernity and its postcolonial aftermath, revealing that we have yet to reckon fully with the history of Westphalia. In his engagement with imperial theology, Aslam makes the postcolonial aftermath visible as convergent with the theological struggles of Europe in the era of colonial modernity and the Cold War exacerbation and exploitation of the colonial reorganization and stabilization of religion, culture, and identities as facilitating a historical continuation, however spatially displaced, of those struggles. My point is not that the postcolonial world is repeating a colonial history as yet another iteration of its belatedness but, instead, that this trajectory of history remains to be interrupted or (if that is even possible) resolved—in postcolony *and* metropole.

Aslam's novels combine a use of theological thinking with intense poeticism and a profound preoccupation with the body. What facilitates this fusion is a sustained use of Sufi aesthetics, which, though it is not adequately addressed by the word *theological*, nonetheless invites it. For Aslam reveals aesthetic practice that engages and interprets scripture and religious law—simply by manifesting a response to either in habits of devotion and the aesthetic forms that comprise them—to be "theological." Aslam addresses the chronotopic challenge of novelistic narrative, of finding a formal correlative for the particular kind of time/space compressions required by the stories he wishes to tell, by putting Islamic (theological, aesthetic, and social), formal literary, and Cold War histories in play with each other, through the staging of a series of aesthetic confrontations between different understandings of Islam but also between iconoclastic impulses and the most iconic and image-riddled aesthetic forms. The novels are replete with references to broken Buddha heads, smashed dolls, Russian icons, illuminated books, walls frescoed in the manner of Bihzad, love lyric that collapses the distinction between human and divine, nude portraits, *qawwali* with its forms of devotion that insist on the planetary immanence of the divine.

Even as Aslam's practice appears to court anachronism by incorporating Sufi poetics within the Anglophone novel, it is in keeping with the work of Urdu writers such as Faiz Ahmed Faiz and Qurratulain Hyder both of whom use Sufi ideas in their work. Rushdie does so too in *Grimus*. To name just two Arabic novelists, Naguib Mahfouz and Tayyib Salih, too, engage with Sufism. The post–World War II renewal of interest in the Sufi tradition among poets in the Middle

East (some of whom as AnneMarie Schimmel puts it with some coyness "politically are leftists") extends beyond the Middle East. It is an element in the thought and literary practice of the South Asian Left but also in a wider ideological array of literary practice that draws upon Sufi strands in traditions of Urdu and Persian poetry.[7] The transnational element of this interest and its Third Worldist component awaits more scholarship.

The simultaneous address to these histories and the intensity of their chronotopic compression make for the baroqueness of the Cold War Baroque novel. The planetary aspect of this baroque relies on this intensity of compression and on the resurfacing of these struggles in confrontations within modern Islam, in the long afterlife of the colonial restructuring of religion. Perhaps paradoxically, in Aslam's case, the deterritorialized space of the global Anglophone novel provides the conditions of possibility for this intensity.

In this context, the conceptual use of a notion of a baroque novel is perhaps most visible when we attend to the terms *baroque* and *novel* as mutually constitutive of the text. For the novel exerts its own conceptual pressure on the material and forms that can be identified with the baroque, and Aslam appears concerned to exploit that tension. In *Maps for Lost Lovers*, the elements in the novel, which lead Lukacs to designate it the form of "a world deserted by God," allow Aslam to produce a complex formal reflection on Sufi thought itself. In their elegiac address to these histories, to those who have made them and perhaps to those who may yet survive their consequences, the novels produce a reflection on death—as the murder of an aesthetic tradition, of learning, of beauty, of human possibility, of the earth itself—and the finitude of human life, which draws on Sufi aesthetics but which, in turn, reveals the limit, concerning the problem of death, in Sufi thought. In *Maps for Lost Lovers*, the Sufi emphasis on the annihilation of the self as part of its emancipation emerges as itself elegiac, and thus even as Sufi thought provides a critical apparatus in its antinomian and anticonventional aspects, it leads to a hypostatized repetition of loss as the outcome of desire, of suffering as the outcome of love, making redress in the world seem unattainable.[8]

In *The Wasted Vigil*, Sufism, and the Islam of which it is a face, is revealed as a moment in the history of the species and of human civilization. The novel's staging of moments in the history of the region as disparate archaeological strata shows Hyder's *Āg kā daryā* (River of Fire) to be an important influence and precursor.[9] As in *Āg kā daryā*, the shards of different civilizational moments represent and demand a reflection on the very idea of history. In *The Wasted Vigil*, this reflection on history comes in a two-tiered structure. As in *Maps for Lost Lovers*, there is an engagement with and absorption of Sufi thought and aesthetics, most clearly visible in the use of the Bihzad, but also in the effort to imagine the earth as wounded and woundable in the manner of the human body, to imagine Allah as the "artist" and creator (aligning Him with the poet and thus all living creation with aesthetic creation) and in the identification of heroic, even defiant, loss with the female characters, Qatrina, Zameen, and Dunia.[10]

Even as this Sufism is itself shown to be ruined and fragmented through the various iconoclasms of war, working from below, the Buddha head represents a stratum of human history that contextualizes even the Sufi moment (now fallen victim to a series of catastrophes, engineered by Empire through the figure of Islam) as merely another stratum in the archaeological layers that comprise the history of the earth. It is as if Aslam has decided to use the fallen Buddha head to concretize a passage from the concluding chapter of *River of Fire*. I mention the English version because the passage does not occur in quite that form in the final chapter of *Āg kā daryā* even if the idea it presents is implicit in the very structure of the novel: "They watched the river ripple past. Words were temporary and transitory. Languages fade away or are forced into oblivion by new tongues. Men also come and go, even the river and the jungle are not eternal."[11] Aslam's use of the Buddha head is in keeping with the structures of Hyder's novel, in which the Buddhist presence in the region called South Asia and the violence of the expansion of the Mauryan Empire, at the very inception of the novel, are used to establish a history, which even as it is only available to the present in the form of ruins nonetheless enables the interrogation of the idea of a national culture, especially one conceived in religious terms. And yet, as in Hyder's novel, Aslam's point is not merely national, even in an antinationalist guise, but instead enables a reflection on the very nature, and parochialism, of human time and its irrelevance to the time of the earth. Such a conception of history (one way of making sense of of human time) offers no comforting vision of redemption.

Aslam's novel achieves its vision of history through an encounter with tragedy and epic, both of which appear commemorative and elegiac in a manner that is inadequate to war. The commemorative elements are hard to sustain in the realist novel, which cannot produce the fanfare of the Iliadic funeral games or the heroic death—such as Antigone's—of tragedy. The realist novel presents the commitment to glory as justification by honor, and thus as attempting an ethical redemption of waste, of unnecessary loss, as glory. *The Wasted Vigil*'s interest in the fate of conscripts refuses the economy of honor and glory. It does so, too, by staging the suggestion that mourning the dead is a luxury unavailable to most in war. The impossibility of mourning the dead properly, the suggestion that there is, to borrow a phrase from Spivak, no response to war, permeates the novel and is strikingly evident in Aslam's play on the stories of Priam and Antigone.[12]

At the same time, Aslam probes the limit of the novel's alignment with history in times of war. As the Buddha head, which is so central, if silent, a presence throughout the novel lies as a reminder of the end of great civilizations in the novel, it yet configures the realist novel as a form that can address the history of the world only as a list of ruins. The broad-canvased realist novel is a social form; war tears societies apart. In its failure, the novel thus enables a historical challenge to the eschatology that might appear licensed by the Baroque that presents ecstatic suffering (Bernini's sculpture of Saint Teresa) as the transformative conduit to heaven, or which presents a muscular power that produces grandiose monuments (Bernini's additions to St. Peter's in Rome) as the earthly manifestations of a power that yet awaits its fullest universal and cosmic expression. At the same time, the novel issues a challenge to the teleology of a secular modernity that might be tempted to celebrate progress by presenting a redemptive economy of historical achievement outweighing or perhaps just *earning* a history of human pain.

DEATH AND THE POET

Even as Aslam's oeuvre performs complex acts of retrieval and exposure of disparate histories, the hermeneutic work, the daily cognitive mapping, demanded of the faithful by a conservative piety, both in its domestic and more overtly political guises, is also everywhere present in his novels. In *Maps for Lost Lovers,* the novel in which, as I suggested in chapter 3, the hermeneutic demands and their worldly instantiations are most intensely imagined and in which their representation is most fully achieved—particularly in the detail with which the inner lives of the characters is presented—Aslam stages a confrontation between poetry and the law, represented by those who adhere to more conservative forms of social and religious norms.

The novel's perspective is aligned with poetry and poets, especially with Faiz Ahmed Faiz, whose presence is felt throughout the book, which is dedicated to him along with the painter Abdur Rahman Chughtai, who will become even more significant in *The Wasted Vigil*. It is also aligned with Faiz through the name, Dasht-e-Tanhaii, it adopts for the town in which it is set, given within the novel by the Pakistani immigrants to the corner of Britain in which they find themselves. It is taken from one of his lyrics and translated for the reader as "Desert of Loneliness" or "Wilderness of Solitude." Like Faiz, Aslam, too, has inhabited Sufi tradition for his own literary practice.[13]

Aslam ushers in a Sufi devotional aesthetic in opposition to a more law-bound conception of Islam through the perspective of the Communist poet, Shamas, enraged and despairing about what the Soviet Union has done to communism but yet committed to radical principles, who has refused to move out of the working-class immigrant neighborhood in which he lives and where he continues to work to integrate the local community into the larger political system. Shamas is an atheist who loves the Sufis, and in this love and his political commitments he is clearly allied with Faiz.

Encountering *Maps for Lost Lovers* for the first time can be disconcerting. Intensely image-ridden, almost overwrought, obsessed with tropes of love poetry, elegy, and pastoral, it is as if Aslam has written the novel as poem. The central preoccupation of the novel is the relationship between religious law and human attempts to live by and around it in the presence of the darkest brutalities of history: colonialism, Partition, life under Zia-ul-Haq, the migration of the poorest sections of society from Pakistan to England, the savage and unrelenting racism they face there, the violence the rigidly faithful or the opportunistically religious visit upon honest transgressors.

Aslam's use of a self-consciously poetic voice allows him to write a profoundly aesthetic meditation on the encounter between faith, religious law, and the world. The novel is unusual in its unapologetic romanticism and relatively straightforward realism, and in its eschewal of the kind of sophisticated reflexivity one finds in Salman Rushdie and Orhan Pamuk (both of whom have written poets as characters in their novels about the foundational narratives of Islam—Baal in *The Satanic Verses*—and Islamism—Ka in *Snow*) and yet, of course, very much a product of the contemporary moment—as the refusal of that sort of reflexive sophistication is precisely part of Aslam's determination to produce a didactic and simultaneously imaginative record of the historical depredations of the never-ending *durée* of the Cold War moment. Shamas's very presence in Britain is a result of the persecution of the Left in a national context of Cold War clientelism. The almost palpable need to produce a historical record of the geopolitics that have led to the current moment are perhaps most unsurprisingly evident in *The Wasted Vigil*, which can seem like an exercise in didactic history.

Poetry enters the novel in multiple ways. First it is filtered into the prose. The pastoralist combines the consciousness of the poet with that of the painter with a meticulous attention to visual detail. Jugnu, a lepidopterist, uses his passport to carry wildflowers picked before a flight; peacocks and butterflies wander through houses. Although the story is set in an ordinary English town, the novel seeks out and describes every trace of nature. Aslam uses free indirect discourse and slips with unfussed omniscience into the heads of his characters, but the consciousness with which the narrative is most clearly allied is that of the a highly visual poet, indeed, of the poet imagined as the painter of life.

Some of Aslam's uses of nature imagery are prompted by impulses that are fairly familiar to readers of immigrant fiction. For *Maps for Lost Lovers* is, among other things, a record of migrant desolation. Aslam's version of the immigrant novel is particularly elaborate, and arguably its most powerful character, Kaukab, Shamas's very conservative wife, is a richly imagined and meticulously represented version of the helpless and angry mother stymied by what the culture into which she has been brought has done to her children. Kaukab's wrenching loneliness is rendered with great care and without irony, as if Aslam has set out to retrieve the voice of the immigrant mother from the silence imposed by metropolitan culture and by rebellious children, who are nonetheless her victims as well. It is a complex choreography.

The immigrant's loss of a land is also the loss of a landscape and, as the novel has told us earlier, of a season, the monsoon. The pastoralist's attention to nature registers the loss of the home world, especially for the rural migrants at the heart of this story. It is their world that Aslam describes with sustained attention to nature in the novel set in the Punjab, *The Season of the Rainbirds*, in which the attention to nature invites the rubric "Punjabi pastoral," with pastoral conceived not as a form of elite idealization but instead as the villager's perception of beauty in quotidian rural life.[14] Recurring to an attempt frequent in immigrant fiction to make the new home less alien, less climatically traumatic, in *Maps for Lost Lovers* Aslam's attention to nature signals an attempt to create a language that recognizes and makes the migrant's own the beauty of the new land.[15] He presents the poet before he dies, two pages from the end of the novel:

> He stretches out an arm to receive the small light snowflake on his hand. A habit as old as his arrival in this country, he has always greeted the season's first snow in this manner, the flakes losing their whiteness on the palm of his hand to become clear wafers of ice before melting to water—crystals of snow transformed into a monsoon raindrop. (*ML*, 377)

The poet's careful attention to the new land is part of the endeavor of making Britain less European, more Asian, and this attempt defies both the whites, who want to repatriate Pakistanis, and those immigrants who want to police the community from within, keep it faithful to practices they claim will keep it more Pakistani, purely Muslim. Here it is a poetic image that makes England less white and more livable, lyric imagery that transforms the English language by making it more South Asian, by describing it in terms taken from a non-European landscape and from Urdu and Punjabi poetry. Aslam's use of the image is of a piece with his larger practice of using Sufi poetics throughout the novel. One of the effects is to de-Anglicize the novel, hook it firmly to a South Asian literary genealogy, and, through that process, claim English literature for Britain's most despised immigrants. Nowhere does the novel shy away from a reckoning with that contempt. There are numerous episodes of racist violence in the novel, but a synoptic history of racist attitudes is presented early:

> It was a time in England when the white attitude to the dark-skinned foreigners was just beginning to go from *I don't want to see them or work next to them* to *I don't mind working next to them if I'm not forced to, as long as I don't have to speak to them*, an attitude that would change again within the next ten years to *I don't mind speaking when I have to in the workplace, as long as I don't have to talk to them outside the working hours*, and then in another ten years to *I don't mind them socializing in the same place as me if they must, as long as I don't have to live next to them*. By then it was the 1970s and because the immigrant families had to live *somewhere* and were moving in next door to the whites, there were calls for a ban on

immigration and the repatriation of the immigrants who were already
here. (*ML,* 11; Aslam's italics)

The nature imagery connects the desolation engendered by such violent exclusion to a larger sense of desolation in the novel, a sense that
is bound up with a more planetary conception of loss and suffering.
Aslam's reflections may begin with the immigrants of the novel, but
his vision of desolation encompasses the earth. In the very first line
of *Maps for Lost Lovers*, the poet watches the snow falling: "Shamas
stands in the open door and watches the earth, the magnet that it
is, pulling snowflakes out of the sky towards itself" (*ML,* 3). A few
pages later, he reflects on Chanda's and Jugnu's deaths: "He is not a
believer, so he knows that the universe is without saviors: the earth is
a great shroud whose dead will not be resurrected" (*ML ,*20).

The poetic imagery that pervades *Maps for Lost Lovers* is connected to the Sufism that is so central to the novel. The earth is magnet, shroud, and a wilderness of solitude and loneliness. The magnet
is also an image of love in Sufi poetry.[16] By calling the earth a magnet
in the opening paragraph of the novel, Aslam locates love as much
as death in the earth itself. Aslam's use of the metaphor is central to
his endeavor. The notion of the earth's inescapability is not merely an
incidental effect of a character's reflections; it is fundamental to the
novel's vision itself. As the source of nourishment as well as the recipi-
ent of the body after death, the world is all. Aslam's honoring of the
earth's attraction even as a final grave (the resonances between grav-
ity and grave are hard to miss) is part of his insistence that the body
is all that humans have. This is, of course, meant to counteract the
denial of the body with which the novel is so concerned. If everything
ends with the grave, there is no reward to be gained by deferring the
body's pleasure, and the idea of resurrection is a cheat, not a promise.
At the same time, an image that figures the earth as a magnet emphasizes the need to see the earth as an object and a subject of love, and as
love itself. This conception demands a mode of being that recognizes
the denial of the world as fundamentally unethical, as a rejection of
the earth as love. Moreover, it sets forth a vision of the worldliness of
love, turning the image of the magnet against its Sufi source by quali-
fying the emphasis on the annihilation of the self.

Despite her law-bound denial of the body, even Kaukab's thoughts
are infused with an awareness of the relationship between the earth
and the human body. In order to come to terms with her loneliness and
sense of exile in England, she thinks of the story of Adam's creation:

> Kaukab knows her dissatisfaction with England is a slight to Allah
> because He is the Creator and ruler of the entire earth . . . She often
> reminds herself that Allah had given Adam his name after the Arabic
> word *adim*, which means "the surface of the earth;" he—and there-
> fore the whole of mankind, his descendants—was created from earth
> taken from different parts of the world. His head was made from the
> soil of the East, his breast from the soil of Mecca, his feet from the
> West. (*ML*, 31)

It is in order to pay due recognition to the earth's pull, its link to the
human body and its capacity to provide for the body, that Aslam
demands the reader's attention to its beauty. The house in *The Wasted
Vigil* serves a similar function. But it is a beauty and plenitude perennially endangered by humans. In the scene where Shamas's father
loses his memory (and Hindu identity) in an aerial bombing, he smells
oranges being "cut open" by the bomb "before he forgot everything,
the last sensation being the flesh-eating heat of his hair on fire against
his scalp" (*ML*, 54). In *The Wasted Vigil*, Aslam returns to this vision
of a cut and wounded earth. Casa remembers that "Once he had seen
a mine detonating in a grove of pomegranate trees with such force
that the skin of every fruit on every branch had cracked, the red seed
spilling out" (*WV*, 59). Human creations and actions make the world
itself bleed, as the world's body, which may indeed be of the same
matter—as even Kaukab's reflections suggest—as the human body, is
torn and burned alongside humans.

Poetry also enters the novel through a depiction of Sufi song. The
rupture between song and lyric has never really taken place in South
Asia, where poetry, old and new, is still sung by *qawwali* singers, classical vocalists, and even modern rock bands. Pakistan's most popular
band, Junoon, calls its music Sufi-rock and has as a hit a poem by the
Punjabi poet Bulleh Shah, which the group names "Bulleya"—one of
the poets, who presides over Aslam's novel. In the current moment,
consciously Sufi forms and themes are ever more visible as practices of
counterculture. Their presence in a mediatized popular culture presents the danger of increasing commodification, as is evident even in
the name of a show that has become a premier site of Sufi song, *Coke
Studio*, which is sponsored by Coca-Cola in Pakistan. Yet the problem
of aesthetic commodification can be overstated if the varieties of economic patronage in global capitalism are not attended to more carefully.[17] To focus on the forms of patronage available to artists without
a sufficient recognition of the forms of economic largesse bestowed

upon those who object to most aesthetic practices is to produce a somewhat skewed account of global capitalism. As different varieties of Islamic neo-orthodoxy, themselves beneficiaries of the economic patronage of oil money and the Cold War U.S. war chest, represent themselves as the only available anti-imperialism on the block, each neo-orthodox revivalism claims to represent all authentic Muslim tradition. Such countercultural assertion both fights the neo-orthodox revival that the Islamists prefer and rejects Western imperialism. Aslam's project is a sophisticated part of this larger historical trend.

The mystical and heretical heritage of lyric is explicitly restored to the novel through Sufi poetics, and dramatizes a distinction between religious law and devotional practice and custom. Aslam describes a performance by Nusrat Fateh Ali Khan at some length. Early in the performance, Khan sings a "love lyric," and "when he comes to the word 'you'—denoting the earthly beloved—he points to the sky with his index finger to indicate and include Allah in the love being felt and celebrated—a lover looking for the beloved represents the human soul looking for salvation" (*ML*, 192–93). One of the ways in which Aslam aligns himself with the Sufi tradition is to give everyone in Shamas's and Kaukab's family a name that translates into a form or source of light: Shamas, Kaukab, Ujala, Mah-jabin, Charag, the lovers Chanda and Jugnu, and Kiran, whose name is explicitly translated for the reader as a "ray of light." One of the names for God is light (Nur), and the novel's implication is that each one of these humans has a spark of a light we might think of as divine. Each one in the end threatened with extinction by the Law and murderous social norms. In this respect, Shamas's name is perhaps most significant for it links the novel very directly to Rumi's mysticism. By giving his protagonist a name that is variation on Shams (sun), which Rumi himself took after his beloved Shamas's death, Aslam plays with the significations of mystical union in the world. The human is lover, beloved, and the most powerful light (almost) visible to humans—seeker, sought, and source of light and thus divine. The "lost lovers" of the title are thus all those whose love is denied, and the novel is a litany of such characters, but they are also those, like Chanda's brothers and murderers, who cannot find the divine spark in every human or in human love; and the very possibility of the salvation the soul seeks (as light attempts to return to itself) is thus destroyed. Aslam aligns his work with this tradition by availing himself of the theology of Sufi thought.[18]

The thought that illuminates Aslam's own practice, that metaphysical concepts need to be available to the imagination, is one that he attributes to Shamas as his father lies dying: "Shamas was no believer, but imagination insists that all aspects of life be at its disposal, the language of thought richer for its appropriation of concepts such as the afterlife (*ML*, 83). God's light as an igniting spark in humans may only be a metaphor to Aslam, but it is a metaphor that is part of the deep structure of imagery which allows an elegy for human (and planetary) waste to permeate the novel.

Later in the performance, Khan sings a song by Bulleh Shah about fabled and doomed lovers. This turns into a meditation on the role of the "poet-saints of Islam":

> [T]hese verses of the saints—because they advocated a direct communion with Allah, bypassing the mosques—were denounced by the orthodox clerics, so much so that when the poet Bulleh Shah died the clerics refused to give him a decent burial, leaving the body outside in the blazing sun until hundreds of his outraged admirers pushed the holy men aside and buried him themselves. Even today the Sufis are referred to as the "opposition party of Islam." (*ML*, 196)

Aslam's decision to align the general style and consciousness of the novel with that of the poet allows him to recover and update a classic confrontation in Muslim history: the confrontation between the mullah and the antinomian religious poet. It is usually a fight in which the Sufi poet excoriates the rigidity of the mullah's adherence to religious law and tries also to provide dissenting interpretations of Muslim foundational texts and traditions to shore up practices considered insufficiently orthodox. It is an antipathy shared by *Maps for Lost Lovers* and *The Wasted Vigil*.

The mullahs are the ones to want to introduce a life-denying dualism into everything, and the Sufis respond with a vitalism that insists that everything in the world is alive. Like many Sufi poets, the seventeenth-century Bulleh Shah's writing brims with stories of famous lovers, a vitalist sense of the earth, anticlericalism, a disdain for religious law, and a contempt for religious sectarianism and bigotry. He is particularly famous for his defense of Hindus and Sikhs against orthodox violence in Mughal India. The pastoralism of the novel and the image-riddled sensitivity of its prose mark Aslam's own honoring of Sufi vitalism. There is a glimpse of this in the passage about the snowflake that I quoted earlier: a world of transformations is a living world in which everything is perpetually in process. Ultimately that vitalism underpins the entire structure of imagery and the commit-ment to chronicling that other life of the planet, perpetually at risk from the dark side of human creation—bombs and land mines.

The use of Sufi thought is perhaps most explicitly visible in the way Aslam takes a story about doomed lovers, the kind of story one finds repeatedly in South Asian vernacular Sufi verse, and weaves a novel out of and around it. The novel is both a principled stand against a form of violence that is sometimes presented as peculiar to Muslims and a literary convention inherited from a branch of Mus-lim literature. The retelling of this Sufi story is also a solution to the ideological quandary that we have seen as a pervasive problem in "West"-"Islam" relations, and also more largely of the postcolonial double bind. Aslam replaces the chivalric idiom of the humanitarian romance of imperial rescue—where white men save brown women from brown men, to recur to Spivak's usually decontextualized line—with an actual tradition of romance, which is used here to provide a critique of misogyny. In other words, Aslam does not match the imperial line with what Spivak calls the "nativist patriarchal" coun-ter and "parody of the nostalgia for lost origins: 'The woman actually wanted to die.'" Instead he turns to a tradition that foregrounds the pain, loss and violence of misogyny.[19]

In the West, honor killings (though not unique to Muslims) are usually greeted with a kind of hushed despair over Muslim dysfunc-tion, sometimes as a sign that Muslim migrants are irretrievably for-eign, pressed by their religion into a barbarism that will never allow them to live comfortably in Europe or the United States. Internal cri-tique is always in danger of being taken to endorse an imperialism or racism that has seized the language of opposition for its own, and the dilemma is in part rhetorical, requiring its own temporospatial compression: How can one register a simultaneous distance from all elements in the bind? How can one circumvent the usual lag in the unfolding of a narrative, an utterance, a judgment, and forestall it being received in a way that reduces the complexities of double cri-tique? How does one find a language to condemn such cruelty that does not seem borrowed from Europe, and thus cannot be manipu-lated by neo-Orthodox Islamists or the chivalric knights of the West? The impasse is grave and disabling.[20]

By turning to the Sufi poetic tradition, by incorporating it into his own literary practice, Aslam makes it clear that he is claiming a critical position that comes from within Islam's history and that this is first and foremost an internal fight. Muslims have their own historical resources for dealing with such social challenges; Empire does not need to gallop to the rescue. At the same time, the Sufi valuation of the annihilation of the self and its dissolution into the divine, and concomitant valuation of loss in the world as a conduit to that annihilation, can turn into a perpetual postponement of the possibility of betterment in the world and an aesthetic addiction to loss, unable to deliver or imagine any actual improvement in the condition of women, unable to overcome the impasse generated around them by empire, but also to overcome a choice between body and soul, unable to overcome circumstance. The women repeatedly fail for the "poet-saints of Islam [expressed] their loathing of power and injustice always through female protagonists in their verse romances" (*ML*, 195); "always it was the very vulnerability of women that was used by the poet-saints to portray the intolerance and oppression of their times; in their verses the women rebel and try bravely to face all opposition and they—more than the men—attempt to make a new world. And, in every poem and every story, they fail. But by striving they become part of the universal story of human hope" (*ML*, 196). To some extent Aslam overturns the relationship presented in these lines, because in the novel, in contrast to the poetry he describes, women are also the *bearers* of the law. If Chanda, like Sassi and Heer, is killed, Kaukab and Suraya are themselves committed to the law and terribly lonely in their entrapment by it. The realist novel as conceived by Aslam does not permit simply a lyrical lament for the dead beloved and for the inevitable Sisyphean failure of the attempt at love but instead also presents a meditation on the *social relations* that produce that death and such failure. The lingering of hope cannot be as simple as these lines suggest.

Poetry persists in this realist novel as the force of utopian possibility. Sufi poetry is the voice both of autonomy and of an earlier literary tradition. On the terms of the novel, the woman lover/beloved is aligned with poetry, and that the women always fail suggests that poetry itself fails. This implication is important to *Maps for Lost Lovers*. At the end of the penultimate chapter Shamas dies as a result of being beaten up by thugs for hire because he has threatened to expose a local mullah's pedophilia. As he lies dying he calls the entire world by the name borrowed from Faiz, Dasht-e-Tanhaii, the "desert of loneliness." This is why Aslam has withheld the English name of the town he describes: he wants to make the tragedy of the migrants represent all human suffering—returning us to the theological problem of evil.

It seems that Aslam ends *Maps for Lost Lovers* with Shamas's death (imaginable as a metaphor for the death of poetry) and asserts the primacy of the novel so firmly because, in a story of so much suffering, a literary mode that celebrates beauty and love, that enshrines an autonomy that is usually denied to most, risks being socially obtuse and turning misery into theodicy, into an apology for suffering as part of God's plan. To the extent that the Sufi lyric, or indeed any lyric, can slot the story of destroyed lovers into a universal history of hope, to the extent that it risks redeeming that suffering within some larger scheme of human history it can turn utopian hope into theodicy. The generic encounter tugs, thus, in contrary directions. The poet represents a necessary Sufism. But his is also, on the novel's terms, a Sufism that is already defeated, as he has not been able to understand his own injunction to his painter-son: you must represent society. He has not switched over to writing novels. He has also not understood his own central insight about the importance of understanding systems. Earlier on in *Maps for Lost Lovers*, he describes Islam as an administered order:

> A system conditions people into thinking it is never to blame, is never to be questioned. We have to beg, say the beggars, the accursed belly demands food: it is the fault of the belly, not the unjust world that doesn't allow enough sustenance to reach the bellies of everyone through dignified means. (*ML*, 242)

The novel issues an invitation to think in Lukacsian terms and prompts its readers, explicitly, to conceive of the world as "system." Yet where a Lukacsian might think of European capitalism as the only system worth narrating, Aslam makes law-bound conceptions of Islam and global capitalism visible as analogous systems.

To the extent that Sufism provides the immanent structure of lyric in the novel it, too, is defeated. And so, in the end, Aslam's relationship with Sufism and the kind of poetic consciousness that underpins it is ambivalent. However much *Maps for Lost Lovers* might be allied with its poet's way of perceiving the world, and however lyrical that perception might be, the fact is that he no longer writes poetry. Poetry turns you back to the world, forces you to reckon with its beauty and the possibilities for love it offers, and yet the world remains governed by law. Sufism might push toward its cancellation, but in a world governed by the law, poetry like people is crushed into lifelessness.

On the one hand, the realist novel's worldliness makes it antitheodicy; on the other, its absorption of lyric allows its worldliness to
become a demand for human emancipation, for a genuine human
autonomy. It is almost as if Aslam has arranged a confrontation
between Lukacs and Adorno in his novel. The novel reveals the utopian quality of lyric, which erupts into the narrative with the demand
for a better world, as if dramatizing Adorno's thoughts about the
lyric: "the [lyric's] distance from mere existence becomes the measure of all that is false and bad in the latter. In its protest the poem
expresses the dream of a world in which things would be different."[21]
Yet the fusing of the realist novel and the utopian lyric risks a backfire
to the extent that it asks one to experience the actually existing world
as already utopian—that is, it risks representing demand as actual-
ity. At the same time, the big novel's realism pulls it in another direction: realism must be antitheodicy if it is not to be mere romance, if
it is not to turn pain and risk into adventure and reward, shut down
by marriage plots that end just where new sorts of difficulty begin. In
the face of this danger, the realist novel keeps faith with the utopian
demand by terminating the premature utopianism of poetry.

Yet Aslam ends the novel away from the hypostatized commitment
to loss represented by Shamas's death. Two pages later, the narrative
shifts to conclude with a focus on a new minor character: the brother
of the immigrant killed in the condemned building decides to come
out of hiding. He stops at a news agent's and then walks into the
street.

> He hasn't been able to sleep much thinking some calamity is immi-
> nent, dreaming again and again of rocks and stones being hurled at
> butterflies. But at dawn today he had told himself to go out into the
> world again. If a calamity is coming then where else would he rather
> be than with his fellow humans? What else is there but them?
>
> He moves away from the newsagent's window and resumes his
> journey along the snow-covered street. (*ML*, 379)

Aslam is austere, then: by aligning himself with the novel in this way,
he refuses a redemptive account of suffering. He refuses what is, in
effect, an aesthetic vindication of human pain.

WARLORDS AND IMAGE MAKERS

The recalcitrance of human pain is at the very heart of *The Wasted Vigil*
and infuses the repetition, which is the novel's structuring principle.

Early in the novel the reader is told, "Up there Priam begged Achilles for the mutilated body of his son Hector. And Antigone wished to give her brother the correct burial, finding unbearable the thought of him being, unwept, unsepulchred" (*WV*, 15). "Up there" is the library of books nailed to the ceiling, to protect them from being detected by the Taliban. Marcus's search for his daughter, Zameen, and his ongoing search for his grandson, Bihzad, recalls Priam's devastating fate: to watch the young die and have only the hope of granting their bodies a dignity they lost in the particularly cruel forms of their dying. The Russian, Lara, seeks to find and bury her brother, the conscript who raped Zameen every night while she was held prisoner and impregnated her with Bihzad, who, of course, in turn, will become Casa, the militant, and as we learn a different kind of conscript.

The novel is framed by these two figures. Lara opens the novel, "Her mind is a haunted house. The woman named Lara looks up at an imagined noise. Folding away the letter she has been rereading" (*WV*, 5); and Marcus concludes it, "He enters the building and asks if someone would be kind enough to take him to the city centre in a while. He is meeting someone there who could be Zameen's son" (*WV*, 319). Marcus continues a search the reader knows to be futile, one of the wasted vigils suggested by the novel's title, which is itself taken from Abdur Rahman Chughtai's wistful neo-Orientalist painting. That painting feminizes loss and waiting in a way that resonates with Aslam's use of Sufi poetics.

Priam and Antigone are not just arbitrary borrowings from a Western tradition but instead part of the novel's insistence on the history of the Greek presence in the regions bounded by the borders of present-day Afghanistan and Pakistan. It is a history, along with that of the Gandharan civilization that produced the statue of Buddha that is a broken presence throughout the novel, lost through the destruction wreaked by war and, more systematically, by the Taliban's ideologically motivated assault on all forms of unacceptable learning, art, and worship. Aslam may well be particularly sensitive to this because of the analogous precursor banishment of the history of the region now bounded by the map of Pakistan, in which the national narrative required by the creation of the Muslim state sits in tension with the history of the many ancient civilizations, and even relatively recent histories, that have preceded the achieved state—a state, moreover, whose secret service has had a significant hand in Afghanistan's present condition, precisely because of the paradoxical embrace and denial of the borders that are an aftermath of the colonial presence. The state's machinations are represented through the hugely unpleasant character of Fedallah, the rogue ISI agent. The nationalism of the ISI signals a commitment to these borders, whereas the meddling in Afghanistan—based on a resentment of the Durand line dividing Pakistan and Afghanistan and the desire to be able to win a war with India—is, of course, predicated on a denial of those very borders.

The image of the books nailed to the ceiling is a fundamental part of the novel's commitment to repetition. In *The English Patient*, the novel of war that presides most immediately over *The Wasted Vigil*, making it seem, as Pankaj Mishra has said, "an extended tribute" to Ondaatje's novel, Hana nails books to the floor and to each other so she can step on them to reach something.[22] Although the most powerful citation of *The English Patient* in *The Wasted Vigil* is the very conceit of a house partially ruined by war, in which the wounded and the grieving congregate, providing a central organizing principle for the convergence of places and histories, Aslam's sustained elaboration of the image of the nailed books is crucial to his staging of the eruption of inconvenient histories into a violently resistant antiaesthetic, anti-intellectual, and iconoclastic present.

The fundamental antagonism in the novel—the confrontation or, perhaps more daring, "converse" between the warlord and the poet, between the iconoclast and the maker of images—is set up with the epigraphs. The second epigraph from Daulat Shah of Herat's *Tazkirat-ush-Shaura* (Lives of the Poets) pulls the first one from Zbigniew Brzezinski's canonical interview regarding U.S. "strategy" in Afghanistan into its ambit in a gently surprising way:

> And the poet in his solitude
> turned towards the warlord a corner of his mind
> and gradually came to look upon him
> and held a converse with him.

Even as the epigraph sets a precedent for Aslam's own "converse" with the warlord, it performs a confrontation with Brzezinski whose inscription on the page sets him up as the warlord at whom Daulat Shah looks across time and space and with whom he is in dialogue. The address from across centuries to this most modern of warlords invites the question of what kind of converse one might have with someone who can say with magnificent dismissive arrogance:

> What is more important to the history of the world—the Taliban or
> the collapse of the Soviet Empire? A few agitated Muslims or the lib-
> eration of Central Europe and the end of the Cold War. (*WV*, 1)

The epigraph reveals a didacticism—recurrent in the novel—that seems born of despair. Unable to rely on the reader's knowledge of the speaker of the utterance, the novelist needs to introduce the speaker without the subtle omission of information that may make its literariness more deft. The author's inability to count on such knowledge is a symptom of the historical amnesia, which allows the former allies of the United States to become historyless "terrorists" in the metropolitan imagination. It marks, moreover, the burden upon the author in the global Anglophone marketplace—the task of overcoming the metropolitan audience's investment in forgetting its own collusion in this history, an amnesia that Khalid Hosseini's *The Kite Runner*, with its veneration of Ronald Reagan, facilitates marvelously. The pressure to bring that knowledge to the reader is evident throughout the novel, as is the pressure to bring the knowledge of the Muslim past to Muslim readers, metropolitan and otherwise, who may be in danger of forgetting that history in the face of iconoclastic assaults from fellow Muslims. Aslam introduces Brzezinski's words, thus, in a rather explanatory introduction, with a framing that borders on the clumsy. The epigraph is followed by the words below.

> ZBIGNIEW BRZEZINSKI,
> President Jimmy Carter's National Security Advisor, asked if he
> regretted "having supported Islamic fundamentalism, having given
> arms and advice to future terrorists." from *Le Nouvel Observateur*,
> 15–21 January 1998. (*WV*, 1)

If the author cannot rely on his reader to have or desire this knowledge, because of the complex redactions and revisions of history after September 11, 2001, and because of the assault on the signs of history that the war has produced, he must also find a way to address this particular warlord in a manner that circumvents the cavalier dismissal of Muslim "agitation" and find the craft that can manage a converse with the monumental arrogance of that phrase "to the history of the world." The structure of repetition in the novel is in part a response to the challenge it poses. Aslam's repetitions might be read as a meditation on precisely that phrase and as a nonteleological response to it that stages a different conception of history, as a series of repetitions of loss, destruction, and human suffering.

The war between erasure and broken remembrance is the human history of the planet, endlessly set to repeat itself—waiting for the dead, the end of those who can survive it. The history of the world, as a history of loss, does not enable a redemptive reading of the fall of the Soviet Empire. In other words, the history of the world is not consonant with any teleological understanding of "the end of history" as the desirable outcome of that fall. In fact one allegory of the end of history is to be found in the death of Casa, the disappearance of Dunia, and the mutilation of James. The three young people caught in a triangle, products of the Cold War machinations Brzezinski defends, the planet's future on the novel's terms, die, disappear, or are terribly wounded. Dunia's name is at the heart of this allegory. One end of history is the disappearance of the world (Dunia).

Aslam's formal response, already foregrounded by the epigraph from Daulat Shah, is to set the poet, but more broadly the image maker and the made image, against the warlord and the violence of war. On the very first page of the novel the reader is presented with the wistful image of Lara dragging a large round mirror so that she can read the titles on the ceiling without straining her neck:

> The mirror is large—if it was water she could dive and disappear
> into it without touching the sides. On the wide ceiling are hundreds
> of books, each held in place by an iron nail hammered through it. A
> spike driven through the pages of history, a spike through the pages
> of love. A spike through the sacred. The words are reversed but that is
> easier than looking up for entire minutes would be. . . . She slides the
> mirror along the floor as though visiting another section of a library.
> (*WV*, 5)

It is significant that these spikes have been driven through the books by a character who has lost her reason upon being confronted with the terrible atrocity of having to cut off her husband's hand as a punishment for his having ostensibly stolen paintings that she painted. Her attempt to protect the books from the Taliban by nailing them to the ceiling repeats the violence she has had to inflict on her husband in order to protect him from being murdered. But the spikes also represent an assault on love, the sacred, and history that is the tally of the quarter century of war in Afghanistan. The passage intimates a connection that will get developed over the course of the novel between God's creation (humans) and human creation (a variety of images and words). In the description of Qatrina's paintings the connection gets extended to God Himself, who is enfolded into the circle of creation and being. Each painting of one of his ninety-nine names provides a quandary for the Taliban, who want to destroy them all but are unable to separate word from image:

> The Taliban did not know how to deal with the pictures—each bore one of Allah's names in Arabic calligraphy, the Compassionate One, the Immortal One—but the words were surrounded by images not only of flowers and vines but of other living things. Animals, insects and humans. They wanted to tear out these details but couldn't because the various strokes and curves of the name took up the entire rectangle, reaching into every corner, every angle. (*WV*, 179)

If the paintings represent the impossibility of separating divinity from creation, the description of Qatrina's process in creating the paintings shows an almost devotional reverence. The description is slow and prayerlike in its repetition, and so, too, is the process described at leisurely length:

> She would paint a picture, allow the paper to dry, and then dip it into a tray of water to dissolve away some or all of the colour. After it had dried she would paint for a second time and again take away part or the whole of the pigment in the water bath. The process could be repeated as many as ten or twelve times. On occasion she added an amount of colour to the trayful of water before lowering the picture into it, so that the entire composition was suffused by a very pale redness or by a reticent haze of saffron. A sustained shimmer of blue. Layer by layer she would build a complex painting over many weeks (*WV*, 178)

The process bears some resemblance to the layering of Aslam's own style and at the same time figures artistic creation as itself carrying a devotional quality. The way the paintings are made suggests creation and divine manifestation cannot be separated in them, and as the Taliban's dilemma reveals, neither can word, image, script(ure), being, and body.

The other side of the potential for creation is the steady recurrence of atrocity, which itself represents the insidiously inventive (and ecumenical) creativity of human cruelty. Throughout the novel both forms of creation are tortured, assaulted, and broken; word, image, body, and earth are all torn, sometimes in the name of the sacred. Paradoxically the very litany of horror calls the sacred into question by prompting again and again the question: what kind of an eschatological notion of the human future could possibly justify this atrocity?

The confrontation between the warlord and the image maker is present in its most concentrated form in the play on Bihzad's name, a central though not solitary part of which is the plot around the eponymous character in the novel. The novel refers to the artists who have painted in the manner of Bihzad and whose work has been defaced or destroyed. The walls decorated in this way in Marcus's house are either covered with mud for their protection or lying in fragments on the floor. The frescoes are themselves evidence of human creativity, in their dedication to the senses, a metaphor for the shattering of the body and violation of senses by the war, and also for the attack on the Sufi past by the Taliban.

Bihzad's illuminated manuscripts and the style he continues to inspire across the centuries haunt the book with the memory of the Muslim past and offer a reproach—in name and form—to the destructively iconoclastic vision of the Muslim future. The character Bihzad's transformation into Casabianca then stages an allegorical contest between two different conceptions of the Muslim future and performs their attachment to different moments in the past. Bihzad/ Casa is turned into a cipher that represents the possibilities of history and of being at its center. If Bihzad represents Muslim creation and the possibilities of an open future that yet bears some connection to customary forms and thus the paradoxical possibility of nurture from the past, his transformation into Casa, as a truncated Casabianca (from the Felicia Hemans poem), represents a child loyal to elders who, if one follows the poem, are going down with a sinking ship, or, in the case of the new Casa, are busy betraying their young by turning them into cannon fodder. That the character who names Casa is able to remember the reference to the poem and later turn against the education that made that act of naming possible is, on the novel's terms, one of the ironies of the history the imperial encounter has produced. For Casa's very name suggests a transformation—marked by mirroring and mimicry of the imperial fleet and its conscripts—rather than a historically pure resistance by the militant Islamist imagination to imperial encroachment.

The future signified by a Bihzad as opposed to one represented by a Casabianca comes attached to different conceptions of the past. One conception imagines the past as capable of producing an (antinomian) creativity from within the structures of Islam, and another replaces that generative yet paradoxically customary creativity with a modern necropolitics, shaped by imperial defeat, and now mimicking the morbidity of the Western empires that are the cause of that defeat.

SPIES IN LOVE AND THE ENDS OF FREEDOM

The Wasted Vigil's structure of repetition contributes to its density of allusion. Aslam has said that this is a book about other books. The suggestion in the opening lines is that like Lara rereading her letter, we, too, are caught in a cycle of rereading. Lara's name itself seems an allusion to the heroine of *Dr. Zhivago*.[23] Another book about a doctor-poet, or healer–image maker, caught (like Qatrina) in the brutalizing maelstrom of war, a novel, like *The Wasted Vigil*, of lovers and children lost to historical events. Like Lara, who is herself a product of the history her name ushers in, dragging the mirror that could have been pulled down from the wall in Jorge Luis Borges's "The Library of Babel," the reader, too, must read these stories in their many iterations, discerning continuities, as through the inversions and reversals of a mirror.[24]

A significant reworking in the novel is of the figure of the CIA agent who falls in love with a native woman and turns her into an object of rescue—interchangeable with the land she inhabits. David's love affair with Zameen is a rewriting, or perhaps a rereading, of Alden Pyle's love for Phuong in Graham Greene's *The Quiet American*.[25] David's character is the figure through whom the American hand in the current crisis can be revealed. The spy is an increasingly ubiquitous figure in contemporary attempts to map the relations between Western power and radical Islamism. On the news, the spy who turns against current policy in order to reveal its bankruptcy and lack of regional understanding is a figure of remarkable authority, guarantor of a presumed access to covert knowledge, the being who holds the key to penetrating the occult mysteries of the covert control of the world. David's own story leads to us to see the connections between the United States, the Taliban, and the history of the United States itself in the form of the Vietnam War in which he lost his brother, which has fortified his conviction that the world has to be saved from communism; as if the Vietnam War has entirely counterintuitively convinced him of the need to continue the enterprise undertaken there.

David enables the figuration of the tormented spy's need for absolution as a reminder of the cost of American "innocence," perhaps the greatest symbol of American exceptionalism. If Pyle is the "quiet" American, David is more explicitly a "nice" one, operating always under the best of intentions and, decades later, wracked by guilt and eager to make restitution. Within the novel, his niceness is an extension of the innocence that places the burden of absolution upon its many victims. The likability of the American spy, his good intentions, his or her (usually his) capacity to mask his violence even to himself, by a focus on the goodness of his intentions and the logic of rescue, stages the drama of American exceptionalism by displacing the ethical burden upon those on whose bodies that drama is enacted. Such "innocence" and "likability" are themselves predicated on a complex national amnesia, which frees David from the ethical burden of the early history of the United States, a relation in which Native American lifeworlds are fractured and then absorbed in the very process of decimation, of which the canoe he builds is a symbol. David's almost pastoral appreciation for the disappearing practices—as when he remembers with languid wistfulness the Ojibwa woman harvesting wild rice—of Native American life is poised on a suppression of the ethical rage that should attend such witness:

> This time he had brought with him from the United States the basic materials to construct a birch-bark canoe, having contemplated spending a week or so building it here. . . . Visiting the lakes of the northern United States as a child, in the company of his brother Jonathan and an uncle, he had seen a sea of wild rice engulf an Ojibwa woman seated in a canoe. A slide into harvest: she gently bent the slender stalks that were sticking out of the water's surface and knocked the grain into her vessel, to sell for twenty-five cents a pound. The last armed conflict between the United States and military forces and the Native Americans had taken place right there on Leech Lake in 1898. (*WV*, 73)

It is left to Casa's thought to reveal the terrible and habitual violence of that national history as he wonders to himself with an unknowingly ironic awe:

> The missiles that landed in Casa's jihad training camp were named after an American Indian weapon—Tomahawk. Casa knows other words too like Comanche and Apache and Chinook. First the Americans exterminate the Indians, then name their weapons and warplanes after them.
>
> What did those Indians do to make the white Americans respect them?" (*WV*, 159)

Casa's fascination with the American capacity to forget the violence inflicted in the service of the American imperium reveals another mirroring. His appreciation of the violence, innocent in its own right, represents the dispersal of American innocence, the global spread of mimic exceptionalisms. On the novel's terms, the combination of destruction and a disdain for history are America's Cold War gift to the planet. The final and most decisive metaphor for that relationship is the shared grave in which Casa and David end up, entwined to the death. The embrace in which they find themselves as they die represents what the novel imagines as an outcome of America's spread of its particular varieties of violence. The intimacy will continue unto death and beyond.

David's relationship with Zameen follows the more familiar logic of imperial rescue in which women become alibis for political adventures driven by other motives. David's determination to keep her from her first love, the communist Afghan, simply repeats Pyle's conviction that he is the right person to save Phuong. The question of the woman's choice is more clearly foregrounded by Aslam; for Zameen is a much more active figure, attempting to rescue children and lead them to refugee camps across the border, working secretly with refugee women in Peshawar. Yet David is unable to see her as a being capable of making choices. Although she is no longer in love with the young communist and is, in fact, in love with David, he cannot trust her to make her own choice. She *must*, in other words, be saved from her imagined self.

However, Zameen's name (land) overdetermines the allegory in a slightly distasteful manner. To figure the woman as land is to invite the image of woman as that which can be tilled, the source of fertility, indeed the earth itself. Zameen's captivity under the Soviets and her repeated rape by Benedikt does little to upset that gendered cliché. The allegory might be seen as a way of addressing the problem of a response to the Taliban's misogyny, which is completely bound with the perceived impossibility of separating the support of groups such as the Feminist Majority in the buildup to the war in Afghanistan from any other critique of Taliban misogyny. By contrast Northern Alliance misogyny can be useful. That is, a systematic critique can very quickly be assumed to be part of the imperial project and the result, as I suggested in chapter 2, is a series of politically aphasic concessions to the impasse.

In a response to the attempted assassination of Malala Yusufzai, the Pakistani child activist, by the Tehreek-t-Taliban of Pakistan, the novelist Kamila Shamsie described the stalemate with striking clarity. What she wrote is worth quoting at length:

> Yes, of course, the Taliban exists because of political decisions dating back to the 1980s; and of course the mess that is the "war on terror" has only added to the TTP's ranks.
>
> There's no need for the Taliban to invent propaganda against the American and Pakistan state (although they do)—both governments supply an excess of recruitment material for those who hate them. So if you view the Taliban simply through the prism of the war on terror and Pakistan and the United States, it's possible to think the process can be reversed; policies can be changed; everyone can stop being murderous and duplicitous.
>
> But then there's Malala Yousafzai, standing in for all the women attacked, oppressed, condemned by the Taliban. What role have women played in creating the Taliban? Which of their failures is tied to the Taliban's strength? What grave responsibility, what terrible guilt do they carry around which explains the reprisals against them?[26]

Shamsie's questions demand an attention to the evasions that attend a focus on the way women have been used to motivate the war, which repeatedly subsume the questions of what is being done to women, and why it is being countenanced, to the question of how the Western media, policy circles, and the wider apparatus of bellicose justification together manipulate that issue.

The apparent conceptual stress produced by such manipulation can lead to a number of prophylactic moves, which include a quick distancing of oneself by showing one's contempt for Madonna (or some other celebrity's) "discovery" of an issue, a knowing distancing from Ayaan Hirsi Ali or Irshad Manji if one is a Muslim woman or one from a Muslim-majority society, a throwing of any woman who produces a feminist critique of Islamism under the bus by equating her with Hirsi Ali. For all Muslim women are only one degree of separation from Hirsi Ali, and they must at all times lead with the proof that they are not her, or supporters of war against Muslim-majority societies, just as Palestinians and their "sympathizers" always have to lead with their condemnation of suicide bombings in order to earn the right to speak. The more difficult task of questioning the bigotry by which every Muslim woman is always already the same as every other Muslim woman, and the even more complex task of producing an understanding of the stabilization of a discourse of collaboration that homogenizes Muslims through their division only into collaborators and noncollaborators is yet to be undertaken. Indeed the very question of collaboration in the age of transnationalism, globalization, and massive immigration and its relationship with internationalism requires more sustained analysis.

Aslam's response to this impasse in *The Wasted Vigil* is in line with his turning to Sufism as a discourse internal to Islam that provides resources for critique in *Maps for Lost Lovers*. Like the women whose "vulnerability" was used by Sufi poets to represent the "intolerance and oppression of their times" the female characters in *The Wasted Vigil,* too, attempt to remake their world and repeatedly fail. Unlike *Maps for Lost Lovers, The Wasted Vigil* provides little by way of a "universal history of hope." The title of the novel obviates the possibility of hope and presents any waiting that might attend it as simply a devastating waste. Within the world designated by the title, the burden on the women appears as a terrible expectation and marks, at the same time, the gendered limits of interpolating women into such a role.

To imagine Zameen as land is very much in keeping with a variety of nationalist identifications of women with land or nation, destined to bear the burden of identity and honor and to become ciphers for the violation of the land by the invaders. If Zameen, like Phuong in *The Quiet American*, bears those allegorical markings, the burden on Dunia is greater. Her disappearance signifies the end of the world, but her romance with Casa presents the other side of that figuration. Her task—as representation of world—is to love Casa out of his rejection of humanity and the world, to persuade him yet of the humanity of women. This produces a new impasse: in order to understand—and thus recuperate—Casa's humanity the novel has to displace the burden of love onto the woman, whose healing power lies in her being a redemptive figure of self-erasing love who, if one follows the logic of the various allegories, could, but for the vicious brutality of the American apparatuses of torture, return Muslim history to its own self-determining and humane self. Ultimately, however, all is lost: world, history, in Aslam's words, "the planet's future."

When confronted with the brutally inventive varieties of annihilation offered by war, the annihilation of the self may seem trivial, and yet this war reveals that annihilation as a reiteration of the destruction, not as its emancipatory other. Dunia, the world—what is usually taken to be the very antinomy of a Neoplatonic conception of love—is turned into a Neoplatonic and thus abstract and world-erasing entity, through the reduction of the woman simply to a symbol of redemptive love. In her capacity as cipher, the burden of her gender upon the woman is that of providing the illusion of emancipation through love while being interpellated into an ever-expanding economy of annihilation.

INTRODUCTION

1. On the increasing equation of Islam with Sunni juridical forms, see Aamir Mufti, "Why I'm Not a Postsecularist," *boundary 2* 40.1 (Spring 2013): 12.

2. For a study of the politics of Islamophobia, see Deepa Kumar, *Islamophobia and the Politics of Empire* (Chicago: Haymarket Books, 2012).

3. I take my terms here from Mahmood Mamdani, *Good Muslim, Bad Muslim: America, the Cold War, and the Roots of Terror* (New York: Three Leaves Press, 2005).

4. The turning of matters is even more evident after the Arab revolutions. Even the media, especially the *New York Times*, the great bellwether of the intersection of liberal and state opinion, has adopted this vision of Islam. Societies in which Muslims are a majority are now divided into religious "masses" and "secular" dissidents. See, for instance, the *New York Times* article regarding the protests in Istanbul about the government grab of Taksim Square, which states, "Mr. Erdogan still has great support among Turkey's religious masses, but secular critics cite his government's sweeping prosecution and intimidation of journalists as evidence of its intolerance of dissent." Tim Arango and Ceylan Yeginsu, "Peaceful Protest over Istanbul Park Turns Violent as Police Crack Down," *New York Times*, May 31, 2013, http://www.nytimes.com/2013/06/01/world/Europe/police-attack-protesters-in-istanbul-taksim-square.html?emc=eta1, accessed May 31, 2013. The presumption here is that no religious person could be environmentally conscious or appalled by mallification of his or her city and home, or object to authoritarian governance. It might indeed be that the protesters are secular or have secular (not primarily motivated by religion) motives for the protests, but surely what is at stake is the issue at hand and what is being protested. When, unnoticed by most, did the *New York Times* become populist? See two wonderful alternatives: Evran Savci, "On the 'Turkish Model': Neoliberal Democracy with Teargas," *Jadaliyya*, June 4, 2013, http://www.jadaliyya.com/pages/index/12008/on-the-turkish-model_neoliberal-democracy-with-tea, accessed June 4, 2013; Emrah Yildiz, "Alignments of Dissent and

Politics of Naming: Assembling Resistance in Turkey," *Jadaliyya*, June 4, 2013, http://www.jadaliyya.com/pages/index/12001/alignments-of-dissent-and-politics-of-naming_assem, accessed June 4, 2013.

5. See chapter 4.

CHAPTER 1

1. See C. L. R. James, *Beyond a Boundary* (Durham, NC: Duke University Press, 1993). The scene is from *Spooks/MI-5*, "Who Guards the Guards?," 3:3, BBC ONE, October 25, 2004, writer Rupert Walters, dir. Cilla Ware, streaming video, http://movies.netflix.com/WiPlayer?movieid=70110301&trkid=3326878. Hereafter cited in the text as *WGG*.

2. On historical amnesia in the context of the special relationship, see Hazel Carby, "US/UK's Special Relationship: The Culture of Torture in Abu Ghraib and Lynching Photographs," *Nka: Journal of Contemporary Art* 20 (Fall 2006): 60–71.

3. Stuart Hall, *The Hard Road to Renewal: Thatcherism and the Crisis of the Left* (London: Verso, 1988), 2.

4. Hall, *Hard Road to Renewal*, 2.

5. *Spooks/MI-5*, "The Suffering of Strangers," 3:10, BBC ONE, December 13, 2004, writer Ben Richards, dir. Alrick Riley, streaming video, http://movies.netflix.com/WiPlayer?movieid=70110308&trkid=13633959.

6. Hall, "New Ethnicities," in *Stuart Hall: Critical Dialogues in Cultural Studies,* ed. David Morley and Kuan-Hsing Cheng (New York: Routledge, 1996), 449. For critiques of the limitations regarding feminism in the thought of some adherents of the idea of Black Britain and their production of a stable antiracist identity, see Ashley Dawson's fine chapter on Rushdie, "Heritage Politics of the Soul: Immigration and Identity in Salman Rushdie's *The Satanic Verses*," in *Mongrel Nation: Diasporic Culture and the Making of Postcolonial Britain* (Ann Arbor: University of Michigan Press, 2007).

7. *My Beautiful Laundrette*, dir. Stephen Frears, scene 4 (Santa Monica, CA: MGM Home Entertainment, 1985), DVD; hereafter cited in the text as *MBL*.

8. Gayatri Spivak, *An Aesthetic Education in the Era of Globalization* (Cambridge, MA: Harvard University Press, 2012).

9. Spivak, *An Aesthetic Education*, xi, xiv, x, xvi.

10. Gayatri Gopinath, *Impossible Desires: Queer Diasporas and South Asian Public Cultures* (Durham, NC: Duke University Press, 2005), 3, 2.

11. Talal Asad, *Genealogies of Religion: Discipline and Reasons of Power in Christianity and Islam* (Baltimore, MD: Johns Hopkins University Press, 1993), 257.

12. For more on Modood, see chapter 4. Of course, Modood constructs the distinction between racism and antireligious feeling with an elaboration of a notion of religious injury, in which religious pain and identity will reveal themselves as inextricable, indeed as mutually constitutive. Tariq Modood, "Muslims, Race, and Equality in Britain: Some Post-Rushdie

Affair Reflections," *Third Text* 11 (Summer 1990): 127–34; reprinted as "Reflections on the Rushdie Affair: Muslims, Race, and Equality in Britain," in Tariq Modood, *Multicultural Politics: Racism, Ethnicity, and Muslims in Britain* (Minneapolis: University of Minnesota Press, 2005), 103–12.

13. Hall, "New Ethnicities," 446

14. Hall, "New Ethnicities," 447.

15. Asad, *Genealogies of Religion*, 299.

16. Talal Asad, "Freedom of Speech and Religious Limitations," in *Rethinking Secularism,* ed. Craig Calhoun, Mark Jurgensmeyer, and Jonathan van Antwerpen (Oxford: Oxford University Press, 2011), 6918 of 7924 to 6931 of 7924 (ebook location). Asad's antipathy to aesthetic practice leads him to write rather astonishing passages such as the following, which seems to indicate so deep an animosity that the argument disappears into the vortex of hostility. Even by the standards of précis, the passage is reductive: "Paranoia is the condition that some literary historians have, interestingly, identified as integral to modernist aesthetics. It denotes a range of affective states, including horror, loathing and nausea, generated by uncontrolled migration, by movement not from Europe to non-Europe but from non-Europe to Europe. As such, aesthetics, no less than theology, is a dimension of all modern politics, national and international. Modernism—the aesthetics accompanying modernity—engages with powerful feelings of visceral disgust. And it is in *mimesis* that modernism finds one of the most potent sources of revulsion and of paranoia, revulsion because modernism values only independence of judgment and despises imitation, paranoia because modernism seeks to penetrate disguises that make things (people, action, words) appear normal and innocent and shows them to be really meaningful and hostile" (6931 of 7924, ebook location).

17. On a notion of *adab* that does not erase its history, see Ronald A. T. Judy, "Some Thoughts on Naguib Mahfouz in the Spirit of Secular Criticism," *boundary 2* 34.2 (2007): 32–33.

18. On the Urdu *mar̲siya*, see C. M. Naim, "The Art of the Urdu Marsiya," in *Urdu Texts and Contexts: The Selected Essays of C. M. Naim* (Delhi: Permanent Black, 2004). In this essay, Naim also suggests that *mar̲siya* is the closest thing in Urdu to an epic.

19. Saba Mahmood, "Secularism, Hermeneutics and Empire: The Politics of Islamic Reformation," *Public Culture* 18.2 (2006): 346.

20. Mahmood, "Secularism," 346. See the special issue *Critical Secularism, boundary 2* 31.2 (2004).

21. Mahmood's accusation against Gourgouris—that he draws on a "liberal romantic imaginary through which we are routinely asked to recognize our most profound commitments (to autonomy, creativity, imagination and freedom)"—is in the same vein. See "Is Critique Secular? A Symposium at UC Berkeley," *Public Culture* 20.3 (2008): 447. See also Gourgouris's trenchant response, "Antisecularist Failures: A Counterresponse to Saba Mahmood," *Public Culture* 20.3 (2008): 453–59.

22. For the author function, see Michel Foucault, "What Is an Author?," trans. Josué V. Harari, in *The Foucault Reader*, ed. Paul Rabinow (New York: Pantheon, 1984), 101–20.

23. Asad, *Genealogies of Religion*, 221.

24. "Talal Asad and Abdullahi An-Naim in Conversation," 2009, http://blogs.ssrc.org/tif/wp-content/uploads/2009/11/Talal-Asad-and-Abdullahi-An-Naim-in-conversation.pdf, accessed January 19, 2011. Asad appears to be engaging a version of Syed Qutb's account of theological slavery in *Social Justice* and repeating Qutb's response to historical liberalism, letting, in other words, the theology be repositioned entirely within the grid of liberalism. Asad's account is more explicitly based on a collapse between the worldly *institution* of slavery and the theological notion. On Qutb and liberalism, see Ronald A. T. Judy, "Sayyid Qutb's fiqh al-waqi'I, or New Realist Science," *boundary 2* 31.2 (2004): 113–48, esp. 121–22.

25. Saba Mahmood, *Politics of Piety: The Islamic Revival and the Feminist Subject* (Princeton, NJ: Princeton University Press, 2005), 11.

26. For a response to the resuscitation of a variation on the idea of the happy slave, the happy slave family, in "The Marriage Vow," a document endorsed by Rick Santorum and Michele Bachmann, see Tera Hunter, "Putting an Antebellum Myth to Rest," *New York Times*, op-ed, August 1, 2011. Hunter's conclusion is worth quoting in full: "Why does the ugly resuscitation of the myth of the happy slave family matter? Because it is part of a broad and deliberate amnesia, like the misleading assertion by Sarah Palin that the founders were antislavery and the skipping of the 'three-fifths' clause during a Republican reading of the Constitution on the House floor. The oft-repeated historical fictions about black families only prove how politically useful and resilient they continue to be in a so-called post-racial society. Refusing to be honest about how racial inequality has burdened our shared history and continues to shape our society will not get us to that post-racial vision." http://travel.nytimes.com/2011/08/02/opinion/putting-an-antebellum-myth-about-slave-families-to-rest.html?_r=0, accessed February 16, 2013.

27. Mahmood, *Politics of Piety*, 11.

28. Saba Mahmood, "Secular Imperative?," *Public Culture* 20.3 (2008): 463.

29. Domenico Lusordo, *Liberalism: A Counter-History* (London: Verso, 2011); Robin Blackburn, *The American Crucible: Slavery, Emancipation and Human Rights* (New York: Verso, 2011). See also Simon Gikandi, *Slavery and the Culture of Taste* (Princeton, NJ: Princeton University Press, 2011).

30. Of course not all philosophers are prone to such historical blindness; see, for instance, Bernard William's rejection of philosophical reflections on slavery that hide its historical violence: "Seminar with Bernard Williams," *Ethical Perspectives* 6 (1999): 255.

31. On the use of the happy slave, see Gikandi, *Slavery and the Culture of Taste*, 190–91.

32. Moira Ferguson, *Subject to Others: British Women Writers and Colonial Slavery, 1670–1834* (New York: Routledge, 1992), 219.

33. Sarah More, "A True Account of a Pious Negro," in *Cheap Repository Tracts: Sorrowful Sam; or, The History of the Two Blacksmiths* (Philadelphia: B&J Johnson, 1800), 33. *Early American Imprints, Series I: 1639–1800*, http://infoweb.newsbank.com.proxy.libraries.rutgers.edu/iw-search/we/Evans/?p_product=EAIX&p_theme=eai&p_nbid=D58A59XP MTM3ODY2NzY5My4zNDEzODY6MToxMjoxMjguNi4yMTguNzI&p_action=doc&p_queryname=1&p_docref=v2:0F2B1FCB879B099B@EAIX-0F30140A0F718978@37137-100C834C6F864668@33, accessed May 13, 2013. The story is here misattributed to Sarah More but is regarded to be by Hannah More.

34. Sarah More, "A True Account of a Pious Negro," 34. http://infoweb.newsbank.com.proxy.libraries.rutgers.edu/iw-search/we/Evans/?p_product=EAIX&p_theme=eai&p_nbid=D58A59XPMTM 3ODY2NzY5My4zNDEzODY6MToxMjoxMjguNi4yMTguNzI&p_action=doc&p_queryname=1&p_docref=v2:0F2B1FCB879B099B@EAIX-0F30140A0F718978@37137-100C93639B4BC718@34, accessed May 13, 2013.

35. Maria Edgeworth, "The Grateful Negro," in *Tales and Novels*, vol. 5 (New York: Harper and Brothers, 1850), 159.

36. Edgeworth, "The Grateful Negro," 159–60.

37. Edgeworth, "The Grateful Negro," 160.

38. Alan Richardson, "Slavery and Romantic Writing," in *A Companion to Romanticism*, ed. Duncan Wu (Oxford: Blackwell, 1998, 1999), 466.

39. Blackburn, *American Crucible*, 483.

40. Ronald A. T. Judy, "Reflections on Straussism, Antimodernity, and Transition in the Age of American Force," *boundary 2* 33.1 (2006): 40.

41. Judy, "Reflections on Straussism," 40.

42. Carby, "US/UK Special Relationship"; Colin Dayan, *The Story of Cruel and Unusual* (Cambridge, MA: MIT press, 2007); Anthony Bogues, *Empire of Liberty: Power, Desire, and Freedom* (Hanover, NH: Dartmouth College Press, 2010). For a striking history of the historical development of the American prison system, see Robert Perkinson, *Texas Tough: The Rise of America's Prison Empire* (New York: Henry Holt, 2010).

43. Marnia Lazreg, *Torture and the Twilight of Empire: From Algiers to Baghdad* (Princeton, NJ: Princeton University Press, 2008); Graeme Harper, ed., *Colonial and Postcolonial Incarceration* (New York: Continuum, 2001).

44. For a wonderful corrective, see Nadje Al-Ali and Deborah al-Najjar, eds., *We Are Iraqis: Aesthetics and Politics in a Time of War* (Syracuse, NY: Syracuse University Press, 2013).

45. See David Denby, "Anxiety Test: The Hurt Locker and Food, Inc.," *New Yorker*, June 29, 2009, http://www.newyorker.com/arts/critics/cinema/2009/06/29/090629crci_cinema_denby, accessed June 2, 2013; A. O. Scott, "Soldiers on a Live Wire between Peril and Protocol," *New York Times*, June 25, 2009, http://movies.nytimes.com/2009/06/26/movies/26hurt.html?_r=0, accessed June 2, 2013. Scott mentions the

"hyperbolic realism" of the film and (very much in passing) its political evasions but seems unable to link the politics to the deliberate emptiness, made to pass for stylish "realism." The rave reviews of the film are puzzling. For another instance, see David Edelstein's "Explosive Material," June 21, 2009, http://nymag.com/movies/reviews/57462/, accessed June 2, 2013. For a refreshingly critical review, attentive to the "erasure" of politics in the film, see Seth Colter Walls, "All Pain, No Gain," *Newsweek*, January 21, 2010, http://www.thedailybeast.com/newsweek/2010/01/21/all-pain-no-gain.html, accessed June 2, 2013.

46. Kathryn Bigelow, "High Explosive: Kathryn Bigelow Talks to James Bell about Her Iraq Drama, '*The Hurt Locker*,'" *Sight and Sound* 19.9 (2009): 8.

47. Describing a different moment, Edelstein notices that James looks like a spaceman: "Explosive Material," *The Hurt Locker*, dir. Kathryn Bigelow (Universal City, CA: Summit Entertainment, 2013).

48. *Zero Dark Thirty*, dir. Kathryn Bigelow, scene 1 (Burbank, CA: Sony Pictures Home Entertainment, 2013), DVD; hereafter cited in the text as *ZDT*.

49. Jeremy Waldron's introduction to Dayan, *The Story of Cruel and Unusual* (Cambridge, MA: MIT Press, 2007), 44 of 486 (ebook).

50. Nadeem F. Paracha, "Zero IQ Thirty," *Dawn*, January 31, 2013, http://dawn.com/2013/01/31/zero-iq-thirty/, accessed May 28, 2013. See also Susan L. Carruthers, "Zero Dark Thirty," *Cineaste* 38 (2013): 50. Carruthers, too, seems to agree that the film invites mockery; and Deepa Kumar's detailed critique of the film's varieties of bigotry, "Rebranding the War on Terror for the Age of Obama: 'Zero Dark Thirty' and the Promotion of Extra-Judicial Killing," *Mondoweiss*, January 15, 2013, http://mondoweiss.net/2013/01/rebranding-promotion-judicial.html, accessed June 2, 2013.

51. Fayes T. Kantawala, "Very Dark, Very Zero," *Friday Times* 25.1 (February 15–21, 2013), http://www.thefridaytimes.com/beta3/tft/article.php?issue=20130215&page=13, accessed May 28, 2013. On the assassination, see "Cry, the Beloved Country," *Friday Times* 25.3 (March 1–7, 2013), http://www.thefridaytimes.com/beta3/tft/article.php?issue=20130301&page=13, accessed May 28, 2013.

52. The oscillations are very clear in the Rand Corporation report (2003), which seems unable to decide which Muslim and what secularist are most useful, if any.

53. Michael Crowley, "Airplane," *New Republic*, May 20, 2009, https://www.newrepublic.com/article/airplane#, accessed March 10, 2013.

54. Tariq Ali, "Waiting for an Islamic Enlightenment," *Guardian*, October 21, 2005, http://www.guardian.co.uk/books/2005/oct/22/highereducation.islam, accessed February 1, 2013.

55. Judith Butler, *Precarious life: The Powers of Mourning and Violence* (New York: Verso, 2004), 142.

56. Butler, *Precarious Life*, 5–6.

57. On African Arabic slave narratives, see Ronald A. T. Judy, *(Dis)forming the American Canon: African-Arabic Slave Narratives and the Vernacular* (Minneapolis: University of Minnesota Press, 1993). According to Judy, one of the earliest narratives dates to 1731 (19). See also Terry Alford, *Prince among Slaves* (Oxford: Oxford University Press, 1977), and *A Muslim American Slave: The Life of Omar Ibn Said,* ed. and trans. Ala Alrryes (Madison: University of Wisconsin Press, 2011). On Muslims and black internationalism, see Sohail Daulatzai, *Black Star, Crescent Moon: The Muslim International and Black Freedom beyond America* (Minneapolis: University of Minnesota Press, 2012).

CHAPTER 2

1. "Individualism Can't Beat a Good Crowd Riot," *Life of Brian*, scene 20, dir. Terry Jones (Burbank, CA: Handmade Films; Warner Home Video, 1979), DVD.

2. Orhan Pamuk, *Snow*, trans. Maureen Freely (New York: Vintage International, 2005).

3. For a quick discussion of the role of Turkey in the discussion of the veil, see Leila Ahmed's "The Discourse of the Veil," in *Women and Gender in Islam: Historical Roots of a Modern Debate* (New Haven, CT: Yale University Press, 1992).

4. See, for instance, Syed Vali Reza Nasr, *Mawdudi and the Making of Islamic Revivalism* (New York: Oxford University Press, 1996); and, on unintended consequences of the reaction to Turkey leading to a strange (very temporary) alliance between Muslim clerics in Iran and the founding of the Pahlavi dynasty, see Nasr, *The Shia Revival: How Conflicts within Islam Will Shape the Future* (New York: Norton, 2007), 123.

5. The project of understanding the veiled or believing Muslim woman is becoming ubiquitous in Anglophone fiction. You see this in Leila Aboulela's *The Translator* and *Minaret*, Laila Lalami's *Hope and Other Dangerous Pursuits*, Monica Ali's *Brick Lane*, Nadeem Aslam's *Maps for Lost Lovers* and *The Wasted Vigil*, and Mohja Kahf's *The Girl in the Tangerine Scarf.*

6. Alain Badiou, *Saint Paul: The Foundation of Universalism*, trans. Ray Brassier (Stanford, CA: Stanford University Press, 2003), 1–2; hereafter cited in the text as *SP*.

7. There is a remarkable list of formerly secular leftists doing penance for an earlier contempt for, or simply indifference to, religion. They frequently manifest a strange quality of surprise, as if theirs has been a startling discovery that the "natives" are, in fact, sentient. But if one were once one of those thought to be insensible, the compulsive declaration of surprised and new understanding itself seems strange . . . and patronizing.

8. Joan Scott, *The Politics of the Veil* (Princeton, NJ: Princeton University Press, 2007), 158, 164; hereafter cited in the text as *POV*.

9. Achille Mbembe, *On the Postcolony* (Berkeley: University of California Press, 2010), 3.

10. Khaled Abou El Fadl, *Speaking in God's Name: Islamic Law, Authority and Women* (Oxford: Oneworld, 2001), 233, 235, 237–42. For Daniel Pipes's campaign against El Fadl, see "Stealth Islamist: Khaled Abou El Fadl," *Middle East Quarterly* 11.2 (Spring 2004), www.danielpipes. org/1841/stealth- islamist- khaled-abou-el-fadl, accessed August 31, 2010; and "Khaled Abou El Fadl Reveals His Islamist Outlook," *Lion's Den: Daniel Pipes Blog,* February 4, 2005, updated December 5, 2005, http://www. danielpipes.org/blog/2005/02/khaled-abou-el-fadl-reveals-his-islamist, accessed August 31, 2010.

11. As quoted in El Fadl, *Speaking in God's Name,* 237.

12. Scott is happy to foreground her own American perspective and to use American understandings of the French case as theoretical counterpoint (*POV,* 93, 8–9).

13. Of course, the neoconservatives will not let up on this. Jamie Glazov, of *Front Page Magazine* (www.frontpagemag.com) has just published a book in which he discusses *fitna* at length.

14. See Saba Mahmood, "Secularism, Hermeneutics, and Empire: The Politics of Islamic Reformation," *Public Culture* 18.2 (Spring 2006): 323–47.

15. John le Carré, *A Most Wanted Man* (New York: Scribner, 2008), 322.

16. Le Carré, *A Most Wanted Man,* 68.

17. Le Carré, *A Most Wanted Man,* 13–14.

18. The sudden ubiquity of the tortured male body in mainstream popular culture has everything to do with this discussion. You can see the preoccupation with torture in films and television shows, ranging from the radically conservative imagination of *24*—whose fundamental formal conceit, the real-time pretext of the show, is an attempt to find a formal correlative of the ticking-bomb scenario so dear to defenders of torture—to *The Bourne Ultimatum*'s liberal vision of the good spy who exposes torture and corruption. *Children of Men, Rendition, Syriana,* to name a few, provide other examples.

19. Hazel Carby, "A Strange and Bitter Crop: The Spectacle of Torture," *openDemocracy.net,* October 10, 2004, www.opendemocracy.net/media-abu _ghraib/article_21, accessed March 29, 2010.

20. Jasbir Puar, *Terrorist Assemblages: Homonationalism in Queer Times* (Durham, NC: Duke University Press, 2007), 98; hereafter cited parenthetically in the text as *TA.*

21. Hiram Perez, "'Going to Meet the Man' in Abu Ghraib" (unpublished paper).

22. Lila Abu-Lughod, "Do Muslim Women Really Need Saving? Anthropological Reflections on Cultural Relativism and Its Others," *American Anthropologist* 104.3 (September 2002): 783–90. Abu-Lughod mentions Iran as a space where women have greater visibility, but she does not discuss the works she cites by people like Haideh Moghissi and Afsaneh Najmabadi. Moghissi, for instance, has been very critical of Iranian theocracy. Najmabadi's article, "(Un)veiling Feminism," is a fascinating attempt to rethink the history of veiling and unveiling in twentieth-century Iranian history. Najmabadi's notion that the discussion of the veil occludes the complexities

of women's presence in the Iranian public sphere, post-1979, is worth serious discussion, but her discussion militates radically against any recuperation of the burqa under the Taliban, for whom women's education itself is an abomination. Afsaneh Najmabadi, "(Un)veiling Feminism," *Social Text* 64 (Autumn 2000): 29–45. See also Gayatri Spivak's emphasis on the education of the girl child in "1996: Foucault and Najibullah," chapter 4 of *Other Asias* (Malden, MA: Blackwell, 2008), 132–60.

23. The reception of this article has been fascinating. In order to argue with a political theorist celebrating the liberation of Afghan women by the American war machine, Judith Butler reports that she heard a talk about "the important cultural meanings of the burka." She goes on to write, "The fear of the speaker was that the destruction of the burka, as if it were a sign of repression, backwardness, or indeed, a resistance to cultural modernity itself, would result in a significant decimation of Islamic culture, and the extension of US cultural assumptions about sexuality and agency ought to be organized and represented." Butler does not name Abu-Lughod in the text, but she cites the article. See Judith Butler, *Precarious Life: The Powers of Mourning and Violence* (New York: Verso, 2004), 146.

24. Valentine Moghadam, "Patriarchy, the Taliban, and Politics of Public Space in Afghanistan," *Women's Studies International Forum* 25.1 (2002): 19–31. See also Moghadam's "Revolution, the State, Islam, and Women: Gender Politics in Iran and Afghanistan," *Social Text* 22 (Spring 1989): 40–61. Currently, Malalai Joya's position is a useful example. She is critical of the U.S. occupation, the Northern Alliance, and the Taliban and has called for secularism—in the sense of a separation of mosque and state. See also *Time* magazine's attempt to tone down her message: Ayaan Hirsi Ali, "Malalai Joya," in "The 2010 Time 100," *Time*, April 29, 2010, http://www.time.com/time/specials/packages/article/0,28804,1984685_1984949_1985238,00.html. For her resistance to being co-opted, see Judy Mandelbaum, "How Time Magazine Hijacked Afghan Activist Malalai Joya," *Open Salon* (blog), May 4, 2010, http://open.salon.com/blog/judy_mandelbaum/2010/05/04/how_time_magazine_hoodwinked_afghan_activist_malalai_joya.

25. Maliha Safri, "The Political Economy of Afghan Migratory Movement" (unpublished paper).

26. For a range of positions on Islam and feminism, see Fatima Mernissi, *The Veil and the Male Elite: A Feminist Interpretation of Women's Rights in Islam*, trans. Mary Jo Lakeland (Reading, MA: Addison-Wesley, 1991), and *The Fundamentalist Obsession with Women: A Current Articulation of Class Conflict in Modern Muslim Societies* (Lahore, Pakistan: Simorgh/Women's Resource and Publication Centre, 1987); and Amina Wadud, *Inside the Gender Jihad: Women's Reform in Islam* (Oxford: Oneworld, 2006). For a more critical reading, see Ghada Karmi, "Women, Islam, and Patriarchalism," in *Feminism and Islam: Legal and Literary Perspectives*, ed. Mai Yamani (New York: New York University Press, 1996), 69–85. For more of an overview, see miriam cooke, "Women, Religion, and the Postcolonial Arab World," *Cultural Critique*, no. 45 (Spring 2000): 150–84; and Ahmed, *Women and Gender in Islam*.

27. On queer as optic, see Puar, *Terrorist Assemblages*, xiii. On links between the turban and terrorist masculinity, see the entire chapter "'The Turban Is Not a Hat': Queer Diaspora and Practices of Profiling."

28. I mean by *telos* a desired endpoint that is also assumed to be a likely outcome if the prohibitions are observed.

29. This discussion, perhaps more conceptually familiar to early modernists and medievalists, replays new historicist analyses of gender and embodiment in medieval and early modern Europe.

30. In an article coauthored with Charles Hirschkind, Mahmood has already pointed out that Jay Leno and Oprah Winfrey lined up behind George Bush to support the war in Afghanistan. The critique of Hollywood liberalism and its moralistic smugness is very welcome. Nonetheless, the piece is far from contrapuntal. For two, tensely balanced, contrapuntal readings, see Spivak's "1996: Foucault and Najibullah" (cited earlier) and "Terror: A Speech after 9-11," *boundary 2* 31.2 (Summer 2004): 81–111. Spivak does not elide the violence of the Islamist Right, or disappear the problem of gender injustice, in order to mount her critique of imperialism.

31. Saba Mahmood, *Politics of Piety: The Islamic Revival and the Feminist Subject* (Princeton, NJ: Princeton University Press, 2005), 8; hereafter in this chapter cited as *PP*. The essay by Abu-Lughod that Mahmood discusses here is "The Romance of Resistance: Tracing Transformations of Power through Bedouin Women," *American Ethnologist* 17.1 (February 1990): 41–55.

32. The choice is not between *La Perla* and the veil. Modern capitalism and consumerism are strangely ecumenical, but neither Mahmood nor Abu-Lughod mentions the growing trend of "designer Islam": special websites for "Muslim" clothes, high-fashion Islamist designer veils, celebrity Islamists like Pakistan's Junaid Jamshed, the former pop star, who also owns and runs an overpriced high-end fabric and clothing store, where he sells a range of clothes in line with people's "social and cultural values" (www.junaidjamshed.info/junaid-jamshed-fashion-outlets.html, accessed September 6, 2010). One can see the fascination with high-end consumption in the following websites: Islamic Design House, www.islamicdesignhouse.com/usa/, accessed September 6, 2010; Designer Hijab Company, www.designerhijabcompany.com//index.php?osCsid=654d4edab2c902b2c403a57ba21 27d4, accessed September 6, 2010. One excited hijabi blogger is delighted that Lacroix is inspired by the hijab. Mariam Sobh, "Christian Lacroix Uses Hijab as Inspiration," Examiner.com, www.examiner.com/muslim-women-s-style-in-national/christian-lacroix-uses-hijab-as-inspiration, accessed September 6, 2010. When I see some of the other images juxtaposed with Lacroix, all I can think of is Malek Alloula's *The Colonial Harem*. There is, of course, also Hijab Barbie.

33. Michel Foucault, *History of Sexuality*, vol. 1, *An Introduction* (New York: Pantheon, 1978); and Judith Butler, *Gender Trouble: Feminism and the Subversion of Identity* (New York: Routledge, 1990), 34.

34. Marnia Lazreg has recently distanced herself from Mahmood's positions and from positions like Mahmood's. See especially the introduction

and "Letter Four: Conviction and Piety," in *Questioning the Veil: Open Letters to Muslim Women* (Princeton, NJ: Princeton University Press, 2009).

35. One might contrast this with the wonderful collection edited by Afsaneh Najmabadi and Kathryn Babayan, *Islamicate Sexualities: Translations across Temporal Geographies of Desire* (Cambridge, MA: Harvard University Press, 2008).

36. In an astonishing passage, Colin Jager extends this aesthetic tendency. He uses Mahmood's comparison of the members of the *dawa* movement with virtuoso pianists to explain how a Wordsworth sonnet works: "In her discussion of women's mosque movement, Saba Mahmood considers the multiple ways in which traditional forms of religious discipline interact with and help to shape Egyptian modernity. In the course of her investigation she offers an analogy that resonates powerfully with Wordsworth's sonnet. A virtuoso pianist, she notes, can achieve excellence only by submitting herself to a rigorous program of drills, lessons, and exercises; the freedom of expertise, accordingly, is not the freedom of an autonomous will but rather the freedom of mastery—the mastery of a certain set of habits, skills, dispositions, or bodily postures. In like manner, the sonnet's speaker imagines that both poet and reader will submit themselves on a regular basis to the rigours of the sonnet form. In this kind of expertise, a certain discipline becomes so ingrained that the self empties out into pure activity; the forms of life enumerated in the sonnet's octave, accordingly, renounce being in favour of doing, striving to become verbs rather than nouns." I am not sure if the analogy is ultimately between the Muslim woman and the sonnet's speaker, or between the woman and the sonnet, but aestheticization turns out to be crucial to postsecularism. More disturbing is the thought that Muslim women might as well be sonnets, so little reality do they seem to have in this conversation. See Colin Jager, *The Book of God: Secularization and Design in the Romantic Era* (Philadelphia: University of Pennsylvania Press, 2006), 214.

37. Khaled Abou El Fadl, for instance, has also published something with the Rand Corporation. He has also written an introduction to a volume on the War on Terror that includes a piece by Noam Chomsky. Daniel Pipes detests him. I am not sure, then, where, on Mahmood's terms, he stands on the spectrum of complicities with empire.

38. Mahmood, "Secularism, Hermeneutics, and Empire," 343 n. 51, 338–39.

39. Lara Deeb, *An Enchanted Modern: Gender and Public Piety in Shi'i Lebanon* (Princeton, NJ: Princeton University Press 2006).

40. See Nancy Armstrong, *Desire and Domestic Fiction: A Political History of the Novel* (New York: Oxford University Press, 1987). Lila Abu-Lughod's adoption of the notion of the burqa as portable seclusion does the same. The idea there is that women ought to carry their houses with them and, in so doing, provide the virtuous domesticity, which is their patrimony.

41. The term is Mahmood's (*PP*, 197).

42. Some of these analyses need to be more global, but Mahmood insists that the local and the particular are conceptually necessary in order to buttress her claims while surreptitiously stretching arguments into a more global

form. See Faisal Devji's brilliant *The Terrorist in Search of Humanity: Militant Islam and Global Politics* (New York: Columbia University Press, 2008) for a powerful study of global and historical discourses and tendencies at play in militant Islam and the War on Terror.

43. Talal Asad, *Genealogies of Religion: Discipline and Reasons of Power in Christianity and Islam* (Baltimore, MD: Johns Hopkins University Press, 1993), 284.

44. One might surmise that it is in order to secure this equation that she attempts to discredit both El Saadawi and, in a more recent piece on the Danish political cartoons, Tariq Ali.

45. Dipesh Chakrabarty, *Provincializing Europe: Postcolonial Thought and Historical Difference* (Princeton, NJ: Princeton University Press, 2000), 254.

46. Gayatri Chakravorty Spivak, "Acting Bits/Identity Talk," *Critical Inquiry* 18.4 (Summer 1992): 770–803, esp. 803.

47. Gayatri Chakravorty Spivak, "Use and Abuse of Human Rights," *boundary 2* 32.1 (Spring 2005): 136.

CHAPTER 3

1. For an account of the cultural and political trends that contributed to the death of the project of Black Britain and replaced it with an identitarian politics conceived in religious terms, see Chetan Bhatt, "The Fetish of the Margins: Religious Absolutism, Anti-Racism and Postcolonial Silence," *New Formations* 59 (2006): 102–8.

2. Talal Asad, *Genealogies of Religion: Discipline and Reasons of Power in Christianity and Islam* (Baltimore, MD: Johns Hopkins University Press, 1993); hereafter cited in the text as *GR*.

3. For a sympathetically critical discussion of Asad, see Gauri Viswanathan, *Outside the Fold: Conversion, Modernity, and Belief* (Princeton, NJ: Princeton University Press, 1998), xiv–xvi.

4. Saba Mahmood, "Secularism, Hermeneutics and Empire: The Politics of Islamic Reformation," *Public Culture* 18.2 (2006): 346. This version of antisecularism mutates into a kindly attempt to rescue Said from himself in Gil Anidjar's "Secularism," *Critical Inquiry* 33.1 (2006): 52–77.

5. Mahmood, "Secularism," 346.

6. Aamir Mufti, "The Aura of Authenticity," *Social Text* 18.3 (2000): 87, 88.

7. The word *perfection* is curiously important to Arnold: "Certainly we are no enemies of the Nonconformists; for, on the contrary, what we aim at is their perfection. But culture, which is the study of perfection, leads us, as we in the following pages have shown, to conceive of true human perfection as a harmonious perfection, developing all sides of our humanity; and as a general perfection, developing all parts of our society. For if one member suffers, the other members must suffer with it; and the fewer there are that follow the true way of salvation, the harder that way is to find." Matthew Arnold, *Culture and Anarchy: An Essay in Cultural and Political Criticism,*

ed. Ian Gregor (New York: Merrill, 1971), 7–8; hereafter cited in the text as *CA*. In the chapter on sweetness and light, he writes: "Culture is then properly described not as having its origin in curiosity, but as having its origin in the love of perfection; it is a study of perfection. It moves by the force, not merely or primarily of the scientific passion" (34).

8. For some versions of this view, see Talal Asad, *Formations of the Secular: Christianity, Islam, Modernity* (Stanford, CA: Stanford University Press, 2003), and *Genealogies of Religion*; Ashis Nandy, *The Intimate Enemy: Loss and Recovery of Self under Colonialism* (Delhi: Oxford University Press, 1983); and Saba Mahmood, *Politics of Piety: The Islamic Revival and the Feminist Subject* (Princeton, NJ: Princeton University Press, 2005), and "Secularism." For an opposing view, see Aamir Mufti, "Critical Secularism: A Reintroduction for Perilous Times," *boundary 2* 34.1 (2007): 17–23; and "The Aura of Authenticity," 87–103.

9. Asad, *Genealogies of Religion*, 285–91; and *Formations of the Secular*, 8–9.

10. For histories of the development of the novel, see Michael McKeon, *The Origins of the English Novel, 1600–1740* (Baltimore, MD: Johns Hopkins University Press, 1987); and Ian Watt, *The Rise of the Novel: Studies in Defoe, Richardson, and Fielding* (Berkeley: University of California Press, 1957).

11. Leila Aboulela, *The Translator* (New York: Black Cat, 1999), 89; hereafter cited in the text as *T*.

12. Leila Aboulela, "Leila Aboulela: Author Statement," *British Council/ Literature,* British Council, http://literature.britishcouncil.org/leila-aboulela, accessed October 23, 2011.

13. Leila Aboulela, "Moving Away from Accuracy," *Alif: Journal of Comparative Poetics* 22 (2002): 198–207.

14. Nancy Armstrong, *Desire and Domestic Fiction: A Political History of the Novel* (New York: Oxford University Press, 1987), 109–32.

15. The influence of Martin Luther on Jamaluddin al-Afghani, himself a model for Muhammad Abduh, is well known. See, for instance, Aziz Al-Azmeh's *Islams and Modernities* (London: Verso, 2009), 104, 109. The point of the book is not to elide the differences between a range of Muslim reformers but to track some general trends, which Al-Azmeh does brilliantly even as he resists the tendency to homogenize Islam.

16. Olivier Roy, *Globalized Islam: The Search for a New Ummah* (New York: Columbia University Press, 2004), 2–3.

17. The marshaling of women who defend polygamy with Islamist rhetoric can be found in a range of contexts. For an example in Pakistan, see Abbas, "Itineraries of Conversion: Judaic Paths to a Muslim Pakistan," in *Beyond Crisis: Re-evaluating Pakistan,* ed. Naveeda Khan (New Delhi: Routledge, 2010), 344–69. For an account of a defense of conservative positions on women in the Egyptian context, see also Leila Ahmed's discussion of Zeinab al-Ghazali in chapter 10 of *Women and Gender in Islam: Historical Roots of a Modern Debate* (New Haven, CT: Yale University Press, 1992).

18. Aboulela, "Moving Away from Accuracy," 206.

19. "Surah *An-Nisa* 4, 34," in *Qur'an*, trans. Marmaduke Pickthall (London: Ta'ha Books, 1930).

20. For a history of these developments, see Jay Spaulding, *The Heroic Age in Sinna'r* (East Lansing: Michigan State University Press, 1985), 154, 223–24, 238–39, 252. For an account of the rewards for the Islamist middle class in the current Sudanese situation, see Salma Ahmed Nageeb, *New Spaces and Old Frontiers: Women, Social Space, and Islamization in Sudan* (Lanham, MD: Lexington Books, 2004), 16–17.

21. Quoted in Susan Mansfield, "Bridging the Culture Gap," *Aberdeen Press and Journal*, December 4, 1999, 13, *LexisNexis*, accessed August 16, 2011.

22. Leila Aboulela, *Minaret* (New York: Black Cat, 2005); hereafter cited in the text as *M*.

23. For a very useful discussion of postcoloniality and Muslim feminism, see Miriam Cooke, "Women, Religion, and the Postcolonial Arab World," *Cultural Critique* 45 (2002): 150–84. For the offering up of female consent in answer to imperialism, see Saba Mahmood and Charles Hirschkind, "Feminism, the Taliban, and the Politics of Counter-Insurgency," *Anthropological Quarterly* 75.2 (2002): 339–54; see also Mahmood, *Politics of Piety*.

24. See Marie-Aime'e Helie-Lucas, "Women, Nationalism and Religion in the Algerian Liberation Struggle," in *Opening the Gates: A Century of Arab Feminist Writing*, ed. Margot Badran and Miriam Cooke (Bloomington: Indiana University Press, 1990), 104–14, for an exemplary treatment of this problem.

25. See, for instance, John O. Voll, ed., *Sudan: State and Society in Crisis* (Bloomington: Indiana University Press, 1991); and Alex De Waal, *Islamism and Its Enemies in the Horn of Africa* (Bloomington: Indiana University Press, 2004). For the effects of Islamization in present-day Sudan, see Nageeb, *New Spaces and Old Frontiers*.

26. Aboulela does this in *The Translator* as well (69). There are, of course, complexities surrounding this, given the discourse of Western intervention. See Alex De Waal, "Tragedy in Darfur: On Understanding and Ending the Horror," *Boston Review*, October–November 2004, accessed August 20, 2011; and Mahmood Mamdani, "The Politics of Naming: Genocide, Civil War, Insurgency," *London Review of Books*, March 8, 2007, 5–8.

27. Wai'l Hassan, "Leila Aboulela and the Ideology of Muslim Immigrant Fiction," *Novel* 41.2–3 (2008): 316–17.

28. For an argument that connects the two, see Hassan, "Leila Aboulela and the Ideology of Muslim Immigrant Fiction," 305.

29. Salman Rushdie, *Shame* (New York: Picador, 1983), 23.

30. I am using an argument made by Rosemond Tuve, "Sacred 'Parody' of Love Poetry and Herbert," *Studies in the Renaissance* 8 (1961): 249–90.

31. Hassan has argued that this remark indicates that Coetzee does not expect restraint from a Muslim woman, but I think that to understand this remark one needs to revisit the tensions between Rushdie and Coetzee. Coetzee's aversion to magical realism is well known. Rushdie's novels are also, according to Coetzee, too baggy. Aboulela may well be, laudably, the

polar opposite of Rushdie for him. Hassan, "Leila Aboulela and the Ideology of Muslim Immigrant Fiction," 309. See also J. M. Coetzee, "Palimpsest Regained" [Review of *The Moor's Last Sigh*, by Salman Rushdie], *New York Review of Books*, March 21, 1996, accessed April 25, 2007. For the description "halal fiction," see Ferial Ghazoul, "Halal Fiction" [Review of *Coloured Lights* and *The Translator* by Leila Aboulela], *Al-Ahram Weekly Online*, http://weekly.ahram.org.eg/2001/542/bo4.htm, accessed April 25, 2007.

32. Ghazoul, "Halal Fiction."

33. Mike Philips, "Faith Healing" [Review of of *Minaret* by Leila Aboulela], *Guardian*, June 11, 2005, accessed April 26, 2007.

34. Anita Sethi, "Keep the Faith," *Guardian*, June 4, 2005, http://www.theguardian.com/books/2005/jun/05/fiction.features2, accessed April 26, 2007.

35. For a quick and useful overview of this history, see Albert Hourani, *A History of the Arab Peoples* (New York: Warner, 1992), 257–58, 348–49. For a thoughtful account of variants of revivalist reformism, see Ahmad Dallal, "The Origins and Objectives of Islamic Revivalist Thought, 1750–1850," *Journal of the American Oriental Society* 113. 3 (1993): 341–59. It is often argued that the doctrinal differences between different, variously modern revivalist groups makes it difficult to speak of them together, but such reasoning would imply that the separate existence of Quakers, Methodists, and Anabaptists means that there is no such thing as Protestantism.

36. For a discussion of this development, see Mufti, "Fanatics in Europa," *boundary 2* 34.1 (2007): 17–23.

37. Nadeem Aslam, *Maps for Lost Lovers* (New York: Knopf, 2005).

38. Aslam, *Maps for Lost Lovers*, 276.

39. See the first chapters of Asad's *Genealogies of Religion* and *Formations of the Secular.*

CHAPTER 4

1. Michel Foucault, "Nietzsche, Genealogy, History," trans. Donald Bouchard and Sherry Simon, in *The Foucault Reader*, ed. Paul Rabinow (New York: Pantheon, 1984), 79.

2. Tariq Modood, "Muslims, Race, and Equality in Britain: Some Post-Rushdie Affair Reflections," *Third Text* 11 (Summer 1990): 127–34; reprinted as "Reflections on the Rushdie Affair: Muslims, Race, and Equality in Britain," in Tariq Modood, *Multicultural Politics: Racism, Ethnicity, and Muslims in Britain* (Minneapolis: University of Minnesota Press, 2005), 103–12. Hereafter cited in the text as *MP*.

3. Saba Mahmood, "Religious Reason and Secular Affect: An Incommensurable Divide?," in Talal Asad et al., *Is Critique Secular?Blasphemy, Injury, and Free Speech* (Berkeley: University of California Press, 2009); hereafter cited in the text as *RR*. See also the entire volume *Is Critique Secular?*

4. This sense of what I am calling "the redundancy of secularism," the tendency, that is, to add secularism to any set of failures, including Protestant Christian ones, that mark the disenchanted aridity of the contemporary

world is also to be found in Judith Butler's "Sexual Politics, Torture and, Secular Time," *British Journal of Sociology* 59.1 (2008): 1–23; reprinted in Elzbieta H. Oleksy, ed., *Intimate Citizenships: Gender, Sexualities, Politics* (New York: Routledge, 2009), 17–39; and Judith Butler, *Frames of War: When Is Life Grievable?* (London: Verso, 2009), 101–35.

5. On sources for Asad's views regarding religion and belief see Chapter 3, note 39. The same conflation is evident in the following line, "From the Cargo Cults of Melanesia to the Islamic Revolution in Iran, they merely attempt (hopelessly) 'to resist the future' or 'to turn back the clock of history.'" Talal Asad, *Genealogies of Religion: Discipline and Reasons of Power in Christianity and Islam* (Baltimore, MD: Johns Hopkins University Press, 1993), 19.

6. On Mahmood's use of Byzantium, see Dimitris Krallis, "The Critics Byzantine Ploy: Voltairean Confusion in Postsecularist Narratives," *boundary 2* 40 (2013): 223–45.

7. I find the use of the noun *icon* odd, given that the adjectival "iconic" would do the work as well without doing so much violence to the language. How would one talk about a Muslim's relation with Muhammad, on Mahmood's terms? Would one say the Muslim is icon to Muhammad or icon with Muhammad. At the risk of being pedantic, I simply don't see the gain in the adjectival sacrifice. Is it a verbal noun? How would it be used?

8. See, for instance, Amelie Blom, "The 2006 Anti-'Danish Cartoons' Riot in Lahore: Outrage and the Emotional Landscape of Pakistani Politics," *Samaj: South Asia Multi-Disciplinary Journal* 2 (2008), http://samaj.revues. org/1652, accessed June 4, 2013.

9. On the terms of Mahmood's argument regarding agency, abjection, and subjectivation it might be worth asking what ought to prevent someone from asking whether choosing to live with religious pain might not be a form of producing agency and a condition of subject formation.

10. Vali Nasr, *The Shia Revival: How Conflicts within Islam Will Shape the Future* (New York: Norton, 2006), 97.

11. On varying and intersecting impulses on the question, see Barbara Metcalfe, "Travelers' Tales in the Tablighi Jamaat," *Annals of the American Academy* 588 (July 2003): 138.

12. Gauri Viswanathan, *Outside the Fold: Conversion, Belief, and Modernity* (Princeton, NJ: Princeton University Press, 1998), 13.

13. Viswanathan, *Outside the Fold*, 13.

14. Viswanathan, *Outside the Fold*, 251.

15. Viswanathan, *Outside the Fold*, 251.

16. *The Bhagvat-Geeta or Dialogues of Kreeshna and Arjoon, in Eighteen Lectures with Notes*, trans. Charles Wilkins (London: Printed for C. Nourse, 1785), 13.

17. Nicholas B. Dirks, *Castes of Mind: Colonialism and the Making of Modern India* (Princeton, NJ: Princeton University Press, 2001); Shabnum Tejani, *Indian Secularism: A Social and Intellectual History, 1890–1950* (Bloomington: Indiana University Press, 2008); and Bernard Cohn, *Colonialism and Its Forms of Knowledge: The British in India* (Princeton, NJ: Princeton University Press, 1996).

18. *The Bhagvat-Geeta or Dialogues of Kreeshna and Arjoon, in Eighteen Lectures with Notes*, 12.

19. Cohn, *Colonialism and Its Forms of Knowledge*, 60.

20. Sara Suleri, *The Rhetoric of English Rule in India* (Chicago: University of Chicago Press, 1992); Betsy Bolton, "Imperial Sensibilities, Colonial Ambivalence: Edmund Burke and Frances Burney," *English Literary History* 72.4 (2005): 871–99.

21. The code was subsequently revised by Sir Barnes Peacock, the first chief justice of the Calcutta High Court.

22. All quotations from the Indian Penal Code are taken from J. O'Kinealy, B.C.S., "Chapter XV (Of Offences Relating to Religion)," *The Indian Penal Code [Act XLV. Of 1860] And Other Laws of and Acts Of Parliament Relating to the Criminal Courts of India, With Notes, Containing the Rulings of the Nizamut Adawlut on Points of Procedure and Decisions of the High Court of Calcutta* (Calcutta: Messsrs. Thackeray, Spink and Co., 1869), 138–39; hereafter cited in the text as *IPC*. The Pakistani amendments are quoted from "Chapter XV (Of Offences Relating to Religion)" of the *Pakistan Penal Code [Act XLV of 1860]*, http://www.pakistani.org/pakistan/legislation/1860/actXLVof1860.html, accessed August 20, 2011. The five Pakistani amendments are also quoted in their entirety in note 8, Osama Siddique and Zahra Hayat, "Unholy Speech and Holy Laws: Blasphemy Laws in Pakistan—Controversial Origins, Design Defects, and Free Speech Implication," *Minnesota Journal of International Law* 17.2 (2008): 303–86, 311.

23. For a short account of the history of the pamphlet, see Deepak Mehta, "Words That Wound: Archiving Hate in the Making of Hindu-Indian and Muslim-Pakistani Publics in Bombay," in *Beyond Crisis: Re-evaluating Pakistan*, ed. Naveeda Khan (New Delhi: Routledge, 2010), 326.

24. For some critical analyses of these tendencies, see Chetan Bhatt, "The Fetish of the Margins: Religious Absolutism, Anti-Racism and Postcolonial Silence," *New Formations* 59 (2006): 98–115; Kenan Malik, *From Fatwa to Jihad: The Rushdie Affair and Its Aftermath* (New York: Melville House, 2010). For Dahl's reaction see Rachel Donadio, "Salman Rushdie: Fighting Words on a Knighthood," *New York Times*, July 4, 2007.

25. Osama Siddique and Zahra Hayat, "Unholy Speech and Holy Laws: Blasphemy Laws in Pakistan—Controversial Origins, Design Defects, and Free Speech Implication." In its entirety 295-B reads: Defiling, etc., of Holy Qur'an: "Whoever willfully defiles, damages, or desecrates a copy of the Holy Qur'an or of an extract therefrom or uses it in any derogatory manner or for any unlawful purpose shall be punishable with imprisonment for life" (PPC).

26. The history of the addition of the death penalty is fascinating in its own right as it attests to the growing power of the conservative lobby. Aasia Bibi, whose case prompted political interventions that led to the assassinations of the governor of Punjab, Salman Taseer, and the Christian federal minister, Shahbaz Bhatti, was charged under 295-C. I shall return to her case in the next section.

27. The true precariousness of the status of minorities revealed itself when Bhutto's government introduced the second amendment to the constitution,

declaring Ahmadis non-Muslims, in 1974. Although the usual account, figuring the Bhutto government's adoption of the amendment as a response to pressure from the Jamaat-i-Islami party, mirrors American narratives of hapless Democrats, hobbled by a powerful Right, it underplays (as in the American case) the temptations of triangulation. It is unclear why an authoritarian leader who refused to accept the outcome of a democratic election, thereby enabling a civil war, and who subsequently had no trouble turning against his own party members and squashing the demands of trade unions would feel the need to countenance *these* demands. Bhutto's self-presentation as the true representative of the people is radically undermined by the authoritarian nature of his regime and, foundationally, by his complicity with the military and the religious Right in the suppression of the democratic aspirations of the East Pakistanis.

The acceptance of the demands of the anti-Ahmaddiya campaigners is both an index of the nation's anxieties in those years and a part of the larger matrix of Bhutto's consolidation of his own power. Thus the introduction of the amendment and the hosting of the OIC summit also appear to be an attempt to occlude the atrocities against fellow Muslims in the newly formed Bangladesh and Bhutto's complicity in that loss. What was enacted was a recourse to a stabilized Islamic identity that could enable a forgetting of the atrocities committed against fellow Muslims in the former East Pakistan, atrocities, moreover, in which the Jamaat-i-Islami was known to have colluded with the army. In 1974 the Muslim World League also declared Ahmadis non-Muslims.

28. See, for instance, Khalid B. Sayeed, "The Jama'at-i-Islami Movement in Pakistan" *Pacific Affairs* 30.1 (March 1957): 59–68. Osama Siddique and Zahra Hayat remark the objection of the minorities to the Objectives resolution as well, see note 300, "Unholy Speech and Holy Laws: Blasphemy Laws in Pakistan—Controversial Origins, Design Defects, and Free Speech Implication," 368.

For a discussion of the implications of the debates at the Constituent Assembly for the consolidation of the nation-state, see Saadia Toor, *The State of Islam: Culture and Cold War Politics in Pakistan* (London: Pluto Press, 2011), especially chapter 2. For readings of the status of religion in the Pakistani Constitution, see Fazlur Rahman, "Islam and the Constitutional Problem of Pakistan," *Studia Islamica* 32 (1975): 275–87; and "Islam and the New Constitution of Pakistan," *Journal of Asian and African Studies* 8.3–4 (1973): 190–204.

29. Constitution of Pakistan (Second Amendment) Act 1974, art. 3, http://www.pakistani.org/pakistan/constitution/amendments/2amendment.html, accessed August 20, 2011.

30. Ayesha Jalal, *Self and Sovereignty: Individual and Community in South Asian Islam since 1850* (London: Routledge, 2000); Antonio R. Gualtieri, *Conscience and Coercion: Ahmadi Muslims and Orthodoxy in Pakistan* (Montreal: Guernica, 1989). See also Asad Ahmed, "The Paradoxes of Ahmadiyya Identity: Legal Appropriation of Muslim-ness and the Construction of Ahmadiyya Difference," in *Beyond Crisis: Re-evaluating Pakistan,*

ed. Naveeda Khan (New Delhi: Routledge, 2010), 273–314; Spencer Lavan, *The Ahmadiyyah Movement: A History and Perspective* (Delhi: Manohar Book Service, 1974).

31. The Shia, who are numerically a minority, are not yet a *legal* minority in the country.

32. Significantly, they are happy to use this media representation on their own website. "Shahi Imam Decries Nawaz Sharif's Statement on Ahamadiyas," *Ahrar News,* http://archives.dawn.com/archives/36323, accessed August 29, 2011. See also "Sharif's Statement on Ahmadis Angers Clerics," June 7, 2010, archived on The Persecution.org., http://www.thepersecution.org/news/10/eto607.html, accessed August 29, 2011; "PML-N Defends Nawaz's Remarks about Ahmadis," June 10, 2010, http://archives.dawn.com/archives/36323, accessed August 29, 2011.

33. Gualtieri, *Conscience and Coercion,* 102.

34. On "posing," see also Gualtieri, *Conscience and Coercion,* 30–34.

35. *Qadianis* is a derogatory term for Ahmadis. Sayyid Abu'l A'la Mawdudi, *The Qadiani Problem* (Lahore: Islamic Publications, 1979).

36. Mawdudi, *The Qadiani Problem,* 18.

37. Muhammad Iqbal, "Qadianis and Orthodox Muslims," and "Reply to the Questions Raised by Pandit J. L. Nehru," in *Speeches and Statements of Iqbal,* comp. A. R. Tariq (Lahore: Ghulam Ali & Sons, 1973), 91–104, 109–39. See also in the same volume "Rejoinder to the 'Light'" (99–104) and "Letter to the 'Statesman'" (104–8). "Qadianism and Orthodox Muslims" hereafter cited in the text as *QM*; "Reply to the Questions Raised by Pandit J. L. Nehru"/"Islam and Ahmadism," cited as *RQ.* For a subtle reading of the complexity of Iqal's positions, see Naveeda Khan, *Muslim Becoming: Aspiration and Skepticism in Pakistan* (Durham, NC: Duke University Press, 2012).

38. Jalal, *Self and Sovereignty.* See particularly the chapters "Contested Sovereignty in the Punjab: The Interplay of Formal and Informal Politics," 262–319; and "Between Region and Nation: The Missing Centre," 320–85.

39. My view grants more importance to Iqbal's insistence on Muhammad as the seal of the prophets than does Khan. See Khan, *Muslim Becoming,* 92.

40. Aamir Mufti, *Enlightenment in the Colony: The Jewish Question and the Crisis of Postcolonial Culture* (Princeton, NJ: Princeton University Press, 2007), 136.

41. Jalal, *Self and Sovereignty,* 369.

42. Jalal, *Self and Sovereignty,* 356.

43. Jalal, *Self and Sovereignty,* 369.

44. On some of the ironies of the current situation of Ahmadis in relation to concepts of orthopraxy and orthodoxy, see Gualtieri, *Conscience and Coercion,* 102–7.

45. Jawaharlal Nehru, "The Solidarity of Islam," in *Jawaharlal Nehru on Communalism,* ed. Nand Lal Gupta (Delhi: Hope India Publications, 2006), 84–87.

46. On the Jewish Question in relation to minority and secularism in South Asia, see Aamir Mufti, "Secularism and Minority: Elements of a Critique," *Social Text* 45 (1995): 75–96.

47. Mufti, *Enlightenment in the Colony,* 132. The current struggles surrounding religion in Pakistan, sometimes refer to the "Arabization" of Pakistani culture, where the word is usually a code for the rise of right-wing religious actors and their attempts to reshape society by de-vernacularizing it. As a term of critique, "Arabization" must be understood within the history of Urdu and regional progressive thought, because it attempts to retain a social connection with customary social forms, conceived in terms of Indic culture.

48. That it has become a sort of informal national test is evident from Imran Khan's statement that he will not contest the amendment regarding the Ahmadis in the days leading to the 2013 Pakistani elections. Khan's statement: http://www.youtube.com/watch?v=fHw1_nL7Dew and http://www.youtube.com/watch?v=GUe9rit9vxU. Faiza Rahman, "1973 Constitution: Imran Opposes Repeal of Ahmadi Laws," *Express Tribune,* May 3, 2013, http://tribune.com.pk/story/543862/1973–constitution-imran-opposes-repeal-of-ahmadi-laws/. See also the press release, dated May 1, 2013, on the Tehreek-i-Insaf website "PTI Denies Seeking Ahmadis Support in Polls." An excerpt from the release: "Khan said he had an absolute belief in the finality of Prophet Muhammad PBUH. Anyone claiming prophethood after him is a liar. This belief of mine is the same at the entire Muslim ummah. PTI totally subscribes to the article in the Constitution of the Islamic Republic of Pakistan on Qadianis." http://www.insaf.pk/News/tabid/60/articleType/ArticleView/articleId/15820/PTI-denies-seeking-Ahmadis-support-in-polls.aspx., accessed June 6, 2013.

49. Talal Asad, *Genealogies of Religion: Discipline and Reasons of Power in Christianity and Islam* (Baltimore, MD: Johns Hopkins University Press, 1993), 210.

50. Talal Asad, "Free Speech, Blasphemy, and Secular Criticism," in Asad et al., *Is Critique Secular?,* 36. Edward Said, *The World, the Text, and the Critic* (Cambridge, MA: Harvard University Press, 1983).

51. Asad, *Genealogies of Religion,* 293.

52. It is worth asking whether in Shia theocratic Iran Shia thought and practice are both Islamic and *state* orthodoxy? If so, how would the example work within the broader antinomies of "Islamic orthodoxy"/religious criticism and Western intellectual thought/liberalism/state power?

53. For a useful history of the Jihadi groups, see Ayesha Jalal, *Partisans of Allah: Jihad in South Asia* (Cambridge, MA: Harvard University Press, 2008).

54. See also the website thepersecution.org. I'm grateful to Biju Matthew to pointing out the tones of Bollywood gangsterism in the pamphlet.

55. I am using "writer" in the singular here for economy and convenience, but its declared association with a larger group might equally easily indicate a more corporate hand.

56. As the groups desire to connect with, and draw on the authority of, groups like the Taliban and the Lashkar-Jhangvi makes clear, the extrajudicial persecution that is also now part of the Pakistani juridical order cannot be separated from the Cold War context in which the Zia regime

was bankrolled by the United States, as Pakistan became an ally in the war in Afghanistan. As is well known, in the process of fighting various proxy wars (America's) as well as Pakistan's own against India, the regime also created a series of militias. Many of these groups have had their own religio-political agendas for almost a quarter of a century now. The power of these groups suggests that the crisis of the postcolonial state needs to be theorized in terms of both military usurpation of constitutional and judicial processes and of paramilitary state-complicit but increasingly state-hostile groups. The oscillation between complicity and hostility itself requires further documentation and analysis. The hostility appears to emanate from the proximity to segments of the military, itself increasingly fissured, and the fact that such proximity does not guarantee the militias recognition at the political table. These paramilitary groups are also paralegal and yet secure enough, and thus fully juridical, to be able to engage in the process of declaring minorities such as the Ahmadis and Shias non-Muslim. This history of collusion is unintelligible without a recognition of the role of the United States in enabling the institutions and actors in Pakistan most committed to the most reactionary brands of modern Islam in the war against the global Left and communism. The current normativity of this persecution must be seen as an effect of global and local convergences. Yet, as evinced by the resistance* of political agents ranging from human rights activists to the members of the government willing to challenge the laws and a cleric such as Javed Ahmed Ghamidi, combined with initiatives on the ground such as those launched after the murders of the governor of Punjab, Salman Taseer, and the only Christian in the federal cabinet, Shahbaz Bhatti, the normative is also a site of contest and resistance. (*The word *resistance* here seems important precisely because the more theoretically palatable, and less binary, *negotiation* seems not to capture the intensity of the polarization around the attempt to normalize these laws and also risks suggesting the necessity of some mode of acceptance of the way these laws frame minorities.)

57. Shahid Alam, "A Political Murder or War," *Counterpunch*, Weekend Edition, January 15–16, 2011, http://www.counterpunch.org/2011/01/14/a-political-murder-or-war, accessed September 15, 2011.

58. Alam, "A Political Murder or War."

59. Alam, "A Political Murder or War."

60. Alam, "A Political Murder or War."

61. See Linda Walbridge's very important account of the fate of Christians under the Blasphemy law(s), *The Christians of Pakistan: The Passion of Bishop John Joseph* (New York: Routledge, 2009), ix, 89-90.

62. Michel Foucault, "What Is an Author?," trans. Josué V. Harari, in *The Foucault Reader*, 101–20.

63. My terms here are drawn from Judith Butler, *Precarious Life: The Powers of Mourning and Violence* (London: Verso, 2004).

64. Asiya Nasir, "Speech in Parliament following Shahbaz Bhatti's murder," "Dedicated to Shaheed Shahbaz Bhatti," http://www.youtube.com/watch?v=cT4oGIWXfQ4, accessed August 10, 2011.

65. Faiz Ahmad Faiz, "Ham jo tārīk rāho<u>n</u> me<u>n</u> māre ga'e," *Nuskha hā-yi vafā* (Lahore: Maktabah-i Kārvā<u>n</u>, 1984), 262–64.

66. Nasir, "Speech."

67. It is worth pointing out that this claim has ostensibly non-"extremist" proponents. The arch-Orientalist, Muhammad Asad, who made little distinction between the stillness of the Arab desert and the Arab mind in his conversion narrative, *The Road to Mecca*, claimed quite remarkably, in the immediate aftermath of Independence, that only a good Muslim could be a good Pakistani. Asad was, of course, prominent in the Pakistan government before he decamped to Spain—as if because monumentally disappointed by the present of which he had been a fervent proponent, he could only find comfort in the shade of Al-Andalus. He was invited back by Zia-ul-Haq. It is worth wondering why a man who could be disappointed by the Zionism of the Jews in Palestine, because of the indifference to the Arabs it encoded, could not see the consequences of such an assertion for the new minorities in the new state carved out for India's Muslims. See my "Itineraries of Conversion: Judaic Paths to a Muslim Pakistan," in Khan, *Beyond Crisis*, 344–69.

68. Nasir, "Speech."

69. Nasir, "Speech." "Shān me<u>n</u> gustā<u>kh</u>ī" is very difficult to translate. "Shān" is grandeur and glory, and *gustaaqi* is insolence and rudeness but very much with the connotation of an insult to a social superior. Literally, it means "insolence in grandeur," but more broadly it means insolence or insult against someone above one in a hierarchy. Its connotation is of offense against someone immeasurably superior, and the phrase partakes fully of worldly structures of discrimination and inequality.

70. Sahir Ludhianvi, "<u>Kh</u>ūn phir <u>kh</u>ūn hai," in *Ā'o ke ko'ī khvāb bune<u>n</u>* (Bombay: Alavi Book Depot, 1971), 24–26. It might be interesting to note that this poem of Ludhianvi's was written on the occasion of Patrice Lumumba's assassination and that it has for its epigraph Nehru's famous declaration: "Ek maqtūl Lumumba ek zindah Lumumba se kahī<u>n</u> zīadah tāqatvar hotā hai" (A slain Lumumba is much more powerful than a living one).

71. *Burning Alive*, dir. Leonard D'Souza and Anjum James Paul, Youtube, http://www.youtube.com/watch?v=R8VGOakfH8 (part 1) and http://www.youtube.com/watch?v=BQoUofhQeYQ (part 2), accessed Aug 10, 2011. The documentary is narrated in Urdu with a little text (the quotation from the Bible and the title) in English. I have been in touch with Anjum James Paul regarding its availability here. According to Paul (who is from the same village as Shahbaz Bhatti and was his classmate), two of the makers of the documentary, Leonard Dsouza and Nosheen Dsouza, have left the country after being attacked for making it (email correspondence, October 2011).

72. *Burning Alive*.

73. *Burning Alive*.

74. *Burning Alive*.

75. Nasir, "Speech."

76. Faiz, "Ham jo tārīk rāho<u>n</u> me<u>n</u> māre ga'e," 262–64.

77. Ludhianvi, "<u>Kh</u>ūn phir <u>kh</u>ūn hai."

78. Faiz, "Lahū ka surāgh," *Nus<u>kh</u>a hā-e vafā*, 395–96.

79.. Butler, *Precarious Life*. On ongoing trauma, see Anthony Bogues, *Empire of Liberty: Power, Desire, and Freedom* (Lebanon, NH: Dartmouth College Press, 2010), 38–65.

80. Nasir, "Speech."

81. Nasir, "Speech."

82. "Arguments of the Christians (Joint Christian Board)," in *The Partition of the Punjab 1947: A Compilation of Official Documents,* vol. 2, ed. Mian Muhmamad Sadullah et al. (Lahore: National Documentation Centre, 1983), 225.

83. "Arguments of the Christians (Joint Christian Board)," 225.

84. "Arguments of the Christians (Joint Christian Board)," 235.

85. It is significant that the town of Gojra is not far from "Toba Tek Singh," the name of which Saadat Hassan Manto used in his devastating, and oft-translated, story about Partition.

86. Nasir, "Speech." I am tempted to translate "hamen̲ sāth le līya," which I have rendered as "you gathered us with you," as "took us into the fold" but do not want to exaggerate the religious aspect of that phrase, which has such historical resonance in this context.

87. Nasir, "Speech."

88. Nasir. "Speech."

89. Mufti, *Enlightenment in the Colony*, 262.

CHAPTER 5

1. Carl Schmitt, *Political Theology: Four Chapters on the Concept of Sovereignty,* trans. George Schwab (Chicago: University of Chicago Press, 1985), 36.

2. Seyyid Qutb, *Milestones* (Damascus, Dar al-Ilm). The edition is not dated.

3. For a subtle discussion of the question of sovereignty in Syed Qutb, see Ronald A. T. Judy, "Sayyid Qutb's fiqh al-waqi'I, or New Realist Science," *boundary 2* 31.2 (2004): 113–48. See also William E. Shepard, *Sayyid Qutb and Islamic Activism: A Translation and Critical Analysis of Social Justice in Islam* (New York: E. J. Brill, 1996).

4. For an example, see Wendy Brown, *Regulating Aversion: Tolerance in the Age of Identity and Empire* (Princeton, NJ: Princeton University Press, 2006), 7.

5. Tim Mitchell, "McJihad: Islam in the U.S. Global Order," *Social Text* 20.4 (Winter 2002): 1–18.

6. Mohammed Hanif's *A Case of Exploding Mangoes* (New York: Knopf, 2008); hereafter cited in the text as *CM*.

7. Rene Wellek, "The Concept of the Baroque in Literary Scholarship," *Journal of Aesthetic and Art Criticism* 3.2 (December 1946): 77–109; Mario Praz, "The Flaming Heart: Richard Crashaw and the the Baroque," in *The Flaming Heart: Essays on Crashaw, Machiavelli, and Other Studies in the Relations between Italian and English Literature from Chaucer to T. S. Eliot* (New York: Doubleday, 1958); Jose Antonio Maravall, *Culture of*

the Baroque: Analysis of a Historical Structure (Minneapolis: University of Minnesota Press, 1986); Lois Parkinson Zamora and Monika Kaup, eds., *Baroque New Worlds: Representation, Transculturation, Counterconquest* (Durham, NC: Duke University Press); Heinrich Wölfflin, *Renaissance and Baroque,* trans. Kathrin Simon (Ithaca: Cornell University Press, 1964), and *Principles of Art History: The Problem of the Development of Style in Late Art,* trans. M. D. Hottinger (New York: Dover, 1950).

8. Wölfllin, *Renaissance and Baroque.*

9. Wellek, "The Concept of the Baroque in Literary Scholarship."

10. T. J. Clark, *The Painting of Modern Life: Paris in the Art of Manet and His Followers* (Princeton, NJ: Princeton University Press, 1984), xxv.

11. Zamora and Kaup's *Baroque New Worlds* is a magnificent collection, and Zamora's *The Inordinate Eye* is inspiring in its foregrounding of the importance of reading visual and verbal forms together. See Lois Parkinson Zamora, *The Inordinate Eye: New World Baroque and Latin American Fiction* (Chicago: University of Chicago Press, 2006). See also the *PMLA* issue 124.1 (2009) for a collection of essays on Baroque and neo-Baroque.

12. See Mitchell, "McJihad: Islam in the U.S. Global Order."

13. John Guillory, "The Sokal Affair and the History of Criticism," *Critical Inquiry* 28.2 (Winter 2002): 470–508.

14. See, for instance, Chalmers Johnson, "The Largest Covert Operation in History," *History News Network*, June 3, 2009, http://hnn.us/articles/1491.html, accessed June 14, 2013. For a history of the CIA presence in the region, see Steve Coll, *Ghost Wars: The Secret History of the CIA, Afghanistan, and Bin Laden from the Soviet Invasion to September 10, 2001* (New York: Penguin Books, 2004).

15. Mohammed Hanif, *Our Lady of Alice Bhatti* (Noida: Random House, 2011); hereafter cited in the text as *AB.*

16. On Pakistani painting, see, for instance, Akbar Naqvi, *Painting and Sculpture in Pakistan, 1947–1997* (Karachi: Oxford University Press, 1998); Marcella Nesom Sirhandi, *Contemporary Painting in Pakistan* (Lahore: Ferozsons, 1992); Salima Hashmi, *Hanging Fire: Contemporary Art from Pakistan* (New York: Asia Society, 2009); Virgina Whiles, *Art and Polemic in Pakistan: Cultural Politics and Tradition in Contemporary Miniature Painting* (London: I. B. Tauris, 2010). Although Iftikhar Dadi does not call his book a study of Pakistani painting, the contemporary painters it focuses on are either located in Pakistan or members of the Pakistani diaspora: see *Modernism and the Art of Muslim South Asia* (Chapel Hill: University of North Carolina Press, 2010).

17. Conversation with painter, December 28, 2011.

18. A *marsiya* is a long martyrological poem with elaborate descriptions of the incidents at Karbala. It can more generally mean an elegy but becomes martyrological through its subject matter. See C. M. Naim, "The Art of the Urdu Marsiya," in *Urdu Texts and Contexts: The Selected Essays of C. M. Naim* (New Delhi: Permanent Black, 2004), 1–18.

19. Fayes T. Kantawala, "Cry, the Beloved Country," *Friday Times* 25.3 (March 1–7, 2013), http://www.thefridaytimes.com/beta3/tft/article.

php?issue=20130301&page=13, accessed March 20, 2013; and "Mourning Assembly," *Friday Times* 24.42 (November 30–December 6, 2012), http://www.thefridaytimes.com/beta3/tft/article.php?issue=20121130&page=13, accessed March 20, 2013.

20. Hamid Dabashi, *Shi'ism: A Religion of Protest* (Cambridge, MA: Belknap Press, 2011).

21. See Asma Jahangir and Hina Jilani, *The Hudood Ordinances: A Divine Sanction. A Research Study of the Hudood Ordinances and Their Effect on the Disadvantaged Sections of Pakistan* (Lahore: Rhotas, 1990).

22. Georg Lukacs, "Tolstoy and the Development of Realism," in *Studies in European Realism* (New York: Grosset and Dunlap, 1964), 142–43; the edition does not specify a translator, although it has an introduction by Alfred Kazin.

23. There is work to be done on the class politics of the starch and fabric in Pakistan. For, on the one hand, the turn to vernacular, local dress under Bhutto was turn away from colonialism, class is now marked by the condition of cotton *shalwar kameezes* worn by both elite men and women. The white cotton *shalwar-kameez* favored by upper-class men and politicians is itself a sign of privilege. Starch quickly becomes limp in the heat or crumples very quickly in just about any other circumstances. Its absence may indicate the lack of wherewithal required for exceptional amounts of maintenance and also for the greater number of clothes required to stay in such a condition of pristineness. Mixed fabrics can be more convenient for working-class and poor men and women but are also signs of a lower status.

24. Dadi, *Modernism and the Art of Muslim South Asia*, 227. See also Dadi's discussion of the feminist artist Naiza Khan's work in the chapter, "Emergence of the Public Self: Rasheed Araeen and Naiza Khan."

25. Faiz, *Nuskha hā-e vafā* (Lahore: Maktabah-e Kārvān, 1984), 345–46.

26. On the importance of cultural production to politics in Pakistan, see Saadia Toor, *The State of Islam: Culture and Cold War Politics in Pakistan* (London: Pluto Press, 2011).

27. Ayesha Siddiqa, *Military Inc.: Inside Pakistan's Military Economy* (London: Pluto Press, 2007); also, for instance, on Pakistan as a praetorian state, "The Mirage of Middle-Class Revolution" (lecture), December 2011, http://ayeshasiddiqa.blogspot.com, accessed June 4, 2013. Zia Mian and Pervez Hoodhbhoy, "Pakistan, the Army and the Conflict Within," *MERIP: Middle East Research and Information Project*, July 12, 2011, http://www.merip.org/mero/mero071211, accessed June 4, 2013; Nadeem Aslam, *The Wasted Vigil* (New York: Knopf, 2008).

28. Fredric Jameson, "Cognitive Mapping," in *Marxism and the Interpretation of Culture*, ed. Nelson Grossberg and Cary Nelson (Chicago: University of Illinois Press, 1988), 347–57; and *The Geopolitical Aesthetic: Cinema and Space in the World System* (Bloomington: Indiana University Press, 1995).

29 Srinivas Aravamudan, *Guru English: South Asian Religion in a Cosmopolitan Language* (Princeton, NJ: Princeton University Press, 2006), 22, ebook.

30. Laal, *"Umeed-e-Sahar,"* Youtube, http://www.youtube.com/watch?v=G8gJcwh4k88, accessed June 2012.

31. Saadat Hassan Manto, "Toba Tek Singh," in *Kingdom's End: Selected Stories,* trans. Khalid Hasan (New Delhi: Penguin Books, 2007), 9–17.

32. Hanif has become an important commentator on affairs in Pakistan. On the 2013 elections: "Pakistan Elections: How Nawaz Sharif Beat Imran Khan and What Happens Next," *Guardian,* May 13, 2013, http://www.guardian.co.uk/profile/mohammed-hanif, accessed June 7, 2013. On Salman Taseer's murder: "Pakistan Viewpoint: Who Is to Blame for Taseer's Death?," BBC, January 6, 2011, http://www.bbc.co.uk/news/world-south-asia-12129770, accessed June 7, 2013. On blasphemy in Pakistan: "How to Commit Blasphemy in Pakistan," *Guardian,* September 5, 2012, http://www.guardian.co.uk/world/2012/sep/05/pakistans-blasphemy-laws-colossal-absurdity, accessed June 7, 2013. On the floods of 2010: "Pakistan Victims 'Have No Concept of Terrorism,'" BBC, August 21, 2010, http://news.bbc.co.uk/2/hi/programmes/from_our_own_correspondent/8931886.stm, accessed June 7, 2013.

33. Saadat Hasan Manto, *Phundne* (Lahore: Maktabah-e Jadīd, 1955), 8. Hanif says as much regarding the question of love in an NPR interview. See "Mohammed Hanif on Secres and Lies in Pakistan," *NPR,* May 24, 2012, http://www.npr.org/2012/05/24/153303834/mohammed-hanif-on-secrets-and-lies-in-pakistan, accessed June 4, 2013.

34. See "How Injury Travels," particularly the third section of the chapter and the discussion of the boundary commission hearings.

35. Paul Amar, "Turning the Gendered Politics of the Security State Inside Out?," *International Feminist Journal of Politics* 13.3 (September 2011): 299–328.

36. Mulk Raj Anand, *The Untouchable* (London: Penguin Books, 1940), 64.

37. Anand, *The Untouchable,* 65.

38. Fazlur Rahman, "Islam and the Constitutional Problem of Pakistan," *Studia Islamica* 32 (1970): 275–87.

39. Qutb, *Milestones*; Shepard, *Sayyid Qutb and Islamic Activism,* xxv, xl–xli.

CHAPTER 6

1. The poem appears under the title "Wa-yabqā wajhu rabbika," in Faiz, *Nuskha hā-e vafā,* 655–56, from which, in my copy, the lines referring to al-Hallaj's declaration are missing. As what appears to be self-censorship (since the poem does not appear to have been formally banned) this is quite ineffectual because there are so many extant and accessible performances—both sung and recited, including by Faiz himself. (I am grateful to Aamir Mufti for talking to me about the instability of the text across various editions—email correspondence, September 30, 2013). I am grateful to Ali Mir for telling me the story of the performance as related to him by the composer and actor Arshad Mahmood, who was at the performance. For an account of the performance, see also Reginald Massey, "Iqbal Bano: Renowned Pakistani Singer Dies," *Guardian,* May 10, 2009, http://www.theguardian.com/music/2009/may/11/iqbal-bano-obituary, accessed September 30, 2013; and M. Ilyas Khan, "Pakistani Singer

Iqbal Bano Dies," *BBC News*, April 22, 2009, http://news.bbc.co.uk/2/hi/south_asia/8011930.stm, accessed September 30, 2013. The complete poem without the Arabic title and with the more popular title can be found in *O City of Lights: Faiz Ahmed Faiz: Selected Poetry and Biographical Notes,* ed. Khalid Hasan, trans. Khalid Hasan and Daud Kamal (Karachi: Oxford University Press, 2006), 231–33. I have adapted the translation of the title from Abdullah Yusuf Ali's translation of the Qur'an. "*Súra Ar-Rahmán,*" in *Qur'an,* trans. Abdullah Yusuf Ali (New York: Tahrike Tarsile Qur'an, 2012), 55, 27. For a complete recitation of the poem, sans title, see, for instance, *Faiz: Poet in Troubled Times,* dir. Faris Kermani (London: Penumbra Productions, 1986), http://www.youtube.com/watch?v=ps4u_tqefRA, accessed September 25, 2013; Iqbal Bano, "A Tribute to Faiz" (EMI Records, 1988), cassette.

2. Farzana Sheikh, "Will Sufi Islam Save Pakistan," in *Under the Drones: Modern Lives in the Afghanistan-Pakistan Borderlands,* ed. Shahzad Bashir and Robert D. Crewe (Cambridge, MA: Harvard University Press, 2012)

3. On the travails of Sufism in Orientalist, Wahhabi, and media constructions, see Carl Ernst, "Ideological and Technological Transformations of Contemporary Sufism," in *Medium, Metaphor, and Method,* ed. miriam cooke and Bruce B. Lawrence (Chapel Hill: University of North Carolina Press, 2005). See also Ernst's "Between Orientalism and Fundamentalism: Problematizing the Teaching of Sufism," in *Teaching Islam,* ed. Brannon Wheeler (Oxford: Oxford University Press, 2002), 108–23; and Scott Kugle, *Sufis and Saints' Bodies: Mysticism, Corporeality, and Sacred Power in Islam* (Chapel Hill: University of North Carolina Press, 2007).

4. Cheryl Benard, *Civil-Democratic Islam: Partners, Resources, and Strategies* (RAND, 2003), Rand Corporation Report, http://www.rand.org/content/dam/rand/pubs/monograph_reports/2005/MR1716.sum.pdf, accessed March 20, 2013.

5. Aslam is himself perhaps an exemplary product of this history. His very presence in England is a result of his communist father's flight to England during Zia's persecution of the Left. Given his status as a member of the Pakistani diaspora in Britain, it is perhaps unsurprising that he is also preoccupied with crises of Muslim identity.

6. M. M. Bakhtin, "Forms of Time and of the Chronotope in the Novel: Notes toward a Historical Poetics," in *Narrative Dynamics: Essays on Time, Plot, Closure, and Frames,* ed. Brian Richardson (Columbus: Ohio State University Press, 2002), 23.

7. Annemarie Schimmel, *As Through a Veil: Mystical Poetry in Islam* (New York: Columbia University Press, 1982), 47. See also Qurratulain Hyder's introduction to her own translation of *Pat jhar kī āvāz* (The Sound of Falling Leaves) in which she calls her practice "a throwback to the strong Sufi-secular undercurrent and tradition of Persian and Urdu literature." Qurratulain Hyder, *The Sound of Falling Leaves,* trans. Qurratulain Hyder (New Delhi: Sahitya Academy, 1997), v; Qurratulain Hyder, *Pat jhar kī āvāz* (New Delhi: Maktabah-e Jāma, 1970).

8. Nadeem Aslam, *Maps for Lost Lovers* (New York: Knopf, 2005); hereafter cited in the text as *ML*. On the importance of pain and death in the classical Persian poetic Sufi tradition, see Schimmel, *As Through a Veil,* 70–72. On the

complicated relationship with the body in Sufi hagiography, see Shahzad Bashir, *Sufi Bodies: Religion and Society in Medieval Islam* (New York: Columbia University Press, 2011).

9. Qurratulain Hyder, *Āg kā daryā* (Lahore: Maktabah-e Jadīd, 1963).

10. Nadeem Aslam, *The Wasted Vigil* (New York: Knopf, 2008); hereafter cited in the text as *WV*.

11. Qurrutulain Hyder, *River of Fire* (new York: New Directions Books, 1998), 426.

12. Gayatri Spivak, "Terror: A Speech after 9–11," *boundary* 2 31.2 (Summer 2004): 81–111.

13. On Faiz and the Sufis, see the wonderful chapter "Faiz Ahmed Faiz: Towards a Lyric History of India," in Aamir Mufti, *Enlightenment in the Colony: The Jewish Question and the Crisis of Postcolonial Culture* (Princeton, NJ: Princeton University Press, 2007).

14. Nadeem Aslam, *Season of the Rainbirds* (London: Faber and Faber, 1993).

15. The weather, as I suggested in chapter 3, is a recurrent symbol of immigrant displacement. Most responses tend to be close to the sentiment in *The Satanic Verses* that London needs tropicalization.

16. Schimmel, *As Through a Veil*, 105.

17. Tim Mitchell, "McJihad: Islam in the U.S. Global Order" *Social Text* 73, 20.4 (Winter 2002): 1–18.

18. I am tempted to call this mystical thought, but on the problems of calling such thought mystical, see Carl Ernst's "Between Orientalism and Fundamentalism: Problematizing the Teaching of Sufism." Although perhaps what needs to be conceptualized and developed is the ecstatic element across a variety of devotional practices and prayer.

19. Gayatri Spivak, "Can the Subaltern Speak," in *Marxism and the Interpretation of Cultures*, ed. Cary Nelson and Lawrence Grossberg (Urbana: University of Illinois Press, 1988), 217.

20. For an exemplary performance of the impasse, see Lila Abu-Lughod, "Seductions of the 'Honor Crime,'" *differences* 22.1 (2011): 17–63.

21. Theodor Adorno, "On Lyric Poetry and Society" in *Notes to Literature vol. 1*, trans. Shierry Weber Nicholson (New York: Columbia University Press, 1958), 40.

22. Pankaj Mishra, "From a Mansion Near Tora Bora," *New York Review of Books*, October 23, 2008. Michael Ondaatje, *The English Patient* (New York: Vintage International, 1992), 13.

23. Boris Pasternak, *Dr. Zhivago*, trans. Richard Pevear and Larissa Volokonsky (New York: Vintage International, 2011), rpt. ed.

24. Jorge Luis Borges, "Library of Babel," in *Collected Fictions*, trans. Andrew Hurley (New York: Penguin Books, 1998).

25. Graham Greene, *The Quiet American* (New York: Penguin Classics, 2004), rpt. ed.

26. Kamila Shamsie, "What Has Malala Yousafzai done to the Taliban?," *Guardian*, October 10, 2012, http://www.theguardian.com/commentisfree/2012/oct/10/malala-yousafzai-taliban-misogyny, accessed October 20, 2012.